*The man who does not read good books has
no advantage over the man who can't read them.*
Mark Twain

*A library is not a luxury, but one of the
necessities of life.*
Henry Ward Beecher

The Used Book Lover's Guide To Canada

By

David S. and Susan Siegel

Book Hunter Press
P.O. Box 193
Yorktown Heights, NY 10598
www.bookhunterpress.com

The Used Book Lover's Guide To Canada by David S. and Susan Siegel.
© Copyright 1999. Book Hunter Press.

Printed and bound in the United States of America

Library of Congress Catalog Card Number 99-072070

ISBN 1-891379-00-3

Acknowledgments

We would like to thank the over 850 book dealers listed in this Guide who patiently answered our questionnaire, responded to our phone calls, chatted with us during our visits and told us about new dealers in their area. Without their cooperation, this book would not have been possible.

Thanks also to the dealers who compile the local guides for their regions, to the Confrérie de la Librairie Ancienne du Québec for its membership list, to Marvin Post, Hugh Anson-Cartwright and Hannalore Headley who searched through their files for more dealer leads, to Michel Lanteigne who helped us with the Quebec chapter, and to Neil Aitken and Deanna Ramsey who kindly shared their database of dealers with us.

Thanks also to the American Automobile Association and the Canadian Automobile Association for their maps and tour books which helped us plan our trip.

Special thanks to Andrew Edward Macfarlane who graciously translated our Dealer Questionnaire and cover letter into French so that we could reach more dealers in Quebec province.

And special thanks to Constable S.M.Rayworth of the Royal Canadian Mounted Police who, when we found the directions originally given to us by the owner of a shop hard to follow, was kind enough to guide two confused Americans to the street the shop was on—and even recommend a good Canadian read.

Also Available From Book Hunter Press

The Used Book Lover's Guide to New England, a guide to over 750 used book dealers in Maine, New Hampshire, Vermont, Massachusetts, Connecticut and Rhode Island.

The Used Book Lover's Guide to the Mid-Atlantic States, a guide to over 1,000 used book dealers in New York, New Jersey, Pennsylvania and Delaware.

The Used Book Lover's Guide to the South Atlantic States, a guide to over 950 used book dealers in Maryland, Washington, DC, Virginia, North Carolina, South Carolina, Georgia and Florida.

The Used Book Lover's Guide to the Midwest, a guide to over 1,300 used book dealers in Ohio, Indiana, Illinois, Michigan, Wisconsin, Minnesota, Iowa, Missouri, Kentucky and West Virginia.

The Used Book Lover's Guide to the Central States, a guide to over 1,200 used book dealers in the Rocky Mountain, Plains, Southwest and Southcentral States.

The Used Book Lover's Guide to the Pacific Coast States, a guide to over 1,350 used book dealers in California, Oregon, Washington, Alaska and Hawaii.

If you've found this book useful in your book hunting endeavors and would like to order copies of any of the other guides, you will find a convenient Order From at the back of this book. Or, you can call or write to us at:

Book Hunter Press
PO Box 193
Yorktown Heights, NY 10598
(914) 245-6608
Fax: (914) 245-2630
bookhuntpr@aol.com
www.bookhunterpress.com

Table of Contents

2

It's about time I found that book.

List of Maps

Friendly Borders

Long time users of our guides who have taken the time to read our introductions will, by now, be familiar with the stress we describe each time we take to the road to begin another adventure in book hunting. Readers who envy our "life on the road" are soon disabused of such envy when they learn of our travails. Indeed, many wonder if we will ever venture out again.

The existence of this volume, our seventh guide to used book dealers on the North American continent (the first six regional guides covering the 50 United States) is proof either of our continued insanity or of our love for one another (as well as our love for books) and the fact that "the thrill of the hunt" continues to excite us.

Loyal readers may well wonder why we decided to embark on a Canadian venture. The answers are several. In addition to the obvious mountain climber's reply, "Because it is there!" we would add: because we believed initially (and still do) that Canadian readers and collectors have enough in common with their American cousins as to make a guide to that country's used book dealers a valuable asset to bibliophiles on both sides of the border.

Also, from a practical and purely economic point of view, book hunting in Canada can be most rewarding for American collectors. At the time of our visit to Canada, we received $1.45 in Canadian currency for every US dollar we exchanged. While we cannot guarantee that the US dollar will continue to enjoy strong buying power in Canada, it is reasonable to assume that American visitors to Canadian bookstores will pay lower prices for books than they would pay for the same volumes on the American side of the border.

There are, as far as we could ascertain, only two characteristics that make Canadian bookstores different from their counterparts in the USA. One is the display, especially in Quebec, but also in other provinces, of many volumes in the French language. Whether or not we mention this fact in a store's listing, readers can usually assume that stores, particularly in the eastern provinces, will carry a fair number of such volumes.

The second feature unique but not necessarily surprising is the fact that almost every store has shelves marked "Canadian authors" or "Canadian history." At the risk of sounding as if we are patronizing our northern neighbors, American browsers are likely to be surprised when they discover that many of the fine authors they are familiar with are Canadian. They should also be impressed, as we were, by the scope of Canadian scholarship; we saw volume after volume filled with Canadian contributions to the arts, science, literature, the military, sports, etc.

In most other respects, Canadian used bookstores cannot be differentiated from those in the United States. There are winners and losers, pleasures and disappointments, at least from our perspective. We visited many shops which carry a magnificent stock in wonderful condition. Shops that we would rave about regardless of where they were located, and of course, rave we do. We also visited shops that we spent far less time in based on the experience of having visited similar shops in the States. Such shops no doubt serve the local community by providing inexpensive reading but do not generally carry the scope of titles that we believe the traveling book hunter seeks. Clearly we recognize that we are not infallible and that a cache of hard-to-find books could show up at any of these stores the day after our arrival. And, if the owner is wise enough to purchase these volumes, the book hunter who visits these shops, despite our comments, should be in for a treat.

Now that the " business" of visiting Canada to view its used bookstores is behind us, we look forward to returning to that vast country for a more leisurely visit to some of its many non-literary treasures.

David S. and Susan Siegel
August, 1999

How To Get The Most From This Guide

This guide is designed to help you find the books you're looking for, whether you visit used bookstores in person or "browse" by mail or phone from the comfort of your home. It's also designed to help you access the collections of the three categories of used book dealers: open shop, by appointment and mail order.

Open shop dealers maintain regular store hours. Their collections can vary in size from less than a 1,000 to more than 100,000 books and can either be a general stock covering most subject categories or a specialized collection limited to one or more specialty areas.

By appointment or chance dealers generally, but not always, have smaller collections, frequently quite specialized. Many of these dealers maintain their collections in their home. By phoning these dealers in advance, book hunters can easily combine a trip to open shops and by appointment dealers in the same region.

Mail order only dealers issue catalogs and/or sell to people on their mailing list or in response to written, phone or e-mail inquiries.

Antique malls. Many dealers in all three of the above categories also rent space in multi dealer antique malls and some malls have more than one dealer. The size and quality of these collections vary widely from a few hundred fairly common titles to interesting and unusual collections, sometimes as large as what we have seen in individual bookstores. While we include antique malls where we knew there were used book dealers, we have not, on a systematic basis, researched all of the antique malls across Canada.

How this book is organized.
Because we believe that the majority of our readers will be people who enjoy taking book hunting trips, we have organized this guide geographically by province, and within each province by city.

To help the reader locate specific dealers or locations, at the beginning of each provincial chapter we have included both an alphabetical listing of all the dealers in that province as well as a geographical listing by location. At the end of the provincial listings, readers will find a complete list of all the dealers in the guide, arranged alphabetically by the business name.

Within each listing, we have tried to include the kinds of information about book sellers that we have found useful in our own travels.

• *A description of the stock:* Are you likely to find the kinds of books you're searching for in this shop? Are the books reading copies or of collectible quality? Are they fairly common volumes or more difficult-to-find unusual ones? Are they recent publications or do they date back to earlier decades? What condition are the books in? How many volumes does the dealer have? What percentage of the store's stock is paperback? (When collections are a mix of new and used books, and/or hardcover and paperback, we have indicated the estimated percentage of the stock in each category, listing the largest category first.)

• *Detailed travel directions:* How you can get to the shop, usually from the closest major highway exit.

• *Special services:* Does the dealer issue a catalog? Accept want lists? Have a search service? Offer other services? Note that if the dealer issues a catalog, we generally have not listed "mail order" as a separate service.

• *Payment:* Will the dealer accept credit cards?

• *Comments:* Perhaps the most unique feature of this guide is the *Comments* section that includes our personal observations about a shop. Based on our actual visits to the shop, the comments are designed not to endorse or criticize the establishment, but rather to place ourselves in the position of our readers who will want to know: Is this shop likely to have the types of books I'm looking for?

• *Specialty Index:* If you're interested in locating books in specific categories, the *Specialty Index* in the back of the book will help you identify dealers who either deal exclusively in those subjects or who have strong sections in those subjects in addition to a more general collection.

• *Owner's name:* Note that the owner's name is included in each listing only when it is different from the name of the business.

Dealer response

With a few exceptions, only dealers who responded to our questionnaire or who we were able to contact by phone are included in the guide. If the dealer did not respond to our multiple inquiries, and if we could not personally verify that the dealer was in business, the dealer was not listed. In the case of Quebec, letters inviting dealers to be included in the guide were sent in French but because the authors are not fluent in French, telephone follow up was limited.

While we encouraged mail order dealers who sell exclusively on the Internet to let us know about their business so that they could be included in the guide, we did not aggressively seek out all these dealers; our goal in putting together this book is to help readers locate and learn more about dealers who can't be found by other more commonly available means.

Maps

The guide includes a series of 25 provincial, regional and city maps designed to assist readers plan book hunting safaris to open shops and by appointment dealers.

Locations with open shops are shown in regular type while locations that only have by appointment dealers are in italics. Note that the maps are not drawn to scale and are designed to be used in conjunction with actual road maps.

Comments

We're often asked, "Do you actually visit every dealer who appears in your books?" The answer, we must confess, is "No." To do so, would require far more time than one could possibly imagine and would make this book far too expensive.

We try instead to visit the kinds of shops the majority of our readers are most interested in: open shops with a predominately hardcover general collection. We do not normally visit specialty open shops or by appointment and mail order dealers. There are, of course, exceptions, such as when a shop is either closed on the day that we're in the area or is too far off the route we have laid out for ourselves in order to make the most economical use of our travel time. For this reason, we always welcome input from readers who may have personal knowledge of such shops so that we can share the information with other book lovers in future editions.

Some cross cultural issues

This being our first foray out of the USA, we found we had several style issues that needed to be addressed: is the store located in the City Center or in the City Centre? In Quebec, is the store located on Rue St. Denis or St. Denis St? After giving the matter some thought, we eventually decided that as the book was being published in the United States we would use "American" spelling, except when referring to a name or street sign. We hope that this in no way offends our northern neighbors.

A note about Canadian addresses: In many instances, an address has a unit or suite number *in front* of the building address. When this is the case, we have left a space between the two numbers. Also, because we came across so many numbered streets, we have placed a hyphen (–) between the building number and the street name. Example: 23 4564–24th Street. The actual building address is "4564" and the unit number is "23."

Miles versus kilometers: We have tried to used kilometers whenever distances are given. We hope we have done our arithmetic carefully.

A few caveats and suggestions before you begin your book hunting safari.

Call ahead. Even when an open shop lists hours and days open, we advise a phone call ahead to be certain that the hours have not changed and that the establishment will indeed be open when you arrive.

Is there a difference between an "antiquarian" and a "used" book store? Yes and no. Many stores we visited call themselves antiquarian but their shelves contain a large stock of books published within the past ten or fifteen years. Likewise, we also found many pre-20th century books in "used" bookstores. For that reason, we have used the term "antiquarian" with great caution and only when it was clear to us that the book seller dealt primarily in truly antiquarian books.

Used and Out-of-Print. Some used book purists also make a distinction between "used" books and "out-of-print" books, a distinction which, for the most part, we have avoided.

Paperbacks. The reader should also note that while we do not list shops that are exclusively paperback, we do include "mostly paperback" shops, although these stores are generally not described in great detail. While philosophically we agree with the seasoned book dealer we met in our travels who said, "Books are books and there's a place for people who love to read all kinds of books," because we believe that a majority of our readers are interested in hardcover volumes, we have tried to identify "mostly paperback" shops as a caveat to those who might prefer to shop elsewhere. In those instances where we did visit a "mostly paperback" shop, it was because, based on the initial information we had, we thought the percentage of hardcover volumes was greater than it turned out to be.

Size of the collection. In almost all instances, the information regarding the size of the collection comes directly from the owner. While we did not stop to do an actual count of each collection during our visits, in the few instances where we observed a significant difference between the owner's estimate and the size of the collection we saw displayed, we recorded our observation in the *Comments* section. Readers should note, however, that the number of volumes listed may include books in storage that are not readily accessible.

And now to begin your search. Good luck and happy hunting.

The Internet Phenomenon

(And how it has affected the used book world.)

Yes, we have noted that more and more dealers have gone online and are placing a number of their "better" books on the Internet. Other dealers, however, insist that they have no intention of offering their books on the Net.

Some dealers have reduced their hours and several have closed their shops to deal exclusively on the Net. Dealers who used to do searches the old fashioned way can now search for their customers in seconds and at no substantial cost.

While we mourn the loss of some open shops, believe it or not, there are more used book dealers today than there were several years ago.

How all this affects those of us who may be modern enough to use the Internet but who still enjoy the excitement of actually visiting bookstores, examining the books on the shelves, and quite often discovering books we never knew existed, is a matter of individual style.

What it comes down to is this: if you know the title, author, edition and condition of a book you wish to acquire, the Internet can save you countless miles of travel and/or dollars spent on phone calls or postage. Quite often, however, (but not always) such finds can turn out to be more expensive than the same title located on the open shelves in a bookstore.

On the other hand, if like us, you have specific tastes in books, whether they be narrow or broad, we challenge any web site to take the place of wandering through the aisles of a traditional used bookstore, eyeballing title after title, pulling out a volume, thumbing through the pages and, while not quite smelling it, inhaling the book's essence, and ultimately deciding that this is a book you must truly own.

For that thrill of the hunt, we invite you to continue your journey through the pages of this guide.

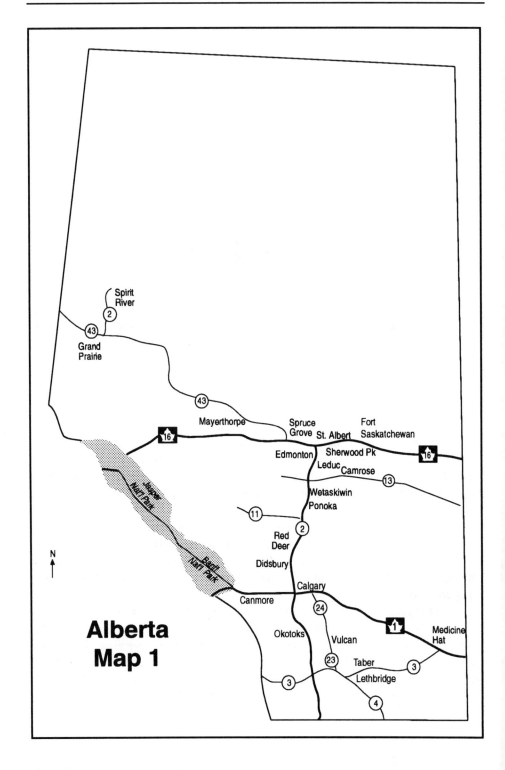

Alberta

Alphabetical Listing By Dealer

Alphabetical Listing By Location

Calgary
(Map 2, page 18)

A Doctor Hook's Used Tapes & Books   **Open Shop**
1235 Macleod Trail SE T2G 2N1   (403) 290-0706

Collection:	General stock of mostly paperback.
# of Vols:	11,000
Hours:	Mon-Sat 10-5:30. Sun & holidays 11-5:30

A Second Look Books   **Open Shop**
3222–28th Street SW T3E 2J6   (403) 240-1719

Collection:	General stock of mostly paperback.
# of Vols:	17,000-20,000
Hours:	Mon-Thu 10-6. Fri 10-8. Sat 10-5:30.

A Why Buy Nu Used Bookstore   **Open Shop**
107 8120 Beddington Boulevard NW T3K 2A8   (403) 275-0717

Collection:	General stock of paperback and hardcover.
# of Vols:	14,000
Hours:	Mon-Fri 10-9. Sat 10-5:30. Sun 12-5.
Travel:	From Hwy 1, turn north on Centre St. Shop is at corner of Centre and Beddington in Beddington Town Centre.
Credit Cards:	Yes
Year Estab:	1998
Comments:	Stock is approximately 70% paperback.

Aaron's Recycled Books   **Open Shop**
1324–17th Avenue SW T2R 0S9   (403) 244-7755

Collection:	General stock of paperback and hardcover.
# of Vols:	40,000
Specialties:	Architecture; art; native studies.
Hours:	Mon-Wed 10-6. Thu & Fri 10-8. Sat 10-5. Sun 12-5.
Services:	Appraisals, accepts want lists, mail order.
Travel:	Between 13th & 14th Sts.
Credit Cards:	Yes
Owner:	Darcy Paladeau
Year Estab:	1989
Comments:	The shop carries a mix of paperbacks and hardcover volumes. While most of the books were of fairly recent vintage, we did note some collectible items, including some early Oz books behind glass. Should you arrive on the right day (after the owner has made a wonderful purchase) you could well leave with a happy smile on your face. Considering the number of quality book dealers in Calgary, unless you're running on a very tight schedule, a stop here could turn out to be lucky for you. At the time of our visit, the number of books on display was far fewer than the number cited above.

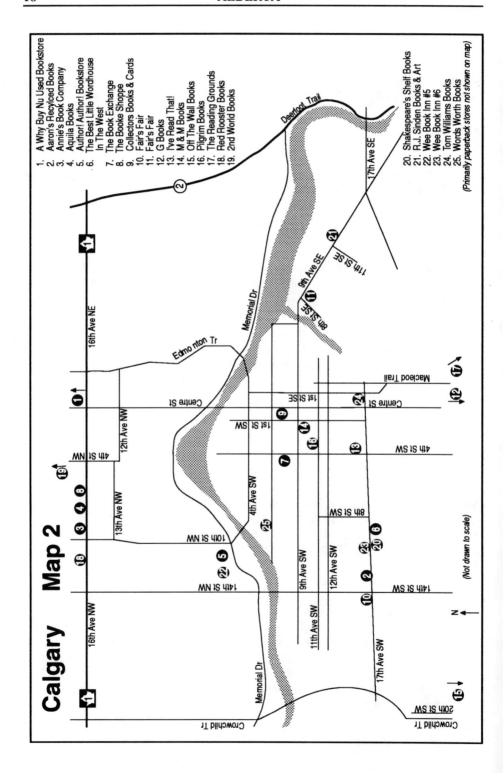

Calgary Map 2

1. A Why Buy Nu Used Bookstore
2. Aaron's Recylced Books
3. Annie's Book Company
4. Aquila Books
5. Author! Author! Bookstore
6. The Best Little Wordhouse In The West
7. The Book Exchange
8. The Booke Shoppe
9. Collectors Books & Cards
10. Fair's Fair
11. Fair's Fair
12. G Books
13. I've Read That!
14. M & M Books
15. Off The Wall Books
16. Pilgrim Books
17. The Reading Grounds
18. Red Rooster Books
19. 2nd World Books
20. Shakespeare's Shelf Books
21. R.J. Sinden Books & Art
22. Wee Book Inn #5
23. Wee Book Inn #6
24. Tom Williams Books
25. Words Worth Books

(Primarily paperback stores not shown on map)

(Not drawn to scale)

Agora Books   **Open Shop**
228–7th Avenue SW T2P 0W6   (403) 294-1449

Collection:	General stock of mostly paperback.
# of Vols:	6,000-8,000
Hours:	Mon-Fri 9:30-6. Sat 10-5.

Annie's Book Company   **Open Shop**
912–16th Avenue NW T2M 0K3   (403) 282-1330
                                                                 Fax: (403) 282-2580
                                                          E-mail: ava@cadvision.com

Collection:	General stock of paperback and hardcover.
# of Vols:	52,000
Specialties:	Art; foreign languages; Canadiana; children's; technology; sci fi.
Hours:	Mon-Sat 10-6, except Tue & Thu till 9. Sun and holidays 12-5.
Services:	Search service, accepts want lists, mail order.
Travel:	16th Ave NW is Hwy 1 (Trans Canada Hwy). Shop is at 9th St.
Credit Cards:	Yes
Owner:	Annie Vigna
Year Estab:	1960
Comments:	A mix of paperback and hardcover books in an attractively decorated shop that also features a cappuccino bar and literary salon which hosts readings and other literary events. Most of the books we saw were of fairly recent vintage and might be considered reading copies.

Aquila Books   **Open Shop**
826–16th Avenue NW   (403) 282-5832
Mailing address: PO Box 75035, Cambrian Postal Outlet Calgary AB T2K 6J8
Web page: www.aquilabooks.com   Fax: (403) 289-0814
                                                      E-mail: aquila@cadvision.com

Collection:	General stock and ephemera.
# of Vols:	30,000
Specialties:	Arctic; Western Canadiana; mountaineering; travel & exploration; first editions; maps.
Hours:	Mon-Sat 10:30-5:30.
Services:	Appraisals, search service, accepts want lists.
Travel:	See Annie's above.
Credit Cards:	Yes
Owner:	Cameron Treleaven
Year Estab:	1985
Comments:	My hat is off to the owner of this shop for the good taste he exercises in purchasing books; the shelves are filled with quality volumes in generally excellent condition. The specialties listed above are represented in quantity and the titles are seldom seen elsewhere. In addition to the fine books, prints and maps, the shop also displays (not for sale) a large array of attractive book ends as well as antique medical and scientific instruments which may be purchased. Considering the quality of the books, we found prices extremely reasonable. The owner also displays good taste in selecting the most helpful employees.

(Calgary)

Author! Author! Bookstore   **Open Shop**
223–10th Street NW   T2N 1V5   (403) 283-9521
                                                            Fax: (403) 283-6990
                                                E-mail: author@netway.ab.ca

Collection:	General stock of paperback and hardcover.
# of Vols:	50,000
Hours:	Daily 10-10.
Services:	Accepts want lists.
Travel:	From 16th Ave NW, turn south onto 10th St NW. Shop is about 12 blocks ahead.
Credit Cards:	Yes
Owner:	Keyvan Nayeri
Year Estab:	1983
Comments:	Stock is approximately 70% paperback.

Bell's Bookstore Cafe   **Open Shop**
1515A–34th Avenue SW   T2T 2B1   (403) 243-3095

Collection:	General stock of mostly paperback.
# of Vols:	15,000
Hours:	Mon-Fri 8-10. Sat & Sun 9-6.

The Best Little Wordhouse In The West   **Open Shop**
911–17th Avenue SW   T2T 0A4   (403) 245-6407
                                                E-mail: tuckerl@cadvision.com

Collection:	General stock of paperback and hardcover.
# of Vols:	50,000
Hours:	Mon-Fri 10-9. Sat 10-5:30. Sun 11-5.
Services:	Accepts want lists.
Travel:	Between 8th and 9th Streets.
Credit Cards:	Yes
Owner:	Lorne Tucker
Year Estab:	1994
Comments:	Stock is approximately 70% paperback.

The Book Exchange   **Open Shop**
4527–8th Avenue SE   T2A 0A7   (403) 272-1828

Collection:	General stock of paperback and hardcover.
# of Vols:	20,000
Hours:	Mon-Fri 10-8. Sat & Sun 10-6.
Travel:	At 4th Street.
Credit Cards:	No
Year Estab:	1979
Comments:	Stock is approximately 65% paperback.

The Booke Shoppe   **Open Shop**
632–16th Avenue NW T2M 0J7   (403) 282-6821

Collection: General stock of mostly hardcover.
# of Vols: 100,000
Specialties: Western Canadiana; Canadian literature; antiques.
Hours: Mon-Sat 10-6.
Travel: See Annie's above. Shop is between 6th & 7th Streets.
Credit Cards: No
Owner: David P. Nicholson
Year Estab: 1970's
Comments: We very much regret not having the opportunity to visit this shop as it
                   seemed clear to us from peering through its front window that there
                   were a large number of hardcover volumes inside that appeared to be
                   in good condition. We arrived at the shop at 10am (the opening time
                   posted in its window). By 10:15 we did not feel it was wise for us to
                   wait any longer for the owner (or an employee) to arrive. If you plan to
                   visit this shop, our advice is to call ahead so that you don't have the
                   same experience. And, if your luck is better than ours, we'd appreciate
                   your sharing your experience with us.

Calgary Book Exchange   **Open Shop**
189 755 Lake Bonavista Dr SE T2J 0N3   (403) 278-1105

Collection: General stock of mostly paperback.
# of Vols: 15,000
Hours: Mon-Wed 10-6. Thu 10-8. Fri 10-6. Sat 10-5:30. Sun 1-4.

Collectors Books & Cards   **Open Shop**
615 Centre Street SW T2G 2C6   (403) 265-3455

Collection: General stock of paperback and hardcover.
# of Vols: 5,000
Specialties: Sports
Hours: Mon-Sat 11-5.
Travel: From Hwy 1, proceed south on Centre St. Shop is between 6th & 7th
                   Avenues SW.
Credit Cards: Yes
Owner: Julie Mailly
Year Estab: 1977
Comments: Stock is 70% paperback.

Fair's Fair   **Open Shop**
1430 1609–14 Street SW T3C 1E4   (403) 245-2778
Web page: www.fairsfair.com   Fax: (403) 236-7460
                                                              E-mail: fairsfair@home.ca

Collection: General stock of paperback and hardcover.
# of Vols: 60,000
Hours: Mon-Sat 10-10. Sun 11-5.
Services: Appraisals, search service, accepts want lists, mail order.

(Calgary)

Travel:	Between 16th & 17th Avenues.
Credit Cards:	Yes
Owner:	George Henderson
Year Estab:	1988
Comments:	A large shop with a heavy emphasis on paperbacks. However, the shop does carry a respectable number of hardcover volumes in mixed condition. Lots of reading copies, a few collectibles and some books that looked almost new. While an erudite don might pass this shop by, those with more popular tastes should be able to find titles here to suit their interests. The owner operates a second shop inCalgary. See below.

Fair's Fair   **Open Shop**
907–9th Avenue SE T2G 0S5   (403) 237-8156
Web page: www.fairsfair.com   E-mail: fairsfair@home.com

Collection:	General stock of paperback and hardcover.
# of Vols:	80,000
Hours:	Mon-Sat 11-6. Sun 11-5
Travel:	Between 8th & 9th Streets.
Credit Cards:	Yes
Owner:	George Henderson
Year Estab:	1988
Comments:	Stock is approximately 60% paperback.

G Books   **Open Shop**
8330 Macleod Trail T2H 2V2   (403) 252-9577
                                                          Fax: (403) 243-6185

Collection:	General stock of paperback and hardcover.
# of Vols:	50,000
Hours:	Mon-Fri 9:30-9. Sat 9:30-6. Sun 12-6.
Travel:	In Heritage Plaza at Macleod Trail and Heritage Dr.
Credit Cards:	Yes
Owner:	Lawrence Gerritsen
Year Estab:	1997
Comments:	Stock is approximately 65% paperback. All hardcover fiction, regardless of condition or edition, is priced at $4.99.

I've Read That!   **Open Shop**
1B 1304–4th Street SW T2R 0X8   (403) 265-6609

Collection:	General stock of paperback and hardcover.
# of Vols:	5,000+
Specialties:	Literature; poetry; military; history; philosophy; biography.
Hours:	Daily 11-6.
Travel:	Between 14th Ave and 13th Ave. On lower level.
Credit Cards:	Yes
Owner:	Roy Yearwood
Year Estab:	1999

Comments: A relatively new, rather modest sized shop with a mix of paperback and hardcover books that included some more recent titles attractively displayed along with some older volumes. Considering the fact that during our visit the owner of a large nearby bookstore walked out with an armful of purchases, we can only hope that the local dealers and other scouts leave a few volumes of interest for you if and when you visit the shop.

Last Word Bookstore   **Open Shop**
201A–4th Street NE T2E 3S1   (403) 237-0638

Collection: General stock of mostly paperback.
# of Vols: 21,000
Hours: Mon-Sat 10-6. Sun 12-5.

M & M Books   **Open Shop**
1001–1st Street SW T2R 0T8   (403) 262-2292

Collection: General stock of paperback and hardcover.
# of Vols: 25,000
Specialties: Business; medicine; true crime; history.
Hours: Mon-Sat 10-6. Sun 11-5.
Travel: At corner of 10th Ave.
Owner: Murray Lott
Year Estab: 1995
Comments: A mix of paperback and hardcover volumes, the majority of which appeared to be of fairly recent vintage, as well as popular titles most of which were reading copies.

Off The Wall Books   **Open Shop**
2042–42nd Avenue SW T2T 2MT   (403) 242-8041

Collection: General stock of hardcover and paperback, videos and CDs.
# of Vols: 50,000+
Specialties: Science fiction; mystery; French language books.
Hours: Most days 10-6, except Thu & Fri till 9. May-Sept: Till 10pm on weekends.
Services: Accepts want lists.
Travel: 33rd Ave exit off Crowchild Trail. Proceed east on 33rd Ave SE, then south on 20th St. Shop is on the corner of 20th St and 42nd Ave.
Credit Cards: Yes
Owner: David & Chris Hall
Year Estab: 1984
Comments: Book snobs approaching this shop will see tons of paperbacks, thousands of CDs, books on tape and magazines and glance around at the hardcover volumes thinking: not much here. Those with a bit more patience might (as we did) spot several serious titles in both literature and the humanities as well as some collectibles, including some pulp magazines and Big Little Books. We do confess, though, that the majority of the hardcover volumes represented more popular titles, practical books and the like.

(Calgary)

Owls' Rook Books   **Open Shop**
712–16th Avenue NW T2M 0J8   (403) 220-9112

Collection:	General stock of mostly paperback.
# of Vols:	40,000
Hours:	Mon-Sat 10-6. Sun 12-5.
Travel:	Between 6th & 7th Streets.
Credit Cards:	Yes
Owner:	Mike & Ronda Vrooman
Year Estab:	1970's
Comments:	We would guess that at least 90% of the stock in this shop was paper-back. Some of the hardcover titles were located on the top shelves above the paperbacks and at least two bookcases filled with older hardcover volumes were also on hand.

Pilgrim Books   **Open Shop**
110–11th Avenue SW, Rm 200 T2R 0B8   (403) 233-2409
                                                                      Fax: (403) 233-0665
                                                          E-mail: pilgrim@cadvision.com

Collection:	Specialty
# of Vols:	45,000
Specialties:	Religion (Christian)
Hours:	Mon-Sat 9:30-5:30.
Services:	Accepts want lists, mail order.
Travel:	Edmonton Trail exit off Hwy 1. Proceed south on Edmonton Trail, then west on 4th Ave, south on 1st St SE and west on 11th Ave. Shop is upstairs in a strip mall. (Use intercom 200 for admission.)
Credit Cards:	Yes
Owner:	Ruth Maconochie
Year Estab:	1990

The Reading Grounds   **Open Shop**
101 14921 Deer Ridge Drive SE T2J 7C4   (403) 271-1192

Collection:	General stock of paperback and hardcover.
# of Vols:	20,000
Hours:	Mon-Fri 7:30am-10pm. Sat 8am-10pm. Sun 10-6.
Travel:	Between Canyon Meadows Dr and Bow Bottom Trail.
Credit Cards:	Yes
Year Estab:	1997
Comments:	Stock is approximately 75% paperback.

Red Rooster Books   **Open Shop**
1708–12th Street NW T2M 3M7   (403) 220-1325

Collection:	General stock of hardcover and paperback.
# of Vols:	10,000-15,000
Hours:	Mon-Sat 9:30-5:30.
Services:	Accepts want lists, mail order.

Travel: See Annie's Book above. At corner of 12th & 16th Avenues.
Credit Cards: No
Owner: Allan Bishop
Year Estab: 1998
Comments: Stock is approximately 55% hardcover.

2nd World Books   **Open Shop**
7 390 Northmount Drive NW T2K 3H5   (403) 282-7522

Collection: General stock of paperback and hardcover.
# of Vols: 10,000
Hours: Mon-Fri 10-9. Sat 10-6. Sun 11-6.
Travel: From 16th Ave, turn north on 4th St NW, then left on Northmount.
Comments: Stock is approximately 75% paperback.

Shakespeare's Shelf Books   **Open Shop**
201 1019–17th Avenue SW T2T 0A4   (403) 245-2440
Web page: www.abebooks.com/home/shelf   E-mail: shelf@cadvision.com

Collection: General stock of hardcover and paperback.
# of Vols: 10,000
Specialties: Modern first editions; Canadian literature and poetry; humanities.
Hours: Mon 12-5. Tue-Sat 10-6. Sun 12-5.
Services: Appraisals, search service, accepts want lists mail order.
Travel: From 16 Ave NW, turn south on 14th St, then east on 17th Ave and
                 south on 9A St. Shop is at corner of 9A and 17th. Parking is available
                 in rear (off 9A St).
Credit Cards: Yes
Owner: Don Gorman
Year Estab: 1996
Comments: One flight up, this shop carries a stock of attractive books, most in excel-
                 lent condition adorned by their original dust jackets. You won't find too
                 many antiquarian volumes here but you will find a nice selection of
                 modern firsts. The shop is modest in size and quite easy to browse.

Shop & Swap Books   **Open Shop**
48 7930 Bowness Road NW T3B 0H2   (403) 286-5246

Collection: General stock of paperback and hardcover, CDs, comics and videos.
Hours: Mon-Fri 10-8. Sat 10-6. Sun 12-5.

Shop & Swap Books   **Open Shop**
135 Whitefield Drive NE T1Y 5X1   (403) 285-8882

Collection: General stock of mostly paperback.
Hours: Mon-Fri 10-8. Sat 10-6. Sun 12-5.

R.J. Sinden Books & Art   **Open Shop**
1336–9th Avenue SE T2G 0T3   (403) 263-5885
                                                        Fax: (403) 263-5899
                                        E-mail: rjsindenbooks@hotmail.com
Collection: General collection of paperback and hardcover and ephemera.

(Calgary)

# of Vols:	10,000+
Specialties:	Art (Canadian); illustrated (by Canadian artists).
Hours:	Mon-Sat 10-5. Sun 12-5.
Services:	Accepts want lists.
Travel:	One half block east of Deerfoot Trail (Hwy 2). Shop is one flight down.
Credit Cards:	Yes
Owner:	Robert J. Sinden
Year Estab:	1995
Comments:	Unlike so many other shops whose stock is at least 50% or more paperback, this shop's hardcover selection is most respectable and consists of a mix in terms of vintage. Most of the books were in good condition. Unless your interests are very narrow, or your schedule very tight, a visit here could be fortuitous. The owner, also an artist, displays framed contemporary art and operates a framing business.

Tramp's CD's Books Games   **Open Shop**
290 9737 Macleod Trail SW T2J 0P6   (403) 255-5652

Collection:	General stock of mostly paperback.
# of Vols:	10,000-15,000
Hours:	Mon-Sat 10am-midnight. Sun 11-10.

Wee Book Inn #5   **Open Shop**
1111 Kensington Rd NW T2N 3P2   Tel & Fax: (403) 283-3322

Collection:	General stock of paperback and hardcover, CDs and videos.
# of Vols:	21,000
Specialties:	Appraisals, search service, accepts want lists..
Hours:	Daily 9am-midnight.
Travel:	From 16th St NW, turn south on 10th St NWand continue to Kensington.
Credit Cards:	Yes
Comments:	Stock is approximately 60% paperback.

Wee Book Inn #6   **Open Shop**
1114–17th Avenue SW T2T 0B4   (403) 228-9774

Collection:	General stock of paperback and hardcover.
# of Vols:	15,000
Hours:	Daily 9-midnight.
Travel:	Northbound on Hwy 2 (Macleod Trail), turn left at 17th Ave SW. Shop is between 11th and 12th Streets SW.

Tom Williams Books   **Open Shop**
122A–17th Avenue SE   (403) 264-0184
Mailing address: Box 4126C Calgary AB T2T 5M9
                                        E-mail: oldtomes@cybersurf.net

Collection:	General stock and ephemera.
# of Vols:	70,000

Specialties:	Canadiana; mountaineering; natural history; hockey; North American natives; maps.
Hours:	Mon-Sat 12-5.
Services:	Appraisals, search service, accepts want lists, mail order.
Travel:	From Hwy 1: Proceed south on Edmonton Trail. When crossing the bridge, keep to the right which will put you on 4th Ave SE heading west. Move quickly to the left and turn left after three blocks onto 1st SE, then right at 17th Ave. Shop is 1/2 block away, one flight down. From Hwy 2 southbound (coming from Edmonton): Memorial Dr exit. Proceed west on Memorial and follow signs to City Centre. Cross bridge and follow directions above.
Credit Cards:	No
Year Estab:	1958
Comments:	This rather large shop should be the answer to the dreams of book people looking for older, often hard-to-find volumes. The books we saw were in mixed condition with more than a few collectibles and indeed some rare items. In addition to the specialties cited above, we noted a nice vintage mystery section, plus records, magazines and other ephemera. To paraphrase the owner: don't look for Stephen King or Dungeons & Dragons here.

Words Books & Cappuccino Bar   **Open Shop**
1715–17th Avenue SW T2T 0E6   (403) 244-4239

Collection:	General stock of mostly paperback.
# of Vols:	10,000
Hours:	Mon 12-11. Tue-Sat 10-11. Sun 12-11.

Words Worth Books   **Open Shop**
928–6th Avenue SW T2P 0V5   (403) 265-0098

Collection:	General stock of hardcover and paperback.
# of Vols:	40,000
Specialties:	Art; religion; philosophy; poetry; psychology; new age.
Hours:	Mon-Sat 11:30-5:30.
Services:	Search service, mail order.
Travel:	Between 9th & 10th Avenues.
Credit Cards:	Yes
Owner:	Keith Sanderson
Year Estab:	1990
Comments:	A healthy mix of hardcover and paperback books offering nice titles, both to folks in the neighborhood who may choose to drop in as well as more serious titles for traveling book people like our readers. Most of the books we saw appeared to be in good condition. The hardcover volumes were a mix in terms of vintage with a majority of the titles being of fairly recent origin.

Camrose

Books For You   **Open Shop**
Duggan Mall, 36 6601–48th Avenue T4V 3G8   (403) 672-1707

Collection: General stock of mostly new and some used (mostly paperback).
# of Vols: 300-400 (used)
Hours: Mon-Wed 9:30-6. Thu & Fri 9:30-9. Sat 9:30-6. Sun 12-5.

Canmore

The Second Story Books/Art/Music   **Open Shop**
713 Main Street T1W 2B2   (403) 609-2368
Web page: www/abebooks.com/home/2ndstory E-mail: secondstory@telusplanet.net

Collection: General stock of mostly paperback.
# of Vols: 12,000
Hours: Daily 10-7. (Winter closing is 6pm.)

Didsbury

Books Then and Now   **Open Shop**
1525–20th Avenue, Box 1912 T0M 0W0   (403) 335-4667
Web page: www.abebooks.com/home/macmackay
                                          E-mail: mackay@mountainview.ab.ca

Collection: General stock of mostly paperback and ephemera.
# of Vols: 7,000
Specialties: Science fiction; Canadiana.
Hours: Wed-Fri 10-2. Other times by appointment.
Services: Search service, accepts want lists, mail order.
Travel: On Hwy 582, six km west of Hwy 2 and two km west of Hwy 2A.
Credit Cards: Yes
Owner: Laurel & Mac Mackay
Year Estab: 1988
Comments: Stock is approximately 80% paperback.

Edmonton
(Map 3, page 31)

Alhambra Books   **Open Shop**
10309–82nd Avenue T6E 1Z9   (780) 439-4195

Collection: General stock of mostly used hardcover and paperback.
# of Vols: 17,000 (used)
Specialties: Canadian history; military; religion; metaphysics.
Hours: Jan-Apr: Mon-Wed 9:30-6. Thu & Fri 9:30-8. Sat 9:30-6. Sun 12-6.
                   May-Dec: Mon-Wed 9:30-6. Thu 9:30-10. Fri & Sat 9:30-11. Sun 12-6.
Services: Search service, accepts want lists, mail order.
Travel: Between 103rd and 104th Sts. The shop is on the second floor.
Credit Cards: Yes
Owner: Tom Monto

Year Estab: 1990
Comments: The labeling on this store's shelves (which makes the shop quite browser friendly) also reveals the interests and specialties of its owner which, in addition to the subjects listed above, also reflect a kind of "beat" approach to our culture. Generally speaking, we were pleased with what we saw but would caution those interested in rare or antiquarian books that this location is not likely to offer the best hunting ground.

Ann–Well Fine Books   Open Shop
11437–124th Street T5M 0K4   (780) 452-4466
Web page: www.abebooks.com/home/awtfinebooks
                                E-mail: awtfinebooks@compusmart.ab.ca
Collection: General stock.
# of Vols: 3,000
Specialties: Literature; military; history; travel.
Hours: Mon-Sat 10-6.
Services: Search service, accepts want lists, mail order.
Travel: On north side of Edmonton, between 114th and 115th Avenues.
Credit Cards: Yes
Owner: Marilyn Wells
Year Estab: 1997
Comments: A very attractive shop with hardcover books that are in excellent condition. Extremely easy to browse. The shop is strong in literature and has a nice selection in travel. A room at the back displays inexpensive paperbacks and bargain books. The owner takes deserved pride in the service she provides and reminds readers that if they can't visit, she will provide swift service via the post.

Athabasca Books   Open Shop
8228–105th Street T6E 4H2   (780) 431-1776
Collection: General stock of hardcover and paperback.
# of Vols: 12,000
Hours: Mon-Fri 11-5:30, except Thu till 8:30. Sat 10:30-5:30. Also Sun during summer.
Services: Mail order, accepts want lists.
Travel: Between 82nd & 83rd Avenues.
Credit Cards: Yes
Owner: Margot Cross
Year Estab: 1988
Comments: An attractive shop with books in quite good condition. Many subject areas represented. Reasonably priced. Generally, more recent editions.

Bargain Books Etc.   Open Shop
12941–97th Street T5E 4C2   (780) 456-6303
Collection: General stock of mostly paperback.
# of Vols: 8,000
Hours: Oct-Mar: Mon-Wed 11-6. Thu & Fri 11-7. Sat 10-6. Sun 12-5. Apr-Sept: Mon-Fri 11-8. Sat 10-6. Sun 12-5.

Belgravia Books & Treasures
7601–115th Street T6G 1N4

Open Shop
(780) 436-4125

Collection:	General stock of hardcover and paperback.
# of Vols:	5,000+
Hours:	Mon-Sat 10-6. Sun 12-5.
Services:	Accepts want lists.
Travel:	From Hwy 2 (Calgary Trail) northbound, continue on 103rd St, then west on 76th Ave. Shop is at corner of 115th St.
Credit Cards:	Yes
Owner:	Lorie White
Year Estab:	1995
Comments:	A cozy corner shop with a mix of hardcover and paperback books. Although many subject categories were covered, most were not represented in great depth. The shelves are nicely labeled and the books were in generally good condition. Whether by chance (the books just happen to come in) or by design, we noted an interesting section devoted to the paranormal.

Bellum Books
5647 Riverbend Road
Mailing address: PO Box 59045 Edmonton AB T6H 5K0
www.abebooks.com/homeBELLUM

By Appointment
(780) 434-2353

E-mail: bellum@powersurfr.com

Collection:	Specialty
Hours:	Military
Services:	Search service, accepts want lists, mail order.
Credit Cards:	No
Owner:	Maurice F.V. Doll
Year Estab:	1994

Bjarne's Books
10533–82nd Avenue T6E 2A3

Open Shop
(780) 439-7133
Fax: (780) 439-3812

Collection:	General stock.
# of Vols:	1,500
Hours:	Tue-Sat 10:30-5:30. Sun 12-5.
Travel:	Between 104th & 105th Streets.
Owner:	Bjarne Tokerud
Comments:	Primarily an antique shop with a modest selection of hardcover volumes. Unlike many other book dealers who display in antique shops, the books here are of a high quality. And, as there are several other used book dealers in the neighborhood, a stop here would not be a mistake. Note: Additional books are available at the dealer's main location in Victoria, BC. See British Columbia section.

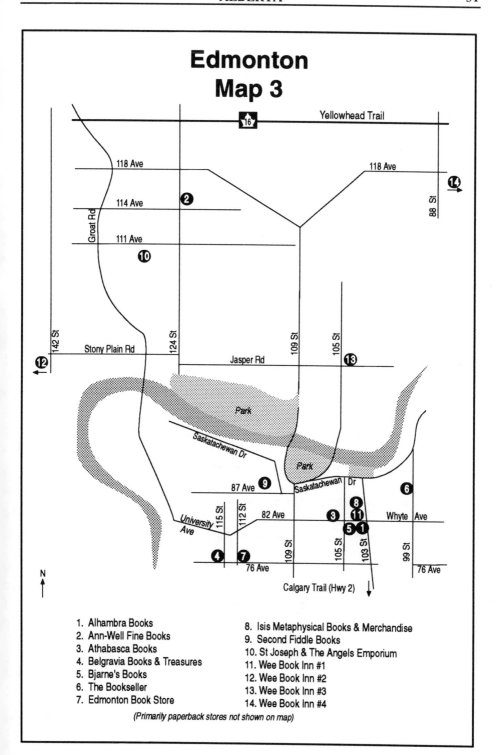

Edmonton
Map 3

1. Alhambra Books
2. Ann-Well Fine Books
3. Athabasca Books
4. Belgravia Books & Treasures
5. Bjarne's Books
6. The Bookseller
7. Edmonton Book Store
8. Isis Metaphysical Books & Merchandise
9. Second Fiddle Books
10. St Joseph & The Angels Emporium
11. Wee Book Inn #1
12. Wee Book Inn #2
13. Wee Book Inn #3
14. Wee Book Inn #4

(Primarily paperback stores not shown on map)

(Edmonton)

Book Nook
6655–178th Street T5T 4J5

Open Shop
(780) 483-9221

Collection: General stock of mostly paperback.
# of Vols: 10,000
Hours: Mon-Fri 10-8. Sat & Sun 11-5.

Books Unlimited
12411–118th Avenue T5L 2K4

Open Shop
(780) 453-1034

Collection: General stock of mostly used paperback.
# of Vols: 50,000
Hours: Mon-Wed 9-6. Thu & Fri 9-9. Sat 9-6. Sun 12-6.

The Bookseller
8904–99th Street T6E 3V4

Open Shop
(780) 496-9193
E-mail: satchwil@direct.ca

Collection: General stock mostly hardcover.
# of Vols: 10,000
Specialties: Literature (ancient and modern); philosophy; theology; reference.
Hours: Mon-Sat 11-5:30.
Services: Appraisals, search service, accepts want lists, mail order, book repair.
Travel: Between Whyte (82nd Ave) and Saskatchewan Dr.
Credit Cards: Yes
Owner: Rod Mattingsley
Year Estab: 1994
Comments: One flight down, this shop stocks a healthy selection of books in the specialties listed above in addition to a modest general stock. Most of the books we saw were in quite good condition and were reasonably priced. The shop is easy to browse.

Booktraders
143 Lake Beaumaris Mall, 15333 Castledowns Road
Mailing address: 17 Kiniski Crescent Edmonton AB   T6L 5E3

Open Shop
(780) 472-1627

Collection: General stock of mostly paperback.
# of Vols: 10,000
Hours: Sun 12-5. Mon-Fri 10-9. Sat 10-5.

Booktraders
Abbotsfield Mall, 32nd Street & 118th Avenue

Open Shop
(780) 414-0247

Collection: General stock of mostly paperback.
# of Vols: 10,000
Hours: Mon-Fri 10-9. Sat 10-5:30. Sun 12-5.

Booktraders
119 Millbourne Mall, 38th Avenue & Millwoods Road

Open Shop
(780) 463-9705

Collection: General stock of mostly paperback.
# of Vols: 10,000
Hours: Sun 12-5. Mon-Fri 9:30-9. Sat 9:30-5:30. Sun 12-5.

Buffalo Book Shop   **By Appointment**
10232 Wadhurst Road T5N 3V1   (780) 454-4329
                                                   Fax: (780) 453-1413
                                    E-mail: donwilliams@powersurfr.com

Collection:	Specialty
# of Vols:	10,000
Specialties:	Canadiana
Services:	Accepts want lists, mail order.
Credit Cards:	Yes
Owner:	Don Williams
Year Estab:	1948

Edmonton Book Store   **Open Shop**
11216–76th Avenue T6G 0K1   (780) 433-1781
Web page: www.compusmart.ab.ca/ebs/   Fax: (780) 433-4569
                                      E-mail: ebs@compusmart.ab.ca

Collection:	General stock of mostly hardcover.
# of Vols:	50,000
Specialties:	Canadiana
Hours:	Mon-Sat 10-6. Sun 12-5.
Services:	Appraisals, search service, mail order.
Travel:	From Hwy 16, turn south on 109th St, west (right) on 76th Ave. Shop is at 112th St.
Credit Cards:	Yes
Owner:	Barbara Ellis
Year Estab:	1978
Comments:	A modest sized shop with an attractive selection of hardcover books and a more modest collection of paperbacks (trade and mass market) intershelved. Most of the books we saw were in quite good condition, sported dust jackets and appeared to be of more recent vintage. There are lots of alcoves, each with its own labeled specialty. Our guess is that at the time of our visit, there were slightly fewer books on display than the number indicated above.

Isis Metaphysical Books & Merchandise   **Open Shop**
8217–104th Street T6E 4E7   (780) 433-9373

Collection:	Specialty. Mostly new and some used.
Specialties:	Metaphysics
Hours:	Mon-Sat 10-10. Sun 11-7.
Travel:	North of Whyte (82nd Ave).

The Jim Corbett Foundation   **Mail Order**
1306–39th Street T6L 2M7   (780) 463-8773
Web page: www.maxpages.com/safaribooks   E-mail: safaribooks@webtv.net

Collection:	Specialty used and new.
# of Vols:	2,500
Specialties:	Big game hunting; travel.

(Edmonton)

Services:	Catalog
Credit Cards:	Yes
Owner:	Jerry Jaleel
Year Estab:	1979
Comments:	Stock is approximately 70% used and out-of-print.

Second Fiddle Books   **Open Shop**
10918–88th Avenue T6G 0Z1   (780) 433-3868
                                                    Fax: (780) 431-1349
                                        E-mail: hunox@telusplanet.net

Collection:	General stock of mostly used paperback and hardcover.
# of Vols:	13,000
Specialties:	Literature; philosophy; history; Canadiana; metaphysics.
Hours:	Daily 10-10.
Services:	Search service, accepts want lists, mail order.
Travel:	From Calgary Trail (Hwy 2/103rd St), turn west on Whyte, right on 109th St, left on 87th Ave and immediate right into lane between 109th & 110th Streets. Store is just ahead.
Credit Cards:	Yes
Owner:	Chris & Kate
Year Estab:	1992
Comments:	Stock is approximately 70% paperback.

St. Joseph & The Angels Emporium   **Open Shop**
10981–127th Street T5M 0T1   (780) 496-7720
                                                    Fax: (780) 496-7721

Collection:	Specialty used and new.
# of Vols:	25,000
Specialties:	Religion (Catholic)
Hours:	Mon-Sat 9-5.
Services:	Search service, accepts want lists, mail order.
Travel:	107th St exit off Hwy 2. Proceed east on 107th Ave then north on 127th St to 109th Ave.
Credit Cards:	Yes
Owner:	Janet Maclellan
Year Estab:	1995
Comments:	Stock is approximately 75% used, 60% of which is hardcover.

Wee Book Inn #1 (Head Office)   **Open Shop**
10310–82nd Avenue T6E 1Z8   (780) 432-7230
                                                    Fax: (780) 439-0641

Collection:	General stock of paperback and hardcover, CDs and videos.
# of Vols:	23,000
Hours:	Daily 9am-midnight.
Services:	Search service, accepts want lists, mail order.

Travel:	Between 103rd and 104th Sts.
Credit Cards:	Yes
Year Estab:	1971
Comments:	Two stores in one. On the street level, one finds an attractive array of mostly colorful "picture" books and the like displayed along the side walls and a quite heavy concentration of paperbacks and comics taking up most of the center space as well as some of the shelves along the side walls. Hardcover volumes are displayed on the very top shelves almost giving one the impression that they lack importance. One flight up, however, the shop does maintain a collection of hardcover volumes in mixed condition. Most were older. Some sets. Quite frankly, though there may well be some winners here, it would take a lot of patient hunting to find them.

Wee Book Inn #2   **Open Shop**
15103A Stony Plain Road T5P 3Y2   (780) 489-0747
Fax: (780) 439-0641

Collection:	General stock of paperback and hardcover, CDs and videos.
# of Vols:	17,000
Hours:	Daily 9am-midnight.
Services:	Appraisals, search service, accepts want lists, mail order.
Travel:	Eastbound on Hwy 16, turn south on 170th St then right on 100th Ave, left on 150th St and right on Stony Plain Rd.
Credit Cards:	Yes

Wee Book Inn #3   **Open Shop**
10428 Jasper Avenue T5J 1Z3   (780) 423-1434
Fax: (780) 439-0641

Collection:	General stock of paperback and hardcover, CDs and videos.
# of Vols:	11,000
Hours:	Daily 9am-midnight.
Services:	Appraisals, search service, accepts want lists, mail order.
Travel:	From Hwy 2/103rd St northbound, turn right on Saskatchewan Dr, then left on Queen Elizabeth Hill. At bottom of hill, turn right on105th St. Take left fork after bridge and turn right on 101st Avenue (Jasper Ave). Parking is available in rear.
Credit Cards:	Yes

Wee Book Inn #4   **Open Shop**
8101–118th Avenue T5B 0R9   (780) 474-7888
Fax: (780) 439-0641

Collection:	General stock of paperback and hardcover, CDs and videos.
# of Vols:	20,000
Hours:	Daily 9am-midnight.
Travel:	Westbound on Hwy 16, turn left on 66th St and right on 118th Ave.
Credit Cards:	Yes

Fort Saskatchewan

Cover To Cover Books   **Open Shop**
9833–104th Street T8L 2E5   (403) 992-1328

Collection: General stock of mostly paperback.
# of Vols: 5,000
Hours: Mon-Fri 9:30-5:30. Sat 9:30-4.

Grand Prairie

Wide Choice Books   **Open Shop**
9924A–100th Avenue T8V 0T9   (403) 539-5622

Collection: General stock of mostly used paperback.
# of Vols: 10,000 (used)
Hours: Mon-Wed 9:30-6. Thu & Fri 9:30-9. Sat 9:30-6.

Leduc

The Bookshop   **Open Shop**
Bay 2 6107–50th Street T9E 7A3   (403) 986-8106

Collection: General stock of mostly paperback.
Hours: Mon-Fri 9-5:30. Sat 9-5.

Lethbridge

Adams Book Corner   **Open Shop**
318–5th Street South T1J 2B5   (403) 320-9131

Collection: General stock of mostly paperback.
# of Vols: 50,000
Hours: Mon-Sat 10-6. Sun 1-5.

David Armstrong, Bookseller   **Mail Order**
PO Box 551 T1J 3Z4   (403) 381-3270
Web page: www.telusplanet.net/public/dabooks   E-mail: dabooks@telusplanet.net

Collection: Specialty books and ephemera.
# of Vols: 2,500
Specialties: Canadiana, especially Alberta; literary first editions, especially Cana-
                  dian.
Services: Appraisals, catalog.
Credit Cards: No
Year Estab: 1996

The Bookcase   **Open Shop**
425–13th Street North T1H 2S3   (403) 320-2262

Collection: General stock of mostly paperback.
# of Vols: 20,000+
Hours: Mon-Sat 10-5:30.

Mayerthorpe

A and M Enterprises   **Open Shop**
4909–50th Street T0E 1N0   (780) 786-4898

Collection: General stock of mostly paperback.
# of Vols: 9,000
Hours: Mon-Fri 9:30-6. Sat 9:30-noon.

Medicine Hat

Robert Block Rare Books   **Mail Order**
334–1st Avenue SE T1A 0A6   (403) 527-8697
                                    E-mail: bobblock@telusplanet.net

Collection: Specialty books and ephemera.
# of Vols: 1,000
Specialties: 19th century English literature; illustrated; fine press; Canadiana.
Services: Appraisals, accepts want lists.
Credit Cards: No
Year Estab: 1984

Mad Hatter Bookstore   **Open Shop**
399 Aberdeen Street SE T1A 0R3   (403) 526-8563

Collection: General stock of paperback and hardcover.
# of Vols: 30,000
Specialties: Comics (collectible)
Hours: Mon-Fri 9:30-5:30. Sat 9:30-5.
Services: Search service, accepts want lists, mail order.
Travel: 1st St SW exit off Hwy 1. Proceed east on 1st St, then right on 5th Ave
                 SE and right on Aberdeen.
Credit Cards: No
Owner: Kathleen Kisinger
Year Estab: 1976
Comments: Stock is approximately 60% paperback.

The Post   **Open Shop**
410 South Railway Street SE T1A 2V5   (403) 526-5677

Collection: General stock of mostly paperback.
Hours: Mon-Sat 10-5.

Reader's Bookshop   **Open Shop**
320 3201–13th Avenue SE T1B 1E2   (403) 528-9474

Collection: General stock of mostly paperback.
# of Vols: 5,000
Hours: Mon-Fri 9:30-9. Sat 10-7. Sun 12-5.

The Reading Room   **Open Shop**
411 North Railway St SE T1A 2Z3   (403) 528-4423

Collection: General stock of mostly paperback.
# of Vols: 20,000
Hours: Tue-Sat 10-5.

Tramp's Music Comics & Games   **Open Shop**
601–2nd Street SE T1A 0C8   (403) 528-8977

Collection: General stock of mostly paperback.
Hours: Mon, Tue, Sat 10-6. Wed-Fri 10-9. Sun 12-5.

Woody's Book Shack   **Open Shop**
669–2nd Street SE T1A 0C8   (403) 527-8094

Collection: General stock of mostly paperback.
# of Vols: 35,000
Hours: Mon-Sat 9:30-5.

Okotoks

Care A Lot Used Books   **Open Shop**
Front 20 McRae Street T0L 1T3   (403) 938-8116

Collection: General stock of mostly paperback.
Hours: Mon & Tue 10-5. Wed 10-8. Thu-Sat 10-5.

Ponoka

Readers Emporium   **Open Shop**
5018–50th Avenue   (403) 783-5511
Mailing address: PO Box 4280 Ponoka AB T4J 1R7

Collection: General stock of paperback and hardcover.
# of Vols: 40,000
Hours: Tue-Sat 10-6.
Services: Search service, accepts want lists, mail order.
Travel: In heart of downtown.
Credit Cards: No
Owner: Bruce Whyte
Year Estab: 1996
Comments: Stock is approximately 70% paperback.

Red Deer

Bookworm's Den   **Open Shop**
5003 Ross Street T4N 1Y2   (403) 346-7505

Collection: General stock of paperback and hardcover.
# of Vols: 5,000

Hours:	Mon-Sat 10:30-5:30.
Travel:	Gaetz Ave exit off Hwy 2. Proceed north on Gaetz then west on Ross.
Year Estab:	1979
Comments:	Stock is approximately 75% paperback.

Red Deer Book Exchange   **Open Shop**
15 6791–50th Avenue T4N 4C9   Tel & Fax: (403) 342-4883

Collection:	General stock of mostly paperback.
Hours:	Mon-Sat 9:30-6, except Wed & Sat to 5.

St. Albert

Keyword Books   **Open Shop**
31A Perron Street T8N 1E6   (780) 458-0565

Collection:	General stock of paperback and hardcover.
# of Vols:	5,000-10,000
Hours:	Tue-Fri 11-7. Sat 11-6.
Travel:	From Hwy 2 in St. Albert, proceed west on St. Anne St then north on Perron.
Credit Cards:	No
Owner:	Michael F. Keyes
Year Estab:	1998
Comments:	Stock is approximately 65% paperback.

Sherwood Park

Recollections Books & Art   **Open Shop**
14 140 Athabascan Avenue T8A 4E3   (403) 464-5522

Collection:	General stock of mostly paperback.
# of Vols:	10,000+
Hours:	Mon-Fri 10-6, except Thu till 8. Sat 10-5.

Spirit River

Beth's Books   **Open Shop**
Spirit River Mall   (403) 864-4515
On Highway 49 & Main Street T0H 3G0

Collection:	General stock of mostly paperback used and new.
# of Vols:	5,000-6,000 (used)
Hours:	Mon-Sat 9:30-5:30.

Spruce Grove

Bookworm Not So Used Books   **Open Shop**
Box 8, King Street Mall T7X 2C7   (403) 962-9686

Collection:	General stock of mostly paperback.
# of Vols:	10,000
Hours:	Mon-Wed 9:30-6. Thu & Fri 9:30-9. Sat 9:30-5:30.

Taber

Never Ending Stories   **Open Shop**
5304–48th Avenue T1G 1S2   (403) 223-0073

Collection: General stock of paperback and hardcover.
# of Vols: 16,000
Hours: Mon-Sat 9-6, except Fri till 9.
Travel: From Hwy 3, turn north on 50th St then right on 48th Ave.
Comments: Stock is approximately 65% paperback.

Vulcan

D & S Books & Cards   **Open Shop**
131 Centre Street T0L 2B0   (403) 485-6544

Collection: General stock of mostly paperback.
# of Vols: 2,000
Hours: Mon-Fri 10-5. Sat 10-4.

Wetaskiwin

Marianne's Book & Craft   **Open Shop**
5208–50th Avenue T9A 0S8   (403) 352-7994

Collection: General stock of mostly paperback used and new.
# of Vols: 5,000-10,000 (used)
Hours: Mon-Wed, Sat 9-6. Thu & Fri 9-8.

British Columbia

Alphabetical Listing By Dealer

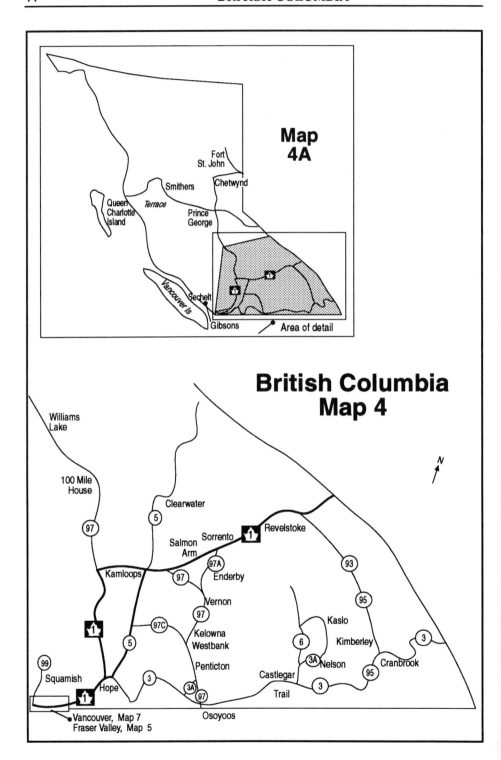

Map
4A

Fort
St. John

Chetwynd

Smithers

Queen
Charlotte
Island

Terrace

Prince
George

Vancouver Is

Sechelt

Gibsons

Area of detail

**British Columbia
Map 4**

Williams
Lake

100 Mile
House

Clearwater

97

5

Sorrento

Revelstoke

Salmon
Arm

N

97A

93

97

Enderby

Kamloops

Vernon

97

95

97C

Kaslo

Kelowna
Westbank

6

Kimberley

3

Penticton

3A

Nelson

Cranbrook

99

Castlegar

95

Squamish

3

Trail

3

Hope

5

3A

97

Vancouver, Map 7
Fraser Valley, Map 5

Osoyoos

Alphabetical Listing By Location

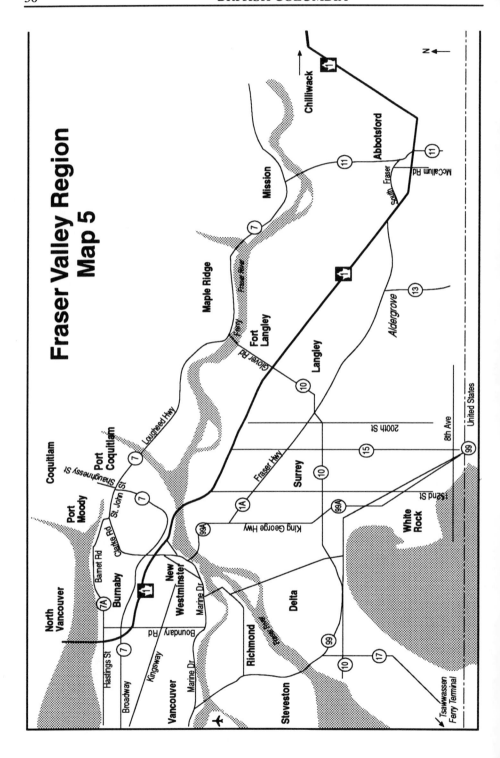

Fraser Valley Region
Map 5

Abbotsford
(Map 5, page 50)

The Book Barrel   **Open Shop**
102 2790 Gladwin Street V2T 4S3   (604) 859-2828

Collection: General stock of mostly paperback.
# of Vols: 10,000
Hours: Mon-Sat 10-5:30.

Hemingway's Used Books   **Open Shop**
33765 Essendene Avenue V2S 2H1   (604) 855-1894

Collection: General stock of mostly used paperback and hardcover.
# of Vols: 55,000-60,000
Specialties: Canadiana; British Columbia; Native Americans; military; sci fi.
Hours: Mon-Fri 10-5:30. Sat 10-5. Sun 12-4. Holidays 12-4.
Travel: Exit 90 (McCallum) off Hwy 1. Proceed north on McCallum then right
                   on Essendene. Parking is available in rear.
Credit Cards: No
Owner: Zee & Gerry Rogers
Year Estab: 1992
Comments: The shop stocks a healthy supply of paperbacks along with a more
                   modest selection of hardcover volumes, some shelved above the paper-
                   backs in the same subject category and others, e.g., fiction, where more
                   titles are available, shelved separately. The books we saw were of
                   mixed vintage and in mixed condition. The shop also sells magazines,
                   sports cards, CDs, cassettes and a variety of non book collectibles.

Spirit & Nature Book Store   **Open Shop**
109 32868 Ventura Avenue V2S 6J3   (604) 864-8581

Collection: General collection of hardcover and paperback.
# of Vols: 13,000
Specialties: Religion; literature; health and self help.
Hours: Tue-Sat 10-6.
Travel: Exit 90 (McCallum) off Hwy 1. Proceed north on McCallum then left
                   on S. Fraser Way, right on Bourquin and left on Ventura.
Credit Cards: Yes
Owner: Wayne Garside
Year Estab: 1993
Comments: Stock is evenly divided between hardcover and paperback.

Aldergrove
(Map 5, page 50)

Anthill Books   **By Appointment**
6775–258th Street V4W 1V3   (604) 856-8088

Collection: General stock of mostly hardcover.
# of Vols: 12,000

Specialties:	Mostly vintage material, including E.R. Burroughs; pulps; magazines; vintage paperbacks; newspaper comics.
Services:	Accepts want lists, mail order.
Credit Cards:	No
Owner:	Nels Myrhoj
Year Estab:	1995

Black Creek
(Map 6, page 61)

Rainy Day Books   **Open Shop**
8268 North Island Highway   (250) 337-1806
Mailing address: RR 5, Site 510 C-31, Comox BC V9N 8B5   Fax: (250) 337-8185
                                              E-mail: ruth-dilts@hotmail.com

Collection:	General stock of mostly paperback.
# of Vols:	8,000
Hours:	Jul & Aug: Daily 10-5. Remainder of year: Tue-Sat 10-5.

Brentwood Bay
(Map 6, page 61)

Pages Used Books   **Open Shop**
1205A Verdier Avenue   (250) 652-4341
Mailing address: 6798 Jedora Drive Brentwood Bay BC V8M 1A6

Collection:	General stock of mostly paperback.
# of Vols:	25,00+
Hours:	Mon-Fri 11-5. Sat 10-5.

Burnaby
(Map 7, page 85 & Map 5, page 50)

Brown's Books   **Open Shop**
3740 East Hastings Street V5C 2H5   Tel & Fax: (604) 294-9311
                                              E-mail: rdavidb@direct.ca

Collection:	Specialty with limited general stock.
# of Vols:	30,000
Specialties:	Mystery; business; self knowledge.
Hours:	Tue-Fri 10-5:30. Sat 10-5. Sun 12-5.
Services:	Search service, accepts want lists, mail order.
Travel:	Hastings St exit off Hwy 1. Proceed east on Hastings for about 10 blocks.
Owner:	Roger Brown
Comments:	Approximately 75% of stock is devoted to mystery, from early first editions to paperbacks.

Burnaby Books   **Open Shop**
4435 East Hastings Street V5C 2K1   (604) 298-0038

Collection:	General stock of hardcover and paperback.
# of Vols:	60,000
Specialties:	Science fiction; literature.

Hours:	Mon-Sat 10-6, except Fri till 9. Sun 12:30-5:30.
Services:	Accepts want lists, mail order.
Travel:	Hastings St exit off Hwy 1. Proceed east on Hastings for about 1½ km. Shop is on the left, just after Rosser.
Credit Cards:	Yes
Owner:	Gerard Knapp
Year Estab:	1983
Comments:	We wish we could have viewed more of the books in this shop as there certainly were a sufficient number of interesting and varied hardcover titles worth more careful examination. Unfortunately though, in order to display more books, several tables with paperbacks were laid out in such a way as to create very narrow aisles making it difficult (but not impossible) to view all of the titles comfortably. If you have the time and the agility, you might be pleased with your visit here.

Campbell River
(Map 6, page 61)

Book Bonanza   **Open Shop**
968 Shoppers Row   V9W 6K6   (250) 287-3212

Collection:	General stock of mostly used paperback.
Hours:	Daily 9:30-5:30, except Fri till 9.

Willow Point Used Books   **Open Shop**
2116F South Island Highway   V9W 1C1   (250) 923-5121

Collection:	General stock of mostly paperback.
# of Vols:	24,000
Hours:	Mon-Sat 10-5.

Castlegar
(Map 4, page 44)

Books & Music   **Open Shop**
1114–3rd Street   V0G 1X0   (250) 365-3399

Collection:	General stock of hardcover and paperback.
# of Vols:	20,000
Hours:	Mon-Sat 9:30-5:30. Sun 11-4.
Travel:	Proceeding east on Hwy 3, turn north on Columbia and right on 3rd St.
Credit Cards:	No
Owner:	Alexander Nicol
Year Estab:	1991
Comments:	Stock is evenly mixed between hardcover and paperback.

Jacquie Hamilton   **Mail Order**
2185 Crestview Crescent   V1N 3B4   (250)-365-8026
Web page: www.abebooks.com/home/JAHAM

E-mail: jahamilt@wkpowerlink.com

Collection:	General collection.
Year Estab:	1997

Cedar
(Map 6, page 61)

Neon Cactus Used Books   **Open Shop**
1694B Cedar Road   (250) 722-0036
Mailing address: PO Box 284 Cedar BC V9X 1W1

Collection: General stock of mostly paperback.
# of Vols: 5,000
Hours: Tue-Sat 12-5.

Chetwynd
(Map 4A, page 44)

Encore Books   **Open Shop**
101 5000 N Access V0C 1J0   (250) 788-3135
Mailing address: 9911–100th Avenue Fort St. John BC V1J 1Y4

Collection: General stock of mostly paperback.
Hours: Mon, Wed, Fri 11-3.

Chilliwack
(Map 5, page 50)

The Book Man   **Open Shop**
45939 Wellington Avenue V2P 2C6   (604) 792-4595
Web page: www.cyberpage.com/bookman/

Collection: General stock of hardcover and paperback.
# of Vols: 500,000
Hours: Mon-Wed 9:30-7. Thu & Fri 9:30-8. Sat 9:30-5:30. Sun 10-5.
Services: Mail order.
Travel: Eastbound on Hwy 1: Chilliwack airport exit off Hwy 1. Proceed east
                   on Yale, right on Princess and left on Young. At next set of lights (five
                   corners intersection) turn left on Wellington. Shop is 1/2 block ahead
                   on right. Westbound on Hwy 1: Young Rd exit. Proceed north on
                   Young, then left on Wellington.
Credit Cards: Yes
Owner: David Short
Year Estab: 1980's
Comments: While we did not count every book in the shop, we certainly believe
                   that the number of volumes quoted above is accurate. The books are
                   very well organized, the shop is easy to browse and hardcover volumes
                   are available in sufficient number. The majority of the books are of
                   fairly recent vintage but there are several shelves labeled "antique
                   books." We always feel good about shops when we make a purchase
                   and in this shop we made four. Book hunters with broad interests
                   should enjoy visiting this shop. If your interests are more specialized,
                   you might want to call ahead to see if the owner carries titles in your
                   field. In addition to its books, the shop also sells magazines and records.

Clearwater
(Map 4, page 44)

Second Story Bookstore & Bistro   **Open Shop**
117 Clearwater Station Road V0E 1N0   (250) 674-2785
                                          E-mail: kpopiel@hotmail.com

Collection:	General stock of mostly paperback.
# of Vols:	20,000
Hours:	Mon-Sat 10-6.

Comox
(Map 6, page 61)

Nearly New Books   **Open Shop**
214 Port Augusta Street V9M 3N1   (250) 339-1278

Collection:	General stock of mostly paperback.
# of Vols:	9,000
Hours:	Mon-Sat 9:30-5:30, except Fri till 9. Sun 12-5.

Coombs
(Map 6, page 61)

Coombs Books   **Open Shop**
Highway 4

Collection:	General stock of paperback and hardcover.
Hours:	May 24-Sept 15: Daily 10-5. (Hours may vary with traffic.)
Travel:	Located on Hwy 4.

Coquitlam
(Map 5, page 50)

Burquitlam Books   **Open Shop**
552C Clarke Road V3J 3X5   (604) 939-6366

Collection:	General stock of mostly paperback.
# of Vols:	17,000
Hours:	Mon-Sat 10-6, except Fri till 7.
Travel:	Hwy 7 exit off Hwy 1. Proceed west on Hwy 7, then right on North Rd (which becomes Clarke) for about four km. Shop is in Burquitlam Plaza on the right.
Credit Cards:	Yes
Owner:	Jo-Anne Sexton & George McLaughlin
Year Estab:	1970
Comments:	We had to look very carefully to find the hardcover volumes in this shop; there were a few. Who knows. Perhaps even the very ones you've been looking for. Most of the stock however can be described as paperback and trade paperback.

Peartree Books   **Open Shop**
500 Marmont Street V3J 7C7   (604) 936-0096
                                                   E-mail: peartree20@aol.com
Collection: General stock of paperback and hardcover.
# of Vols: 70,000
Hours: Tue-Thu 10-6. Fri 10-8. Sat 10-6.
Travel: Malardville exit off Hwy 1. Proceed north on Malardville, then con-
                   tinue north on Marmont. Shop is at corner of Marmont and Austin.
Credit Cards: No
Owner: Mike Poirier
Year Estab: 1998
Comments: Stock is approximately 70% paperback.

Reflections   **Open Shop**
1111D Austin Avenue V3K 3P4   (604) 939-6000
Collection: General stock of mostly new and some used.
# of Vols: 1,000 (used)
Hours: Mon-Thu 10-5:30. Fri 10-8. Sat 10-5:30. Sun 11-5.
Comments: Used stock is approximately 70% paperback.

Courtenay
(Map 6, page 61)

ABC Books   **Open Shop**
324 Fifth Street V9N 1J9   (250) 334-4888
Collection: General stock of mostly used and new paperback.
# of Vols: 10,000 (used)
Hours: Mon-Sat 9:30-5:30, except Fri till 9. Sun 12-5.
Comments: Stock is 75% used, 90% of which is paperback.

Rainforest Books & Stuff   **Open Shop**
1999 Lake Trail Road V9N 9C3   (250) 334-3016
Collection: General stock of hardcover and paperback.
# of Vols: 5,000
Hours: Mon-Fri 9:30-5. Occasional Saturdays.
Travel: From Island Hwy (Hwy 19), proceed west on 17th St, then right on
                   Willimar and left on Lake Trail.
Credit Cards: No
Year Estab: 1996
Comments: Stock is evenly divided between hardcover and paperback.

Second Page Books   **Open Shop**
546 Duncan Avenue V9N 5M7   (250) 338-1144
Collection: General stock of paperback and hardcover.
# of Vols: 3,000+
Hours: Mon-Sat 9:30-5.
Travel: One block off Island Hwy, between 5th & 6th Streets.
Credit Cards: No

Year Estab: 1969
Comments: Stock is approximately 70% paperback.

Cranbrook
(Map 4, page 44)

Pages Book Emporium   **Open Shop**
1011 Baker Street V1C 1A6   (250) 489-3262
Fax: (250) 489-4758

Collection: General stock of new and mostly paperback used, comics, magazines and newspapers.
# of Vols: 20,000
Hours: Mon-Sat 9-5:30, except Fri till 7.
Travel: From Hwy 93, turn south at 9th Ave connector. Proceed one block then left on Baker. From Hwy 95, turn right on 9th Ave connector if north-bound (left if southbound), then left on Baker.
Owner: Doug & Val Pepper
Year Estab: 1981
Comments: We're certain that the folks in this community take advantage of the large number of paperback books as well as the new magazines and newspapers sold at this location. We spotted somewhat fewer than 1,000 hardcover volumes, most of which were reading copies of fairly recent vintage.

Creston

Holly Pender-Love Books   **Mail Order**
516–10th Avenue North   (250) 428-7855
Mailing address: Box 736 Porthill Idaho 83853   Fax: (250) 428-7859
Web page: www.abebooks.com/home/hollypenderlove
E-mail: pepper_71@hotmail.com

Collection: General stock.
# of Vols: 500
Services: Accepts want lists, search service.
Credit Cards: No
Year Estab: 1995

Delta
(Map 5, page 50)

Ainsworth Books   **Mail Order**
PO Box 411 V4E 2A9   (604) 543-7587
Web page: www.abebooks.com/home/ainsworth   E-mail: ainsworth@dowco.com

Collection: General stock.
# of Vols: 6,000
Services: Appraisals, search service, lists by request, accepts want lists.
Credit Cards: Yes
Owner: Betty Kilner
Year Estab: 1939

Bryan's Bookstore   **Open Shop**
5068–48th Avenue V4K 1V8   (604) 946-2678

Collection:	General stock of mostly paperback.
# of Vols:	25,000
Hours:	Mon-Fri 9:30-5:30. Sat 9:30-5.

Denman Island
(Map 6, page 61)

Abraxas Books & Gifts   **Open Shop**
1071 Northwest Road   (250) 335-0433
Mailing address: PO Box 27 Denman Island BC V0R 1T0

Collection:	General stock of mostly new and some used.
Hours:	Mon-Fri 9-5. Sat 10-5. Call for summer Sun hours.
Owner:	Corinne Bjorge & Shaun Woods
Comments:	Small selection of used books, evenly divided between hardcover and paperback.

Duncan
(Map 6, page 61)

Gallowglass Books   **Open Shop**
40 Ingram Street V9L 1N7   (250) 746-4104
Web page: www.gallowglassbooks.com   Fax: (250) 746-4108
                                                   E-mail: gallow@islandnet.com

Collection:	General stock of hardcover.
# of Vols:	20,000
Specialties:	Canadian history; military.
Hours:	Mon-Sat 10-5.
Services:	Search service, accepts want lists, mail order.
Travel:	Trunk Rd exit off Hwy 1 (Island Hwy). Proceed west on Trunk, right on Canada and left on Ingram.
Credit Cards:	Yes
Owner:	Jeff Downie
Year Estab:	1984
Comments:	A spacious shop with books that appear to be uniformly selected for their good to better condition. The shop is easy to browse and the collection offers coverage in most subject areas. Strong in history but not a slouch in some of the more popular areas. Reasonably priced.

Ulla's Bookshop   **Open Shop**
193 Station Street V9L 1M8   (250) 715-1383
                                                          Fax: (250) 746-5372
                                                   E-mail: ravenma@hotmail.com

Collection:	General stock of hardcover and paperback and some ephemera.
# of Vols:	12,000
Hours:	Mon-Sat 10:30-5:30, except Fri till 7:30. Sun by chance.
Services:	Accepts want lists, mail order.

Travel:	Trunk Rd exit off Hwy 1 (Island Hwy). Proceed west on Trunk, then right on Jubilee. Shop is at corner of Station St and Jubilee.
Credit Cards:	Yes
Owner:	Ulla Coulson
Year Estab:	1997
Comments:	Whether or not you make a purchase here (as we did), unless you're impervious to the charm of a well organized bookstore that offers attractive volumes representing many areas of interest and in generally quite good condition at reasonable prices, you should enjoy your visit here.

Enderby
(Map 4, page 44)

Wind Dancer Books   **Open Shop**
706 George Street V0E 1V0   (250) 838-0044

Collection:	General stock of hardcover and paperback.
# of Vols:	6,000-10,000
Hours:	Mon-Sat 9-5.
Travel:	On Hwy 97B.
Credit Cards:	Yes
Owner:	Ed & Jade Varchol
Year Estab:	1997
Comments:	Stock is evenly divided between hardcover and paperback.

Fort Langley
(Map 5, page 50)

Heritage Used Bookstore   **Open Shop**
23295 Mavis Avenue V1M 2S5   (604) 888-8422

At presstime, the store was in the process of being sold and its future was uncertain. (If the store continues in business, it may change its name.) Readers are advised to call the above number before traveling to Fort Langley and/or check with telephone information for a new listing.

Fort St. John
(Map 4A, page 44)

Bill's Books & Bargains   **Open Shop**
9911–100th Avenue V1J 1Y4   (250) 785-2660

Collection:	General stock of mostly paperback.
# of Vols:	60,000+
Hours:	Mon-Sat 11-6.

Encore Books   **Open Shop**
9828–98A Avenue V1J 1S2   (250) 787-0020

Collection:	General stock of mostly paperback.
# of Vols:	21,000
Hours:	Mon-Sat 10-6.

Gabriola

Neil Aitken   **Mail Order**
PO Box 178   V0R 1X0   (250) 247-8685
Web page: www.abebooks.com/home/fogbound   Fax:(250) 247-8116
                                                        E-mail: aitkenn@nanaimo.ark.com

Collection: Specialty. Mostly used.
# of Vols: 1,000
Specialties: Books about books; book arts.
Services: Appraisals, search service, accepts want lists.
Credit Cards: No
Year Estab: 1997

Galiano Island
(Map 6, page 61)

Galiano Island Books   **Open Shop**
76 Madrona Drive V0N 1P0   (250) 539-3340

Collection: General stock of mostly new and some used.
# of Vols: 600 (used)
Hours: Mon-Thu 10-5. Fri-Sun 10-6.

Ganges
(Map 6, page 61)

Brook's Books   **Open Shop**
At Mouat's Mall, 106 Fulford-Ganges Rd.   (250) 537-9874
Mailing address: PO Box 287, Ganges PO, Salt Spring Island BC V8K 2V9

Collection: General stock of hardcover and paperback.
# of Vols: 2,500
Specialties: Women's studies.
Hours: Tue-Sat 10-5.
Services: Accepts want lists, mail order.
Travel: Located on Salt Spring Island. Fulford-Ganges Rd is the island's main
                   road. Turn right at the end of the road. The shop is on the lower level of
                   the mall.
Credit Cards: Yes
Owner: Brook B. Holdack
Year Estab: 1992

Gibsons
(Map 4A, page 44)

Hidden Treasure Used Books   **Open Shop**
459 Marine Drive   (604) 886-7129
Mailing address: RR 5, Site 15, Compartment 26 Gibsons   V0N 1V0

Collection: General stock of mostly paperback.
# of Vols: 10,000
Hours: Oct-Apr: Daily 11-3. May-Sept: Daily 11-4.

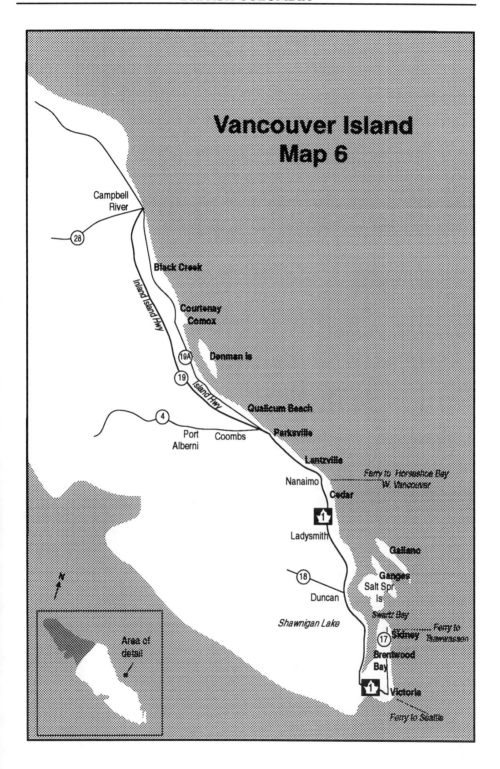

Vancouver Island
Map 6

Campbell
River

28

Black Creek

Inland Island Hwy

Courtenay
Comox

19A Denman Is

19

Island Hwy

Qualicum Beach

4

Port
Alberni

Coombs

Parksville

Lantzville

Ferry to Horseshoe Bay
W. Vancouver

Nanaimo

Cedar

1

Ladysmith

Galiano

18

Ganges

Salt Spr
Is

Duncan

Swartz Bay

Shawnigan Lake

17 Sidney

Ferry to
Tsawwassen

Brentwood
Bay

N

1 Victoria

Area of
detail

Ferry to Seattle

Hope
(Map 4, page 44)

Pages   **Open Shop**
4 895–3rd Avenue   (604) 869-9947
Mailing address: PO Box 2112 Hope BC V0X 1L0

Collection: General stock of mostly paperback.
# of Vols: 10,000
Hours: Tue-Sat 10-5.

Kamloops
(Map 4, page 44)

Avalon Used Books & Music   **Open Shop**
249 Tranquille Road V2B 3G1   (250) 376-7988
                                    E-mail: ptolman@wkpowerlink.com

Collection: General stock of paperback and hardcover.
# of Vols: 25,000
Hours: Mon-Sat 10-5.
Services: Accepts want lists.
Travel: Westbound on Hwy 1: City Centre exit. Bear right and at next fork
                 continue on Lansdown to Overlander Bridge to North Kamloops. At
                 end of bridge, turn right and take overpass onto Tranquille Rd. Shop is
                 three blocks ahead. Eastbound on Hwy 1: Summit Dr exit. Continue
                 downhill to Overlander Bridge and follow above directions.
Credit Cards: No
Owner: Pat Tolman
Year Estab: 1992
Comments: Quite a pleasant shop that offers the community a little bit of every-
                 thing. Heavy in paperbacks, the shop does have a modest number of
                 hardcover volumes, some quite recent and in attractive dust jackets,
                 and others older and representing another age. The shop also carries
                 magazines, cassettes, videos and other sundry items. If you have the
                 time, visit the owner's second shop in Kamloops (see Legends below).

Bainbridge Military Books   **Open Shop**
102 220 Third Avenue V2C 3M3   (250) 851-0416
                                                   Fax: (250) 851-0480

Collection: Specialty
# of Vols: 3,000
Specialties: Military
Hours: Tue-Fri 11-5. Other times by appointment.
Services: Appraisals, catalog, accepts want lists.
Travel: Kamloops exit off Hwy 5. Proceed east on Third Ave to Victoria.
Credit Cards: Yes
Owner: Charles Bainbridge
Year Estab: 1985

Legends Used Books
22 1415 Hillside Drive V2E 1A9

Open Shop
(250) 377-8793
Fax: (250) 579-9367
E-mail: ptolman@wkpowerlink.com

Collection:	General stock of paperback and hardcover.
# of Vols:	15,000
Travel:	Pacific Way exit off Hwy 5. Turn north onto Hillside and proceed 1/2 block, then left into parking lot of Hillside Plaza.
Credit Cards:	Yes
Owner:	Pat Tolman
Year Estab:	1999
Comments:	While we were not able to visit this shop, we were advised that its stock is similar to its sister store (see Avalon above) although with a somewhat larger selection of hardcover items.

Kaslo
(Map 4, page 44)

Onslow & Daisy's
420 A Avenue V0G 1M0

Open Shop
(250) 353-2992

Collection:	General stock of mostly paperback.
# of Vols:	2,000
Hours:	Mon-Fri 8:30-5:30. Sat 10-4.

Kelowna
(Map 4, page 44)

D & D Used Books
170 Highway 33 West V1X 1X7

Open Shop
(250) 765-3371

Collection:	General stock of mostly paperback.
# of Vols:	150,000
Hours:	Mon-Sat 10-5.
Services:	Accepts want lists, mail order.
Travel:	From Hwy 97, turn onto Hwy 33 south. Shop is about 4½ km ahead.
Owner:	Diane Felty
Year Estab:	1986
Comments:	A heavy concentration of paperbacks along with a variety of comic books, magazines (including *National Geographics*), puzzles, LPs and (our estimate) fewer than 1,000 hardcover volumes, many of a practical nature, e.g., auto repair.

First Try Books
426B Bernard Avenue V1Y 6N7

Open Shop
(250) 763-5364

Collection:	General stock of paperback and hardcover, videos and CDs.
# of Vols:	20,000
Hours:	Mon-Fri 9-7. Sat 11-7. Sun & Holidays 12-5.
Travel:	Three blocks north of Hwy 97, between Pandosy and Ellis.
Owner:	Wayne Blackley

Year Estab: 1994
Comments: Stock is approximately 70% paperback.

The Okanagan Bookman   **Open Shop**
2942 Pandosy Street V1Y 1V9   (250) 763-4567

Collection: General stock of hardcover and paperback.
# of Vols: 20,000
Specialties: Literature; military.
Hours: Mon-Sat 10-6. Sun 12-5.
Services: Occasional catalog, appraisals, mail order.
Travel: Pandosy exit off Hwy 97. Proceed east (away from City Centre) on Pandosy.
Credit Cards: Yes
Owner: Bob Ross
Year Estab: 1979
Comments: A modest sized shop with a mix of hardcover and paperback books.
                   Most of the hardcover volumes we saw were of mixed vintage and in
                   mixed condition. We spotted some interesting titles during our brief
                   visit and recognize that we might have missed some others. Indeed,
                   customers who were in the shop at the same time that we were made a
                   purchase and walked out with a smile.

Spellbound Books   **Open Shop**
2974 Pandosy Street V1Y 1W2   (250) 762-7078

Collection: General stock of mostly paperback.
# of Vols: 30,000 (used)
Hours: Mon-Sat 10-5.
Travel: See The Okanagan Bookman above.
Owner: Phyllis Turnell
Year Estab: 1981
Comments: Primarily paperbacks with fewer than 1,000 hardcover volumes of
                   mostly recent vintage.

Ted's Paperbacks & Comics   **Open Shop**
269 Leon Avenue V1Y 6J1   (250) 763-1258

Collection: General stock of mostly paperback.
# of Vols: 100,000
Hours: Mon-Sat 10-5.

Kimberley
(Map 4, page 44)

Bavarian Book Exchange & Gift Shop   **Open Shop**
375 St. Mary's Avenue   Tel & Fax: (250) 427-5165
Mailing address: 345 Deer Park Avenue Kimberley BC V1A 2J7
ww.cyberlink.bc.ca/~hankens   E-mail: hankens@cyberlink.bc.ca

Collection: General stock of paperback and hardcover.
# of Vols: 30,000
Specialties: Children's

Hours:	Tue-Sat 12-6. Closed January.
Services:	Search service, accepts want lists, mail order.
Travel:	Hwy 95A to downtown Kimberley. At traffic light, turn right and proceed one block, then right again. Shop is about 1/2 block ahead.
Credit Cards:	No
Owner:	Hanny Kensington
Year Estab:	1994
Comments:	Stock is approximately 70% paperback.

Owl & Teapot Gently Used Books **Open Shop**
1910 Warren Avenue V1A 1S3 Tel & Fa x: (250) 427-5579
Web page: http://catapault.com/kimberleybc/owlteapo.htm
E-mail: chmackz@rockies.net

Collection:	General stock of paperback and hardcover.
# of Vols:	10,000
Hours:	Tue-Sat 11-6. (Call for Sun & Mon hours.) Jul & Aug: Daily 11-6.
Services:	Search service, accepts want lists, mail order.
Travel:	From Hwy 95A southbound, turn left on Wallinger which becomes Warren.
Credit Cards:	Yes
Owner:	Heather Mackenzie
Year Estab:	1994
Comments:	A charming, easy to browse combination tea shop and bookstore located in a portion of the owner's home. The hardcover volumes were of generally mixed vintage and we spotted a few collectibles. As the collection lacks depth, if you're looking for something special, our suggestion is that you call to determine if the owner is likely to have it.

Ladysmith
(Map 6, page 61)

Fraser & Naylor, Booksellers **Open Shop**
535 First Avenue (250) 245-4726
Mailing address: PO Box 999 Ladysmith BC V0R 2E0 Fax: (250) 245-4786

Collection:	General stock of used paperback and hardcover and some new.
# of Vols:	5,000+
Hours:	Mon-Sat 9:30-5:30.
Services:	Search service, accepts want lists, mail order.
Travel:	From Island Hwy (Hwy 1), follow signs to downtown Ladysmith.
Credit Cards:	Yes
Owner:	Douglas Fraser & Shirley Naylor
Year Estab:	1994
Comments:	A relatively small shop that any small village would be happy to be home to. The shop offers new books as well as used paperbacks and even a few hardcover items but little that a traveling book person could not find elsewhere.

Langley
(Map 5, page 50)

Ambassador Discount Books   **Open Shop**
5490 Salt Lane V3A 5C7   (604) 534-2124

Collection:	General stock of paperback and hardcover.
# of Vols:	15,000
Hours:	Mon-Sat 10:30-5.
Travel:	200 St exit off Hwy 1. Proceed south on 200 St, then east on Fraser Hwy for about one km. Shop is on left in the one way street section.
Credit Cards:	No
Owner:	Mac & Geraldine Desmarais
Year Estab:	1992
Comments:	The majority of the books in this shop are paperback with a modest number of hardcover volumes, many of the "practical" and how-to categories. Some fiction and some serious titles, but hardly a sufficient number to attract serious book people.

The Bookworm   **Open Shop**
20473 Douglas Crescent V3A 4B6   (604) 533-7939

Collection:	General stock of mostly paperback.
# of Vols:	100,000
Hours:	Mon-Sat 10:30-5. Sun 12-4.
Travel:	200th St exit off Hwy 1. Proceed south on 200th St, left on Fraser Hwy, right on 204th St and left on Douglas Crescent.
Credit Cards:	No
Owner:	Terry Walsh
Year Estab:	1993
Comments:	This shop is primarily paperback with a table of hardcover fiction offered at $1.00 each and some additional hardcover practical and how-to titles scattered throughout. The shop also sells used jigsaw puzzles.

Lantzville
(Map 6, page 61)

The Bookworm Cafe   **Open Shop**
1 7221 Lantzville Road   (250) 390-4541
Mailing address: PO Box 27 Lantzville BC V0R 2H0

Collection:	General stock of mostly paperback.
# of Vols:	3,000
Hours:	Mon-Fri 8-4:30. Sat 9-4:30.

Maple Ridge
(Map 5, page 50)

Carolyn's Used Book Store   **Open Shop**
22441 Dewdney Trunk V2X 7X7   (604) 463-2122

Collection:	General stock of mostly paperback.

# of Vols:	40,000
Hours:	Mon-Sat 9:30-5:30. Sun 12-5.

Haney Books   **Open Shop**
22330 Dewdney Trunk Road V2X 3J2   (604) 467-4913

Collection:	General stock of mostly paperback.
# of Vols:	10,000+
Hours:	Tue-Sat 10-5:30, except Fri till 7. Sun 12-4.

Jensen's Bookcase   **Open Shop**
22367–119th Avenue V2X 2Z2   (604) 467-5595

Collection:	General stock of mostly paperback.
# of Vols:	28,000
Hours:	Mon-Sat 8:30-5.

Mission
(Map 5, page 50)

Murdoch's Bookshoppe   **Open Shop**
33078–1st Avenue V2V 1G3   (604) 826-9229
                                       E-mail: brian_murdoch@mindlink.bc.ca

Collection:	General stock of used and new hardcover and paperback.
# of Vols:	25,000
Specialties:	Canadiana; Canadian literature; military; World War II, native studies; literature.
Hours:	Tue-Sat 10-5. Extended hours during Christmas season.
Services:	Catalog, accepts want lists.
Travel:	Abbotsford exit off Hwy 1. Proceed north on Hwy 11 to Mission. Take first exit (City Centre) after the bridge crossing the Fraser River, then west on 1st Ave (Hwy 7). Shop is 3½ blocks ahead.
Credit Cards:	Yes
Owner:	Ann & Brian Murdoch
Year Estab:	1993
Comments:	A relatively small shop which displays a combination of new books, some remainders and used books, most in quite good condition. Most of the used books (located in a second room to the rear of the store) were of fairly recent vintage, although we did note a few older volumes. The books we saw were certainly well cared for and while the stock was modest in number, since the owner is always buying new material there may be books to your liking on the shelves when you arrive.

Nanaimo
(Map 6, page 61)

Arbutus Books   **Open Shop**
85A Nicol Street V9R 4S7   (250) 753-1036

Collection:	General stock of paperback and hardcover.
# of Vols:	5,000+

(Nanaimo)

Hours:	Mon 12-5. Tue-Sat 10-5, except Thu 11-5.
Travel:	From Victoria, continue north on Hwy 1 (Island Hwy) which becomes Nicol St.
Credit Cards:	No
Owner:	Neal Brown
Year Estab:	1993
Comments:	A small shop with mostly paperbacks and a limited number of hardcover volumes, the majority of which were reading copies.

Beaufort Book Exchange   **Open Shop**
11 1588 Boundary Crescent V9S 5K8   (250) 753-2622

Collection:	General stock of mostly paperback.
# of Vols:	20,000
Hours:	Mon-Fri 9-5. Sat 10-5. Sun occasionally.

Bestsellers   **Open Shop**
45 Commercial Street V9R 5G3   (250) 755-1222

Collection:	General stock of paperback and hardcover.
# of Vols:	5,000+
Hours:	Mon-Fri 9-5. Sat 10-5.
Travel:	See Bygone Books below.
Credit Cards:	Yes
Comments:	A few doors away from another bookseller, this shop offers a modest collection of paperbacks and hardcover volumes. If you have the time, you may want to stop by.

Bygone Books   **Open Shop**
35 Commercial Street V9R 5G3   (250) 741-1766
                                        E-mail: bygonebk@island.net

Collection:	General stock of mostly hardcover.
# of Vols:	20,000
Specialties:	Art; military; nautical; native studies; Canadiana.
Hours:	Mon-Sat 10-5.
Services:	Appraisals, accepts want lists, mail order.
Travel:	From Victoria: City Centre exit off Hwy 1, then right on Commercial St. Parking is available in rear. From ferry terminal: Proceed south on Hwy 1, then left on Comox Rd which becomes Front St, then Church, then Commercial.
Credit Cards:	Yes
Owner:	Joel Johnston
Year Estab:	1996
Comments:	A good sized shop with mostly hardcover books and some paperbacks in the rear. The shelves are well labeled and the shop is easy to browse. The books are in generally good condition. Many subjects covered. Worth visiting.

Castro & Cowan
Mail Order

2645 Ritten Road, RR #3 V9X 1W4

(250) 722-3688

Web page: www.abebooks.com/homecastrocowan

E-mail: mcastro@direct.ca

Collection:	General stock.
# of Vols:	3,000-5,000
Owner:	Maria Castro & Bruce Cowan

Good Old Book Exchange
Open Shop

34 1150 Terminal North V9S 5L6

(250) 754-6121

Collection:	General stock of paperback and hardcover.
# of Vols:	10,000
Hours:	Mon-Fri 9-8. Sat 9-5. Sun 11-5.
Travel:	On Hwy 1, in Terminal Park Mall, north of City Centre.
Credit Cards:	Yes
Year Estab:	1984
Comments:	Stock is approximately 70% paperback.

Island Trains & Hobbies
Open Shop

4176 Departure Bay V9T 4B7

(250) 756-9441

E-mail: island_trains@bc.sympatico.ca

Collection:	Specialty new and used.
Specialties:	Railroads; military; photography.
Hours:	Mon-Sat 10-6, except Thu & Fri till 8. Sun 12-5.
Travel:	From Hwy 1, turn east on Norwell Dr then right at next light onto Departure Bay.
Credit Cards:	Yes
Owner:	Michael Kocot
Year Estab:	1996
Comments:	Stock is evenly divided between new and used.

J & D Jelley
Mail Order

6136 Janelle Place V9V 1M7

(250) 756-3659

E-mail: deejay@island.net

Collection:	General stock.
# of Vols:	1,200
Specialties:	Sports
Services:	Accepts want lists, search service.
Owner:	Dawn Jelley
Year Estab:	1997

Literacy Nanaimo Bookstore
Open Shop

202 22 Commercial Street V9R 5G4

(250) 754-8982

Collection:	General stock of paperback and hardcover.
# of Vols:	20,000
Hours:	Mon-Sat 10-5.
Travel:	See Bygone Books above.
Comments:	A non profit shop. Stock is donated and approximately 75% paperback.

Nelson
(Map 4, page 44)

Black Cat Books   **Open Shop**
202 402 Baker Street V1L 4H8   (250) 352-5699

Collection: General stock of mostly used paperback.
Hours: Tue-Sat 9:30-5:30.
Year Estab: 1993

Pack Rat Annie's   **Open Shop**
411 Kootenay Street V1L 1K7   (250) 354-4722

Collection: General stock of paperback and hardcover.
# of Vols: 10,000
Hours: Mon-Sat 9-5.
Travel: From Hwy 3, turn south on Kootenay.
Comments: Stock is approximately 75% paperback.

New Westminster
(Map 5, page 50)

Books, CD's, Tapes, Movies, Comics & Curios   **Open Shop**
520–6th Street V3L 3B4   (604) 520-0866

Collection: General stock of paperback and hardcover, CDs, videos and more.
# of Vols: 30,000
Hours: Daily 12-9.
Travel: From Surrey, going westbound on Hwy 1, take first exit after crossing
                   bridge onto Brunette. Continue south on Brunette which becomes Co-
                   lumbia, then right on 6th St.
Credit Cards: No
Year Estab: 1985
Comments: This shop probably has as many CDs, cassettes, LPs, videos and maga-
                   zines as it does books. The majority of the books we saw were paper-
                   back. Squeezing in between narrow aisles we were able to spot some
                   hardcover books of fairly recent vintage as well as a few oldies.

Charles McKee Books   **Mail Order**
1306–6th Avenue V3M 2C4   (604) 526-0183
Web page: www.abebooks.com/home/housedaddybooks

                                              E-mail: cmbooks@portal.ca

Collection: General stock and ephemera.
# of Vols: 320,000+
Specialties: Science fiction; horror; mystery; fishing; Canadiana; humor; cartoons
                   (strip); cookbooks; Fedogan & Bremer; limited editions; Terminal Fright
                   publications.
Credit Cards: No
Year Estab: 1995
Comments: Formerly associated with Bakka, a science fiction shop in Toronto.

Renaissance Books   **Open Shop**
804–12th Street V3M 4K1   (604) 525-4566
                                    E-mail: lavana_labrey@bc.sympatico.ca

Collection:	General stock of paperback and hardcover.
# of Vols:	70,000
Hours:	Mon-Fri 6:30am-9pm. Sat & Sun 8am-9pm.
Services:	Search service, accepts want lists, mail order.
Travel:	Brunette exit off Hwy 1. Proceed south on Brunette which becomes Columbia, then right on McBride, left on 8th Ave and right on 12th St. From Vancouver: Follow Kingsway which becomes 12th St in New Westminster. Parking is available in rear.
Credit Cards:	Yes
Owner:	John Preston & Lavana La Brey
Year Estab:	1997
Comments:	A potpourri consisting of some interesting older hardcover titles including (at least at the time of our visit) a nice section on spiritualism and the like, plenty of paperbacks, recent popular hardcover titles, both fiction and non fiction, a nice art section and, if you have time to spare, a coffee shop.

Royal Book Mart   **Open Shop**
600 Agnes Street V3M 1G8   (604) 521-3332

Collection:	General stock of mostly paperback.
Hours:	Mon-Fri 11-7. Sat 10-5:30.

Visions Bookstore   **Open Shop**
700 Columbia Street V3M 1A9   (604) 520-0047
                                                        Fax: (604) 527-1133

Collection:	Specialty new and used.
Specialties:	Metaphysics; new age; self help.
Hours:	Mon-Sat 9-5:30.
Travel:	Between 6th & 8th Streets.
Credit Cards:	Yes
Year Estab:	1990
Comments:	Stock is approximately 25% used.

North Vancouver
(Map 7, page 85)

Academic Books   **By Appointment**
709 Westmoreland Crescent V7P 2G8   (604) 980-1810

Collection:	Specialty
# of Vols:	80,000
Specialties:	Canadiana; Arctic; USA; Australia.
Services:	Catalog, accepts want lists.
Credit Cards:	No
Owner:	B. Rowell
Year Estab:	1970

(North Vancouver)

Acanthus Books   **By Appointment**
                                                    E-mail: iancam@bc.sympatico.ca

Collection:	General stock.
Specialties:	Canadiana
Services:	Search service.
Credit Cards:	No
Owner:	Jean Cameron
Year Estab:	1989

Booklovers   **Open Shop**
102 175 East 3rd Street V7L 1E5   (604) 986-9501

Collection:	General stock of hardcover and paperback.
# of Vols:	25,000+ (See Comments)
Hours:	Mon-Sat 11-6:30. Sun 12-5.
Services:	Accepts want lists, mail order.
Travel:	Lonsdale exit off Hwy 1. Proceed south on Lonsdale, then left on 3rd.
Credit Cards:	Yes
Owner:	Duncan Cumming
Year Estab:	1992
Comments:	The owner advised us that his practice is not the refuse any print material brought into his shop for sale. Thus, the shop is overburdened with boxes of unsorted books and magazines in almost every aisle making it a bit difficult to traverse the aisles and view all the books that are shelved. All we can say is that if you visit here, you'll need to be both careful and agile. Most of the hardcover volumes we saw were reading copies of mixed vintage and quite reasonably priced. There's no shortage of paperbacks, magazines of every type and description and LPs.

Carillon Books   **By Appointment**
412 Lyons Place V7L 1Y5   (604) 984-2787
Web page: www.abebooks.com   E-mail: artbooks@portal.ca

Collection:	Specialty
# of Vols:	6,000
Specialties:	Art; architecture; music; photography; fine arts.
Services:	Accepts want lists, mail order.
Credit Cards:	Yes
Owner:	George Carroll
Year Estab:	1993

Carousel Books & Records   **Open Shop**
1830 Lonsdale V7M 2J9   (604) 984-0933
                                                          Fax: (604) 926-8509

Collection:	General stock of hardcover and paperback.
# of Vols:	5,000-10,000
Specialties:	Philosophy; bibles; religion; languages.
Hours:	Mon-Sat 10:30-4:30.

Travel:	Lonsdale exit off Hwy 1. Proceed south on Lonsdale. Shop is at 18th St.
Credit Cards:	No
Owner:	Dr. John Micallef
Year Estab:	1976
Comments:	A modest sized shop with hardcover books of mixed vintage although stronger at the slightly older end of the range. Some paperbacks but not overwhelmingly so. As the specialties above indicate, the collection also includes some scholarly titles.

Caprice Munro, Bookseller   **By Appointment**
2 124 East 19th Street V7L 2Y8   (604) 986-5490
                                                    E-mail: clmunro@direct.ca

Collection:	Specialty. Mostly used
Specialties:	Horses and horse related.
Services:	Appraisals, accepts want lists
Credit Cards:	No
Year Estab:	1991

Serenity Books & Gifts Shop   **Open Shop**
129 West 3rd Street V7M 1E7   (604) 987-8726

Collection:	General stock of new and used hardcover and paperback.
Specialties:	Metaphysics
Hours:	Mon-Sat 10-5:30. Sun 12-5.
Comments:	Stock is approximately 25% used, 80% of which is hardcover.

Westernesse Bookshop   **Open Shop**
152 West 15th Street V7M 1R5   (604) 988-8424

Collection:	General stock of hardcover and paperback.
# of Vols:	20,000
Specialties:	Modern first editions.
Hours:	Tue-Sat 10-5:30.
Travel:	Lonsdale exit off Hwy 1. Proceed south on Lonsdale to 15th, then right on 15th St.
Credit Cards:	Yes
Owner:	Randall Scott
Year Estab:	1990
Comments:	A nice collection of hardcover volumes plus some paperbacks. The majority of the books were in quite good condition, neatly shelved and the shop is easy to browse. While the variety of subjects available is limited, the quality of the books is not.

100 Mile House
(Map 4, page 44)

Trolls Used Books   **Open Shop**
330 Birch Avenue   (250) 395-3596
Mailing address: PO Box 373 108 Mile Ranch   V0K 2Z0

Collection:	General stock of paperback and hardcover.

# of Vols:	10,000
Hours:	Mon-Sat 9-4.
Travel:	First Ave exit off Hwy 97. Proceed east on First Ave, then right on Birch. Shop is on right in a strip mall.
Credit Cards:	No
Owner:	Michael Larkin
Year Estab:	1995
Comments:	Stock is approximately 80% paperback.

Osoyoos
(Map 4, page 44)

The Polka Dot Door   **Open Shop**
8131 Main Street   (250) 495-2226
Mailing address: PO Box 430 Osoyoos BC V0H 1V0

Collection:	General stock of mostly paperback.
Hours:	Mon-Sat 9:30-5:30.

Parksville
(Map 6, page 61)

The Book Collector   **Open Shop**
154 Morrison V9P 1V4   (250) 248-9511
                                                    E-mail: jschef@bcsupernet.com

Collection:	General stock of hardcover and paperback.
# of Vols:	5,000
Hours:	Mon-Sat 10-5:30.
Travel:	From Nanaimo ferry terminal, take Inland Hwy north (Hwy 19). Take second Parksville exit and continue on Alberni Hwy to downtown. Left on Morrison.
Credit Cards:	Yes
Owner:	C. Scheffer
Year Estab:	1987
Comments:	A small shop with a mix of hardcover and paperback books and some interesting titles. (We even left with one.) Whether the books came from buying trips on the part of the owner or were the result of a walk-in purchase, the opportunity for a traveling book person to come across a surprising find at a very reasonable price presents itself here.

Buckshot Books   **Open Shop**
2A 1209 East Island Highway V9P 1R5   (250) 248-5484
                                                          Fax: (250) 248-5498

Collection:	General stock of mostly paperback.
# of Vols:	5,000
Hours:	Mon-Sat 10-5.
Travel:	South of Parksville in the Heritage Park Shopping Center, a small strip mall, on Hwy 19A (Island Hwy).
Credit Cards:	Yes

Owner:	C. Purkis
Year Estab:	1996
Comments:	If this shop had more than 50-100 hardcover volumes we must confess we were unable to spot them. Plenty of paperbacks, both of the pocketbook and trade variety.

Fireside Books   **Open Shop**
122A Craig Street   (250) 248-1234
Mailing address: 536 Rowan Avenue Parksville BC V9P 1H3
                              E-mail: bookbugs@nanaimo.arc.com

Collection:	General stock of paperback and hardcover.
# of Vols:	10,000-15,000
Hours:	Mon-Sat 10-5. Sun (summer only) 11-4.
Services:	Accepts want lists, mail order.
Travel:	From Nanaimo, continue north on Island Hwy (Hwy 19A), then left on Craig. From Hwy 19, see The Book Collector above. Turn right on Hirst, then quick right on Craig.
Credit Cards:	No
Owner:	Stan Wallington
Year Estab:	1996
Comments:	While the stock in the shop is primarily paperback (good vacation reading), 20%-30% of the stock is made up of hardcover volumes, some of the recent bestseller type as well as practical items and a few old classics.

Releaf Books   **Open Shop**
120 Alberni Highway   (250) 248-0620
Mailing address: 215 Chestnut Street Parksville BC V9P 2P7

Collection:	General stock of paperback and hardcover.
# of Vols:	10,000
Hours:	Mon-Sat 9:30-5. Also Sun in summer.
Travel:	See The Book Collector above.
Credit Cards:	Yes
Year Estab:	1996
Comments:	Stock is approximately 75% paperback.

Penticton
(Map 4, page 44)

The Book Shop   **Open Shop**
242 Main Street V2A 5B2   Tel & Fax: (250) 492-6661
Web page: www.abebooks.com/home/bookshop   E-mail: bookshop@vip.net

Collection:	General stock of used hardcover and paperback and remainders.
# of Vols:	250,000
Specialties:	Art; photography; architecture; modern literature; Canadiana; military; wine.
Hours:	Mon-Sat 9-6, except Fri till 9. Sun and holidays 11-5.
Travel:	In downtown.

Credit Cards:	Yes
Owner:	Bruce Stevenson
Year Estab:	1974
Comments:	We were pleasantly surprised to note first, that the number of books claimed above is accurate, and second, that the ratio of hardcover items to paperbacks is at least 50/50. A large portion of the hardcover volumes are of fairly recent vintage. The shelves are well labeled and broken down into numerous subcategories for easy browsing. In addition to the books, we saw lots of magazines, particularly *National Geographics*, but others as well. Reasonably priced. Unless you're looking for esoteric or scholarly items, you could have a lot of fun here.

The Good Stuff Shoppe   **Open Shop**
236 Martin Street V2A 5K3   (250) 492-5335

Collection:	General stock of paperback and hardcover.
# of Vols:	3,000+
Hours:	Mon-Sat 9-5.
Travel:	One block from Main Street.
Comments:	More of a non book establishment carrying used furniture, knick knacks and an assortment of other collectibles with one room devoted to paperbacks and older hardcover items.

Port Alberni
(Map 6, page 61)

The Last Page Book Store   **Open Shop**
2964 Third Avenue V9Y 2A7   (250) 723-2665

Collection:	General stock of new and used paperback and hardcover.
Hours:	"Regular Hours."

Looking Glass Books   **Open Shop**
3550 Johnston Road V9Y 7X1   (250) 724-5433

Collection:	General stock of mostly new and mostly paperback used.
# of Vols:	2,500 (used)
Hours:	Mon-Fri 9:30-5:30, except Fri till 9. Sat 9:30-5:30. Sun 11-5.

Port Coquitlam
(Map 5, page 50)

Poco Books   **Open Shop**
2630 Shaughnessy V3C 3G6   (604) 941-5821

Collection:	General stock of hardcover and paperback.
# of Vols:	5,000
Hours:	Mon-Sat 10-5.
Travel:	Hwy 7 (Lougheed Hwy) exit off Hwy 1. Continue north on Hwy 7, which then turns eastward. Shortly after the road turns to the east, turn left onto Shaughnessy.
Credit Cards:	No

Year Estab: 1990
Comments: Stock is evenly divided between hardcover and paperback.

Port Moody
(Map 5, page 50)

Black Lion Books   **Open Shop**
2605A St. John's Street V3H 2B5   (604) 937-5166
Web page: www.abebooks.com/home/blacklion   E-mail: linday@intergate.bc.ca

Collection: General stock of hardcover and paperback and ephemera.
# of Vols: 11,000
Specialties: Literature (English, French, French Canadian).
Hours: Mon-Sat 10-6. Sun 10-5.
Services: Appraisals, search service, accepts want lists, mail order.
Travel: From downtown Vancouver, proceed east on Hastings St which be-
                   comes Barnet Hwy (Hwy 7A) and then St. John's St in Port Moody.
Credit Cards: Yes
Owner: Linda Young
Year Estab: 1998
Comments: An attractive shop with a modest collection of mostly hardcover vol-
                   umes in good to excellent condition. While the majority of the books
                   we saw were of fairly recent vintage, there were some older volumes
                   and certainly some classics to be seen. The shop has a nice collection
                   of French titles.

Prince George
(Map 4A, page 44)

The Final Chapter   **Open Shop**
1511 Third Avenue V2L 3G3   (250) 564-4114

Collection: General stock of mostly paperback.
# of Vols: 10,000+
Hours: Mon-Sat 10-5:30.

Spruce City Resale   **Open Shop**
1245 Third Avenue V2L 3E6   (250) 563-8222

Collection: General stock of mostly paperback.
# of Vols: 1 million
Hours: Mon-Thu 10-6, except Fri til 8. Sat 10-6.
Travel: From Hwy 97, continue north to 5th Ave, then follow 5th Ave to down-
                   town where it becomes 4th Ave. Left at Victoria, then right on 3rd.

Qualicum Beach
(Map 6, page 61)

Baywater Books   **Open Shop**
6030 West Island Highway   (250) 757-2060
Mailing address: 6030 West Island Highway Qualicum Beach BC V9K 2E1

Collection: General stock of mostly paperback.

# of Vols:	20,000
Hours:	Daily 9-5.

The Bookcase   **Open Shop**
676 Memorial V9K 1S9   (250) 752-2522

Collection:	General stock of mostly paperback.
# of Vols:	25,000
Hours:	Mon-Sat 10-5.

Queen Charlotte
(Map 4A, page 44)

Bradley Books   **Open Shop**
623–7th Street V0T 1S1   (250) 559-0041

Collection:	General stock of new and mostly paperback used.
# of Vols:	4,000 (used)
Hours:	Tue-Sat 12-6.

Northwest Coast Indian Books   **Open Shop**
PO Box 670 V0T 1S0   (250) 559-4681
Web page: www.abebooks.com/home/indianbooks   Fax: (250) 559-8643
                                                                 E-mail: nwcbooks@island.net

Collection:	Specialty new and used.
# of Vols:	5,000
Specialties:	Pacific Northwest Coast Indians.
Hours:	Mon-Fri 8:30-4. Weekends by appointment.
Services:	Catalog, accepts want lists.
Credit Cards:	Yes
Owner:	Bill Ellis
Year Estab:	1984
Comments:	Stock is approximately 75% new.

Revelstoke
(Map 4, page 44)

DJ's New & Used Furniture   **Open Shop**
301 McKenzie Street V0E 2S0   (250) 837-4454

Collection:	General stock of mostly paperback.
# of Vols:	2,500
Hours:	Mon-Sat 10-6, except Fri till 7.

Richmond
(Map 5, page 50)

Steveston Book Store   **Open Shop**
3760 Moncton Street V7E 3A6   (604) 274-3604

Collection:	General stock of new and mostly paperback used.
# of Vols:	5,000 (used)
Hours:	Mon-Sat 10:30-6. Sun 11-6.

Salmon Arm
(Map 4, page 44)

Coulton's Sales   **Open Shop**
310 Ross Street NE V1E 4R9   (250) 832-7822

Collection: General stock of mostly paperback.
# of Vols: 30,000
Hours: Mon-Fri 9:30-5. Sat 10-4.

Sechelt
(Map 4A, page 44)

Ashley's Books & Records   **Open Shop**
5500 Trail Ave V0N 3A0   (604) 885-8952
                                    E-mail: ashleys_books@sunshine.net

Collection: General stock of mostly hardcover.
# of Vols: 100,000
Specialties: Canadiana
Hours: Mon-Sat 10-5.
Services: Appraisals, search service, accepts want lists, mail order.
Travel: From Horseshoe Bay ferry terminal in West Vancouver, take ferry to
                  Gibsons, then continue to Sechelt.
Credit Cards: Yes
Owner: Jeff Talbot
Year Estab: 1994

Shawnigan Lake
(Map 6, page 61)

Bains Books & Militaria   **By Appointment**
3000 Glen Eagle Road, RR 1 V0R 2W0   (250) 743-8016
Web page: www.abebooks.com/home/bainsbooks   E-mail: bains@cbnet.net

Collection: Specialty books and ephemera.
# of Vols: 8,000
Specialties: Military
Services: Appraisals, occasional catalog, accepts want lists, mail order.
Credit Cards: No
Owner: Hal Bryan
Year Estab: 1989

Sidney
(Map 6, page 61)

Beacon Books & Collectables   **Open Shop**
2372 Beacon Avenue V8L 1X3   (250) 655-4447
                                                Fax: (250) 655-5283
                                            E-mail: tanners@pinc.com

Collection: General stock of paperback and hardcover.

(Sidney)

# of Vols:	15,000
Specialties:	Art; nautical; literature; mystery.
Hours:	Mon-Sat 10-5:30. Sun 12-4.
Services:	Accepts want lists, mail order.
Travel:	From Swartz Bay ferry terminal, proceed on Hwy 17 (Patricia Bay Hwy) to Beacon Ave exit. Left on Beacon.
Credit Cards:	Yes
Owner:	Clive & Christine Tanner
Year Estab:	1994
Comments:	A good sized browser friendly shop with a mix of paperback and hardcover books of mixed vintage. Most of the books we saw were in good condition. A separate room (formerly operated as a separate bookstore) houses an exclusively mystery collection, both paperback and hardcover but mostly paperback.

Compass Rose Nautical Books   **Open Shop**
9785 Fourth Street V8L 2Y9   (250) 656-4674
Web page: www.compassrose.ca   Fax:(250) 656-4760
E-mail: compassrose@bc.sympatico.ca

Collection:	Specialty new and used.
Specialties:	Nautical
Hours:	Mon-Sat 10-6. Sun 12-5.
Services:	Mail order.
Travel:	See Beacon Books above.
Credit Cards:	Yes
Owner:	Terry Patten
Year Estab:	1998
Comments:	Stock is approximately 70% new.

Lawrence Eddy Books   **Open Shop**
104 9790 Second Street V8L 3Y8   Tel & Fax: (250) 656-2366
E-mail: lawrence@pinc.com

Collection:	General stock of hardcover and paperback.
# of Vols:	4,000
Specialties:	Modern literature.
Hours:	Mon-Sat 10-3.
Services:	Appraisals, accepts want lists
Travel:	See Beacon Books above. From Beacon Ave turn right on Second St. Shop is on second floor.
Credit Cards:	No
Year Estab:	1966
Comments:	We were looking forward to visiting this shop as it's located in a community that promotes itself as a "booktown." Unfortunately, on the day of our arrival, we found a sign on the door indicating that the shop would be closed for a week.

The Haunted Bookshop **Open Shop**
9807 Third Street V8L 3A6 (250) 656-8805
Fax: (250) 656-3058
E-mail: hbs@inetex.com

Collection:	General stock of hardcover and paperback and ephemera.
# of Vols:	25,000
Specialties:	History; literature; nautical; children's (19th & 20th centuries).
Hours:	Mon-Sat 10-5. Sun 12-5.
Services:	Appraisals, search service, accepts want lists, mail order.
Travel:	See Beacon Books above. From Beacon Ave turn left on Third.
Credit Cards:	Yes
Owner:	Adrian Batterbury & Odean Long
Year Estab:	1947
Comments:	A very nice shop with quality books in most subject areas. While modest in size, in our view, the condition of the volumes on hand and the availability of scarcer volumes makes this shop worth a visit.

Smithers
(Map 4A, page 44)

Mountain Eagle Books **Open Shop**
Third Avenue, PO Box 4306 V0J 2N0 (250) 847-5245

Collection:	General stock of new and mostly paperback used.
Hours:	Mon-Thu 8:30-6. Fri 8:30-9. Sat 9-6.
Comments:	Stock is approximately 65% used.

Sorrento
(Map 4, page 44)

Spirits of Onyx Creek **Open Shop**
2805 Caen Road (250) 675-4200
Mailing address: PO Box 341 Celista BC V0E 1L0

Collection:	General stock of mostly paperback.
# of Vols:	1,000
Hours:	Tue-Fri 9-5:30. Sat 9-4.

South Surrey

John J. King, Bookseller **Mail Order**
2283–129th Street V4A 7V7 (604) 538-7092
Web page: www.abebooks.com/home/alcuin Fax: (604) 538-5223
E-mail: antbook@aol.com

Collection:	Specialty books and ephemera.
# of Vols:	2,000
Specialties:	Books on books; Elzeviers; private press; Vellum indentures.
Services:	Search service, accepts want lists.
Credit Cards:	No
Year Estab:	1998

Squamish
(Map 4, page 44)

Mostly Books   **Open Shop**
38012 Cleveland Avenue V0N 3G0   (604) 892-3912

Collection: General stock of new and used paperback and hardcover.
# of Vols: 5,000 (used)
Hours: Mon-Thu 10-5:30, except Fri till 6. Sun 11-3.
Travel: From Hwy 99, at sign for Squamish town center, turn west on Cleveland.
Comments: Stock is approximately 30% used, 60% of which is paperback.

Steveston
(Map 5, page 50)

Gerry's Books   **Open Shop**
130 3651 Moncton Street V7E 3A5   (604) 272-6601

Collection: General stock of mostly paperback.
# of Vols: 50,000
Hours: Daily 10-6.

Surrey
(Map 5, page 50)

The Book Barn   **Open Shop**
3 5723–176th Street V3S 4C9   (604) 574-9395

Collection: General stock of mostly paperback.
Hours: Mon 12-5:30. Tue-Sat 9:30-5:30.

Books & Things   **Open Shop**
10224–152nd Street V3R 6N7   (604) 585-1448

Collection: General stock of mostly paperback.
# of Vols: 16,000
Hours: Mon-Sat 10-5. Sun 12-4.

Phoenix Books   **Open Shop**
10202–152nd Street V3R 6N7   (604) 584-8738
Web page: www.phoenixbooks.com   E-mail: phoenix@phoenixbooks.com

Collection: Specialty. Primarily new with some used.
Specialties: Metaphysics
Hours: Mon, Tue, Sat 10-6. Wed-Fri 10-8. Sun 12-6.
Travel: Eastbound on Hwy 1: 152nd St exit. Proceed south on 152nd St.
                  Westbound on Hwy 1: 160th St exit. Proceed west on 104th Ave then
                  left on 152nd St.
Credit Cards: Yes
Owner: Arnold Pointer
Year Estab: 1976
Comments: Stock is approximately 85% new.

Sue's Book Shelf   **Open Shop**
106 7380 King George Highway V3W 5A5   (604) 599-8482

Collection: General stock of mostly paperback.
# of Vols: 10,000
Hours: Mon-Sat 9:30-6. Sun 12-4.

Terrace
(Map 4A, page 44)

Grant Hazelwood, Bookseller   **By Appointment**
2711 Skeena Street V8G 3K3   (250) 635-2317

Collection: Specialty
# of Vols: 4,000
Specialties: Fishing; hunting; canoeing; travel & exploration.
Services: Appraisals, accepts want lists, mail order.
Credit Cards: No
Year Estab: 1979

Trail
(Map 4, page 44)

@ Pages   **Open Shop**
1358 McQuarrie V1R 1X3   (250) 368-8078

Collection: General stock of mostly paperback.
Hours: Mon-Sat 10-6.

Vancouver
(Map 7, page 85 & Map 5, page 50)

ABC Book Emporium   **Open Shop**
1247 Granville Street V6Z 1M5   Tel & Fax: (604) 682-3019

Collection: General stock of hardcover and paperback.
# of Vols: 50,000
Specialties: Science fiction (paperback); mystery (paperback); magazines.
Hours: Mon-Thu 11-7. Fri 11-8. Sat 10-7. Sun 12-7.
Travel: Between Davie & Drake.
Credit Cards: Yes
Owner: Skip Mabee
Year Estab: 1988

Abraham's Books   **Open Shop**
1721 Grant Street V5L 2Y6   (604) 253-1952
                                         E-mail: abesbooks@netscape.com

Collection: Specialty
# of Vols: 5,000
Specialties: Metaphysics; eastern and western philosophy; magic; UFOs; Judaica;
                 religion.

Hours: Tue-Sun 12-6. Open some evenings in summer.
Travel: Two blocks north of 1st Ave, just off Commercial Drive.
Credit Cards: No
Owner: Abraham & Laura Krown
Year Estab: 1999

Albion Books   **Open Shop**
523 Richards Street V6B 2Z5   (604) 662-3113

Collection: General stock of hardcover and paperback, LPs and CDs.
# of Vols: 20,000
Hours: Mon-Fri 10-5:30. Sat 10-5:30. Sun 12-5:30.
Travel: Downtown, between Pender and Dunsmuir.
Credit Cards: Yes
Owner: David Beaver
Comments: A mix of hardcover and paperback books, some intershelved, a few
                  new titles and LPs (particularly jazz). The shop's size is such that we
                  saw little evidence of any subjects covered in depth. This does not
                  mean that we did not spot some interesting volumes, including some
                  antiquarian titles.

Antiquarius   **Open Shop**
609 207 West Hastings Street V6B 1H7   (604) 669-7288
Web page: www.abebooks.com/home/antiquarius   Fax: (604) 688-5506
                                                  E-mail: ephemera@axionet.com

Collection: General stock.
# of Vols: 15,000
Specialties: British Columbia; military.
Hours: Mon-Sat 11-5.
Services: Appraisals, accepts want lists, mail order.
Travel: At Cambie.
Credit Cards: Yes
Owner: Bernard Spring
Year Estab: 1985

Antique Map-Print Gallery   **Open Shop**
110 332 Water Street V6B 1B6   (250) 662-8171

Collection: Specialty
Specialties: Maps; mountaineering; skiing; travel & voyages; atlases; Ireland; Brit-
                  ain in pictures; prints.
Hours: Mon-Sat 11-12 & 2-4 but best to call ahead.
Services: Accepts want lists, mail order.
Travel: At the waterfront, on the lower level of Le Magasin mall in Gastown.
Credit Cards: No
Owner: Brendan M. Moss
Year Estab: 1977

1. ABC Book Emporium
2. Abraham's Books
3. Albion Books
4. Amber Bookshop
5. Antiquarius
6. Antique Map-Print Gallery
7. Baehr Books
8. The Blue Heron
9. Booklovers
10. The Bookstall in Ambleside
11. Brown's Books
12. Burnaby Books
13. Carousel Books & Records
14. Carson Books & Records
15. Characters Fine Books & Coffee Bar
16. Criterion Books
17. EP Books
18. Funston's Christian Book Centre
19. Hermit Books
20. Kestrel Books
21. Lawrence Books
22. Macleod's Books
23. Mystery Merchant Book Store
24. Serenity Books & Gifts Shop
25. Stillman Books

26. Tanglewood Books
27. Tanglewood Books
28. Thompson Rare Books
29. Westernesse Bookshop
30. Wilkinson's Automobilia
31. Joyce Williams Antique
    Prints & Maps
    *(Primarily paperback
    stores not shown on map)*

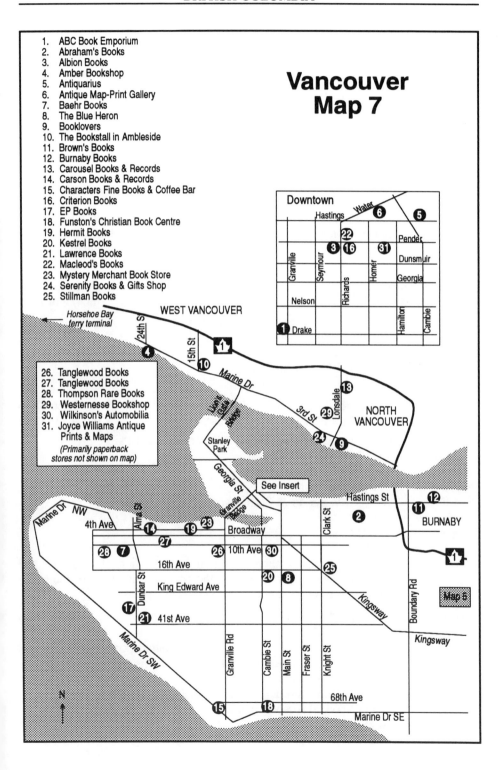

(Vancouver)

Baehr Books   **Open Shop**
3754 West 10th Avenue V6R 2G4   (604) 228-1180

Collection:	General stock of paperback and hardcover.
# of Vols:	30,000
Specialties:	Philosophy; religion; art.
Hours:	Daily 11-6.
Services:	Accepts want lists.
Travel:	Between Alma and Highbury.
Credit Cards:	Yes
Owner:	Scott Baehr
Comments:	A combination of hardcover and paperback books intershelved. Most in good condition. The shelves are nicely labeled with many topics and sub topics on hand. What the shop may lack in antiquarian fare it makes up for in more modern titles.

The Blue Heron   **Open Shop**
3516A Main Street V5V 3N3   (604) 874-8401

Collection:	Specialty. Mostly new and some used.
Specialties:	Antiques and collectibles.
Hours:	Tue-Sat 11-5.
Travel:	Between 19th & 20th Ave.
Comments:	Primarily an antique store.

Carson Books & Records   **Open Shop**
3425 West Broadway V6R 2B4   (604) 739-4041

Collection:	General stock of hardcover and paperback and LPs.
# of Vols:	15,000
Specialties:	Metaphysics; literature; art.
Hours:	Daily 11am-10pm.
Travel:	Between Waterloo & Collingwood.
Credit Cards:	Yes
Owner:	Tim Carson
Year Estab:	1993
Comments:	An easy to browse shop with a strong collection of hardcover and paperback books, particularly in the popular vein. Most of the books we saw were in good condition. Reasonably priced.

Characters Fine Books & Coffee Bar   **Open Shop**
8419 Granville Street V6P 4Z9   (604) 263-4660
                                                    E-mail: kirkwood@axion.net

Collection:	General stock of paperback and hardcover.
# of Vols:	60,000 (See Comments)
Hours:	Mon-Wed 7:30am-6pm. Thu & Fri 7:30am-9pm. Sat & Sun 9-6.
Services:	Search service, accepts want lists.
Travel:	At 68th St.
Credit Cards:	Yes

Owner: Carol Kirkwood
Year Estab: 1992
Comments: It's not often that we sample the food at bookstores that also offer coffee bars. However, as this establishment was our first stop of the day and the coffee bar opened at 7:30am, we decided to get an early start and while Susan munched on a bagel and sipped her coffee, David perused the books. While the majority of the books were paperback, the hardcover volumes were not to be ignored and were certainly respectable for a shop of this type. In addition to literature (including mystery), history, biography, etc., there was also quite a nice children's section. At the time of our visit, only a portion of the collection cited above was on display.

Craig's Books   **By Appointment**
302 2131 West 3rd Avenue V6K 1L3   (604) 737-0530
Web page: www.abebooks.com/home/craigsbks   Fax: (604) 731-2615
                                                E-mail: epic@intergate.bc.ca

Collection: General stock.
# of Vols: 1,000
Specialties: Sports; Canadiana.
Services: Mail order.
Credit Cards: No
Owner: Craig Bowlsby
Year Estab: 1989

Criterion Books   **Open Shop**
434 West Pender Street V6B 1T5   Tel & Fax: (604) 685-2224
Web page: www.abebooks.com   E-mail: crit@direct.ca

Collection: General stock.
# of Vols: 15,000-20,000
Hours: Mon-Sat 11-5:30.
Services: Appraisals, mail order.
Travel: At Richards. Shop is on second floor.
Credit Cards: No
Owner: Lance McCaughran
Year Estab: 1991
Comments: There are at least half as many books laid out on the floor in front of the shelves as there are on the shelves. Don't let this put you off, however. If you have good knees, are willing to bend, and your patience will allow, you may well find some items here not seen elsewhere. We did. The stock is primarily hardcover with many subjects covered. Prices are quite reasonable.

EP Books   **Open Shop**
4495 Dunbar Street V6S 2G4   (604) 222-2780
Collection: General stock of paperback and hardcover.
# of Vols: 10,000

(Vancouver)

Specialties:	Psychology; self help; Christian spirituality and religion; literature; history.
Hours:	Mon-Fri 11-6. Sat 11-5:30.
Travel:	On west side of Vancouver. Proceeding west on King Edward (25th Ave), turn left on Dunbar. Shop is four blocks ahead at West 29th Ave.
Credit Cards:	Yes
Owner:	Ed Peasgood
Year Estab:	1998
Comments:	An even mix of paperback and hardcover volumes, most in quite good condition, displayed nicely in a shop that is small and easy to browse. While most of the volumes were of fairly recent vintage, we did see a few old timers.

First Canadian Used Books   **By Appointment**
152 East 8th Avenue V5T 1R7   (604) 873-4778
                                                    Fax: (604) 873-9112

Collection:	General stock of paperback and hardcover.
# of Vols:	20,000
Specialties:	Canadian literature.
Services:	Accepts want lists, mail order.
Credit Cards:	Yes
Owner:	Peter Anymouse
Year Estab:	1989
Comments:	Stock is approximately 75% paperback.

Funston's Christian Book Centre   **Open Shop**
8146 Cambie Street V6P 3J5   (604) 324-4362
                                                    Fax: (604) 324-4343
                                              E-mail: funstons@beacom.com

Collection:	Specialty new and used.
# of Vols:	40,000+ (used)
Specialties:	Religion
Hours:	Mon-Thu 9-5:30. Fri 9-9. Sat 9-5:30.
Services:	Search service, accepts want lists, mail order.
Travel:	Corner of Cambie and Marine Drive SE.
Credit Cards:	Yes
Owner:	Dave Powell
Year Estab:	1973

Hermit Books   **Open Shop**
2509 West Broadway V6K 2E8   (604) 732-4070

Collection:	General stock of hardcover and paperback.
# of Vols:	5,000+
Specialties:	Literature; poetry; mythology.
Hours:	Sun & Mon 11-6. Tue-Sat 11-7.
Services:	Mail order.

Travel:	Between Larch and Trafalgar.
Credit Cards:	Yes
Owner:	Eileen Hansen & Sharon Johnson
Year Estab:	1996
Comments:	A small shop with both paperback and hardcover volumes, most of recent origin. Stimulating titles. A reasonable balance of subject areas, although the shop's size limits the number of volumes in any one category. The books were in good condition.

Kestrel Books   **Open Shop**
3408 Cambie Street V5Z 2W8   (604) 872-2939
Web page: www.abebooks.com/home/kestrelbks   E-mail: kestrelbks@home.com

Collection:	General stock of hardcover and paperback.
# of Vols:	30,000
Specialties:	Humanities; First Nations; natural history.
Hours:	Daily 12-9:30. Open all holidays except Christmas Day.
Services:	Mail order.
Travel:	Grandview Hwy exit off Hwy 1. Proceed west on Grandview, then left on Cambie. From Hwy 99 north, follow Oak St, then right on 25th Ave (King Edward) and left on Cambie. Shop is at 18th St.
Credit Cards:	Yes
Owner:	Ron Fryer
Year Estab:	1985
Comments:	Some new (mostly children's) books with the vast majority of the stock a combination of hardcover and paperback titles that are intershelved. The books we saw were in generally good condition. Most of the items appeared to be of fairly recent vintage. The shop is easy to browse and offers a pleasant ambience.

Lawrence Books   **Open Shop**
3591 West 41st Avenue V6N 3E7   (604) 261-3812

Collection:	General stock of hardcover and paperback.
# of Vols:	50,000
Specialties:	Military; Canadiana; literature; children's; nautical.
Hours:	Daily 1:30-5:30.
Travel:	At corner of Dunbar.
Credit Cards:	Yes
Owner:	Joan Lawrence
Comments:	We were disappointed when we drove up to this shop at about 2:30 in the afternoon to find a sign in the window indicating that the shop would be closed for a few days; it was only after we returned home that we learned that the owner had died that week and that his widow would be continuing the business. While it would be a disservice to try to describe the shop based on our peering through its windows, at least two area dealers who we visited had good things to say about this shop and we believe that a visit here could be a satisfying experience. If you do get to visit here, we hope you'll share your impressions with us.

(Vancouver)

Stephen C. Lunsford Books   **By Appointment/Chance**
710 207 West Hastings Street V6B 1H5   (604) 681-6830
                                                       Fax: (604) 681-6994
                                                         lunsford@direct.ca

Collection:	Specialty books and ephemera.
# of Vols:	5,000
Specialties:	Western Americana; Americana.
Hours:	By chance, Tue-Sat 10-5.
Services:	Appraisals, catalog, accepts want lists.
Credit Cards:	No
Year Estab:	1977

Macleod's Books   **Open Shop**
455 West Pender Street V6B 1V2   (604) 681-7654
Web page: www.abebooks.com/home/macbks   E-mail: macbks@direct.ca

Collection:	General stock.
# of Vols:	30,000+
Specialties:	Western Canadiana; literature; art; history; military; native studies; classics.
Hours:	Mon-Sat 10-5:30. Sun 12-5.
Services:	Accepts want lists, mail order.
Travel:	At corner of Richards.
Credit Cards:	Yes
Owner:	Don Stewart
Year Estab:	1964
Comments:	Any shop that has two shelves of books on anarchism and a section on Sacco and Vanzetti should be considered worthy of visiting. This establishment has strength in almost every subject we could think of. Its books are in generally good condition, including its antiquarian items. The books are meticulously organized and the paperbacks are scarce. Needless to say, we liked the shop and recommend it to traveling book lovers.

John Meier, Bookseller   **By Appointment**
PO Box 60604 V6H 4B9   (604) 731-6910
                                                       E-mail: jmeier@portal.ca

Collection:	Specialty books and ephemera.
Specialties:	Modern literary first editions; signed; proofs and advance reading copies; manuscripts.
Services:	Appraisals, catalog, accepts want lists.
Credit Cards:	No
Year Estab:	1995

Mystery Merchant Book Store   **Open Shop**
1952 West 4th Avenue V6J 1M5   (604) 739-4311

Collection:	General stock of new and mostly paperback used.
# of Vols:	1,000 (used)

Specialties: Mystery
Hours: Mon-Thu 10-5. Fri 10-8. Sat 10-5. Sun 12-5.
Travel: Between Arbutus and Burrard.

Narnia Books
303 2950 Heather Street   V5Z 3J8
Web page: www.abebooks.com/home/nbks

Mail Order
(604) 266-4857
E-mail: nbooks@msn.com

Collection: General stock.
Specialties: Strong emphasis on British books.
Credit Cards: Yes
Owner: David & Joanne Anderson
Year Estab: 1995

Outsider Enterprises
Centrepoint PO Box 19607   V5T 4E7
Web page: www.abebooks.com/home/phantomstranger/

Mail Order
(604) 874-3199

E-mail: tallnutt@netcom.ca

Collection: Specialty books and ephemera.
# of Vols: 1,000
Specialties: Modern first editions; science fiction; fantasy; comics.
Services: Search service, accepts want lists.
Credit Cards: No
Owner: Thomas R. Allnutt
Year Estab: 1997

Tony Power, Books
813 Sawcut Lane   V5Z 4A2

Mail Order
(604) 877-1426
E-mail: power@vcn.bc.ca

Collection: Specialty
Specialties: Modern first editions; contemporary fiction (Canadian, US and UK, including US born writers in Canada).
Credit Cards: No
Year Estab: 1994

Stillman Books
1321 Kingsway   V5V 3E3
Web page: www.abebooks.com/home/stillmanbooks

Open Shop
(604) 877-1712
E-mail: tsbooks@portal.ca

Collection: General stock of hardcover and paperback.
# of Vols: 20,000
Specialties: Children's; illustrated; aviation; military.
Hours: Mon-Fri, except closed Wed, 11-6. Sat 10:30-5.
Services: Appraisals, accepts want lists.
Travel: From Hwy 1: Grandview exit. Continue west on Grandview which becomes East 12th. Left on Clark which becomes Knight , then right on Kingsway. From Hwy 99: Oak or Granville St to W. 25th Ave (King Edward Ave). Right on King Edward, left on Knight, cross Kingsway and take first left onto 21st St.
Credit Cards: Yes

(Vancouver)

Owner:	Terry A. Stillman
Year Estab:	1981
Comments:	A breath of fresh air in that the shop, while modest in size, offers what we view as a very nice selection of mixed vintage hardcover volumes, some popular, some unusual, most in good to better condition and more than a few that, had it not been for the limitations of our car trunk, we would have smuggled back across the border. Unless your tastes are highly esoteric, you should enjoy a visit here.

Tanglewood Books   **Open Shop**
2932 West Broadway V6K 2G8   (604) 731-8870

Collection:	General stock paperback and hardcover.
# of Vols:	15,000-20,000
Hours:	Mon-Wed 11-8. Thu & Fri 11-9. Sat 11-6. Sun 12-6.
Services:	Accepts want lists, mail order.
Travel:	Between Macdonald and Bayswater.
Credit Cards:	Yes
Year Estab:	1994
Comments:	A mostly paperback shop. The vast majority of the hardcover books we saw were of recent vintage and were in good condition. If your interests are in the antiquarian or scholarly field, this may not be the place for you. The stock in a sister store on Granville Street (see below) offers a similar although larger mix of paperbacks and hardcovers as well as some new books and remainders.

Tanglewood Books   **Open Shop**
2709 Granville Street V6H 3J1   (604) 731-5571

Collection:	General stock of mostly used paperback and hardcover and remainders.
# of Vols:	20-30,000
Hours:	Mon-Wed 10-8. Thu & Fri 10-9. Sat 10-6. Sun 12-6.
Services:	Accepts want lists, mail order.
Travel:	Between 11th & 12th Ave.
Credit Cards:	Yes
Comments:	Approximately 85% of stock is used, 65% of which is paperback.

Thompson Rare Books   **Open Shop**
4376 West 10th Avenue V6R 2H7   Tel & Fax: (604) 224-4832
Web page: www.mjtbooks.com   E-mail: mjt@mjtbooks.com

Collection:	General stock.
# of Vols:	10,000
Specialties:	Literary first editions; detective fiction; science fiction; fantasy.
Hours:	Tue-Sun 12-6.
Services:	Appraisals, mail order.
Travel:	Between Trimble and Discovery.
Credit Cards:	Yes

Owner:	Michael John Thompson
Year Estab:	1986
Comments:	It may be unfair for us to tout shops that are of particular interest to us but that has never stopped us in the past. One of our interests is vintage mystery and fantasy and this shop is particularly strong in both of these areas. This does not mean that the shop lacks strength in the broader fields of literature. Indeed its collection can be said to be general. However, should your interests parallel ours, you'll be especially pleased if you have an opportunity to visit here. At the time of our visit, only a portion of the collection cited above was on display.

Max Weder Books   **By Appointment**
2953 Ontario Street V5T 2Y5   (604) 873-2050
Web page: www.abebooks.com/home/weder   E-mail: ettinger@portal.ca

Collection:	General stock and ephemera.
# of Vols:	1,800
Specialties:	Sports; children's.
Services:	Accepts want lists, mail order.
Year Estab:	1997

Wilkinson's Automobilia   **Open Shop**
2531 Ontario Street V5T 2X7   (604) 873-6242
Web page: www.wilkinsonsauto.com   Fax: (604) 873-6259
                                                                          E-mail: info@wilkinsonsauto.com

Collection:	Specialty new and used.
Specialties:	Automotive; racing; motorcycles, repair manuals.
Hours:	Tue-Fri 11-6. Sat 11-5.
Services:	Subject lists, mail order.
Travel:	Between Broadway and 10th Ave.
Owner:	Bill Wilkinson
Comments:	Stock is approximately 60% used.

Joyce Williams Antique Prints & Maps   **Open Shop**
346 West Pender Street V6B 1T1   (604) 688-7434

Collection:	Specialty
Specialties:	Books about old prints and maps; maps.
Hours:	Tue-Fri 10:30-5. Sat 10:30-3. Other times by appointment.
Services:	Appraisals
Travel:	Downtown, between Hamilton and Homer.
Credit Cards:	Yes
Owner:	Joyce Williams & Don Clark
Year Estab:	1980

Windhover Books   **Mail Order**
1600–925 West Georgia Street V6C 3L2   (604) 631-9166
Web page: www.windhoverbooks.com   Fax: (604) 669-1620
                                                                  E-mail: rklarenbach@lawsonlundell.com

Collection:	Specialty

Specialties:	Modern first editions.
Services:	Search service, accepts want lists.
Credit Cards:	No
Owner:	Randy Klarenbach
Year Estab:	1979

Vernon
(Map 4, page 44)

B.J.'s Books   **Open Shop**
10 1800 Kalamalka Lake Road V1T 6V3   (250) 549-1041

Collection:	General stock of mostly paperback.
# of Vols:	80,000
Hours:	Mon-Sat 11-6. Sun 2-5.
Travel:	Kalamalka Lake Rd exit off Hwy 6. Proceed south on Kalamalka.
Comments:	Stock is approximately 80% paperback.

The Book Nook   **Open Shop**
2908–30th Avenue V1T 2B7   (250) 558-0668

Collection:	General stock of paperback and hardcover.
# of Vols:	30,000
Specialties:	History; modern first editions; Canadiana.
Hours:	Mon-Fri 10-5. Sat 10-4.
Services:	Appraisals, accepts want lists.
Travel:	Northbound on Hwy 97: 30th Ave exit. Turn right on 30th Ave. Southbound on Hwy 97: 27th St exit. Turn left on 30th Ave. Shop is between 29th & 30th Sts.
Credit Cards:	No
Owner:	Alan Frankel
Year Estab:	1991
Comments:	Mostly paperbacks with a fair number of hardcover volumes in mixed condition and of mixed vintage. Most were reading copies of popular or practical titles.

Cornhill Books   **By Appointment**
Box 1871 V1T 8Z7   (250) 260-4119
                                        E-mail: cornhillbooks@bc.sympatico.ca

Collection:	General stock.
# of Vols:	10,000
Services:	Mail order.
Credit Cards:	Yes
Owner:	Bill & Sherry Musselwhite
Year Estab:	1990

Ebenezer's   **Open Shop**
3110–29th Avenue V1T 1Z1   (250) 542-0980

Collection:	General stock of mostly paperback.
# of Vols:	25,000
Hours:	Mon-Sat 9:30-5:30, except Fri till 9. Sun 11-4.

Jim Godin, Bookseller   **By Appointment**
2704–11th Street V1T 6Z7   (250) 542-0612
                                                 E-mail: godin@bc.sympatico.ca

Collection:	General stock.
# of Vols:	1,500
Specialties:	Angling
Services:	Appraisals, search service, accepts want lists, mail order.
Credit Cards:	No
Year Estab:	1994

K & K Bookstore   **Open Shop**
3410–31st Avenue V1T 7L3   (250) 542-8880

Collection:	General stock of new and used paperback and hardcover.
# of Vols:	8,000 (used)
Hours:	Mon-Sat 9:30-5:30.
Travel:	Southbound on Hwy 97. 31st Ave exit. Turn right at exit. Northbound on Hwy 97. 25th Ave exit. Turn left and then quick right onto 34th St. Left on 31st Ave.
Credit Cards:	Yes
Year Estab:	1970
Comments:	Stock is evenly divided between new and used books. Used stock is approximately 60% paperback.

Pages Book Store   **Open Shop**
3012–30th Avenue V1T 2C1   (250) 545-4662

Collection:	General stock of mostly paperback and comics.
# of Vols:	15,000
Hours:	Mon-Sat: 9:30-5:30
Travel:	Between 31st and 30th Streets.
Comments:	While we saw some attractive hardcover volumes in the store's windows, the interior of the shop appeared to be well over 90% paperback and comic books.

Victoria
(Map 8, page 96 & Map 6, page 61)

A-AA-ABA Books   **Open Shop**
1600 Quadra Street V8W 2L4   (250) 389-0777

Collection:	General stock of mostly used paperback.
Hours:	Mon-Wed and Fri-Sat 11-5.

Archie's Books & Antiques   **Open Shop**
145 Menzies Street V8V 2G4   (250) 385-4519

Collection:	General stock of hardcover and paperback.
# of Vols:	10,000
Hours:	Mon-Sat 11-5:30.
Services:	Accepts want lists, mail order.

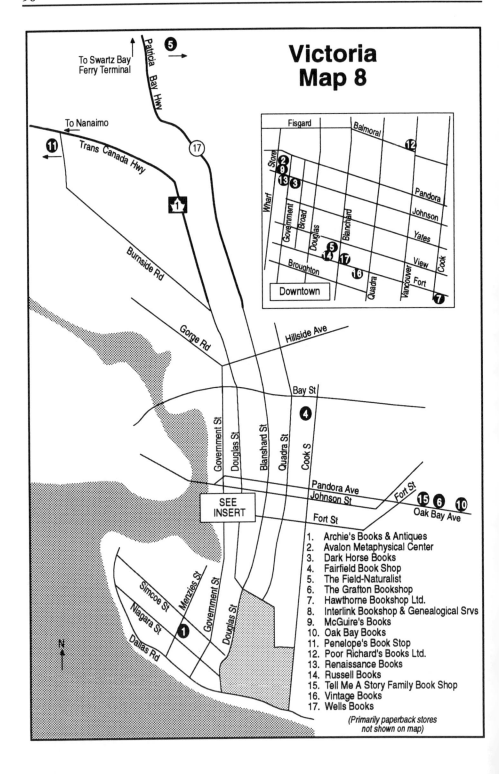

Victoria
Map 8

1. Archie's Books & Antiques
2. Avalon Metaphysical Center
3. Dark Horse Books
4. Fairfield Book Shop
5. The Field-Naturalist
6. The Grafton Bookshop
7. Hawthorne Bookshop Ltd.
8. Interlink Bookshop & Genealogical Srvs
9. McGuire's Books
10. Oak Bay Books
11. Penelope's Book Stop
12. Poor Richard's Books Ltd.
13. Renaissance Books
14. Russell Books
15. Tell Me A Story Family Book Shop
16. Vintage Books
17. Wells Books

*(Primarily paperback stores
not shown on map)*

Travel:	Between Simcoe and Niagara.
Credit Cards:	Yes
Owner:	Archie Wells
Year Estab:	1996
Comments:	Considering the size of the shop and the fact that in addition to its hardcover and paperback books, the shop also sells furniture and assorted antiques, the number of volumes we saw, at least of the hardcover variety, offered some interesting choices for the traveling book person. Not much in the way of depth, but the books were in reasonably good condition and there were enough collectibles to pique one's interest.

Avalon Metaphysical Center   **Open Shop**
62 560 Johnson Street V8W 3C6   (250) 380-1721
Web page: www.metaphysical.bc.ca   Fax: (250) 381-2019
E-mail: avalon@metaphysical.bc.ca

Collection:	Specialty. Mostly new.
# of Vols:	5,000
Specialties:	Occult, magic; astrology; new age; supernatural.
Hours:	Mon-Sat 10-6. Sun 12-5.
Services:	Mail order.
Travel:	Downtown, in Market Square. See McGuire's Books below.
Credit Cards:	Yes
Year Estab:	1998
Comments:	Stock is approximately 80% new.

The Book Prospector   **Mail Order**
748 Lorimer Road   V9E 1G1   (250) 474-5726
E-mail: bookprospector@home.com

Collection:	Specialty
# of Vols:	5,000
Specialties:	Mining; gold rush; Klondike; Arctic; Northern and Western Canadiana; Alaska; Canadiana non fiction; natural history; religion (Christian); Western Americana.
Services:	Catalog (E-mail), accepts want lists.
Credit Cards:	No
Owner:	Gilbert Neufeld
Year Estab:	1995

Dark Horse Books   **Open Shop**
623 Johnson Street V8W 1M5   (250) 386-8736
Fax: (250) 386-8738
E-mail: 75231.3646@compuserve.com

Collection:	General stock of hardcover and paperback.
# of Vols:	10,000
Specialties:	Science fiction; fantasy; Canadian literature; gay and lesbian.
Hours:	Wed-Sat 10-6. (Also Tue from late May-late Sept.) Sun 12-5.
Travel:	Between Broad and Government.
Credit Cards:	Yes

(Victoria)

Owner: Rebekah Johnson & Robert Garfat
Year Estab: 1997
Comments: The owner of this establishment proudly describes it as an "alterna-
                   tive" bookstore that provides its customers with non violent, thought
                   provoking titles. Most of what we observed in the specialty fields
                   noted above were paperback although there were some hardcover vol-
                   umes on hand. "You pays your money and you makes yer cherce."

Empire Books   **By Appointment**
630 Oliver Street V8S 4W3   (250) 598-2317
                                                       E-mail: ibaird@uvic.ca

Collection: General stock.
# of Vols: 2,500
Specialties: G. A. Henty; railroads; British historical fiction.
Services: Mail order.
Credit Cards: No
Owner: Ian Baird
Year Estab: 1987

Fairfield Book Shop   **Open Shop**
247 Cook Street V8V 3X4   (250) 386-9095

Collection: General stock of mostly used paperback and remainders.
# of Vols: 25,000
Hours: Mon-Sat 10-5. Sun 12-5.

The Field-Naturalist   **Open Shop**
1126 Blanshard Street V8W 2H6   (250) 388-4174
Web page: www.pacificcoast.net/~fieldnat   E-mail: fieldnat@pacificcoast.net

Collection: Specialty. Mostly new and some used.
Specialties: Natural history; ornithology; botany.
Hours: Mon-Sat 9:30-5:30.
Travel: Between View & Fort.
Owner: Bruce Whittington

Gorge Centre Books   **Open Shop**
2961 Tillicum Road V9A 2A6   (250) 384-2616

Collection: General stock of mostly used paperback and some remainders.
# of Vols: 20,000
Hours: Mon-Sat 10-6.

The Grafton Bookshop   **Open Shop**
2238 Oak Bay Avenue V8R 1G5   (250) 370-1455

Collection: General stock of hardcover and paperback.
# of Vols: 20,000
Hours: Mon-Sat 10-5:30. Sun 12-4.
Services: Accepts want lists, mail order.

Travel: Between Monterey and Hampshire.
Credit Cards: Yes
Owner: Jill Grafton
Year Estab: 1998
Comments: After dragging Susan away from a charming tea shop two or three doors down from this bookshop, we were both reminded that the bookshop itself had a certain flavor of "past years." Some stores that advertise themselves as having rare and/or antiquarian items use these phrases rather loosely; this store can legitimately claim to offer rare titles. While the stock is modest in size, the shop does offer a healthy number of hard-to-find titles in a number of different subject areas. Even if you don't buy a book, you may want to drop in at the tea shop.

Haultain Books   **Open Shop**
1500 Haultain Street V8R 2K2   (250) 592-1555
Collection: General stock mostly paperback.
# of Vols: 25,000-30,000
Hours: Mon-Sat 12-5.

Hawthorne Bookshop Ltd.   **Open Shop**
1027 Cook Street V8V 3Z7   (250) 383-3215
                                                    Fax: (250) 598-8065
Collection: General stock of mostly hardcover.
# of Vols: 10,000
Specialties: Poetry; Canadiana.
Hours: Mon-Fri 10-5. Sat 10-4.
Services: Appraisals, search service, catalog, accepts want lists.
Travel: From intersection of Douglas (or Blanshard) and Fort, turn east on Fort. Shop is four blocks ahead at Fort and Cook.
Credit Cards: Yes
Year Estab: 1985
Comments: A nice selection of volumes, most in quite good condition. While the stock may be termed general, we noted strengths in some of the more serious subject areas, e.g., religion. Some paperbacks but not a significant number.

Interlink Bookshop & Genealogical Services   **Open Shop**
3840A Cadboro Bay Road V8N 4G2   (250) 477-2708
Web page: www.pacificcoast.net/~ibgs   E-mail: ibgs@pacificcoast.net
Collection: Specialty new and used paperback and hardcover.
# of Vols: 3,000 (used)
Specialties: Genealogy
Hours: Tue-Sat 10-4:30.
Services: Catalog
Travel: McKenzie Ave exit off Hwy 17. Proceed east on McKenzie.
Credit Cards: Yes
Year Estab: 1988

(Victoria)

Langford Book Exchange   **Open Shop**
106 721 Station Road V9B 2S1   (250) 478-0914

Collection: General stock of mostly paperback.
# of Vols: 15,000
Hours: Tue-Sat 10-4.

Lighthouse Books   **Open Shop**
28 Burnside West V9A 1B3   (250) 380-1467

Collection: General stock of mostly paperback.
# of Vols: 10,000
Hours: Tue-Sat 10-5.
Travel: Burnside exit off Hwy 1. Proceed south on Burnside. Shop is between
                   Harriet and Tillicum.
Credit Cards: No
Owner: Connie Baarda
Year Estab: 1994
Comments: Primarily paperback with a thousand or fewer hardcover volumes,
                   most either reading copies of just "old books."

McGuire's Books   **Open Shop**
9 560 Johnson V8W 3C6   (250) 380-0230
                                              E-mail: michaelmcguire@sprint.ca
Collection: General stock of mostly used hardcover and paperback.
# of Vols: 18,000 (used)
Specialties: Literature; mystery; Celtic; nature.
Hours: Mon-Sat 10:30-5. Sun 12-5.
Services: Search service.
Travel: Located on lower level of Market Square between Government and
                   Store.
Owner: Michael McGuire
Year Estab: 1999
Comments: The shop offers a modest selection of hardcover and paperback books
                   that are intershelved. We were surprised to see a number of *Coles
                   Notes* (apparently the Canadian equivalent of *Cliff Notes*) on the shelf,
                   perhaps available so that purchasers need not go through the trouble of
                   reading the classics being summarized therein. Most of the volumes
                   we saw were "ordinary."

Oak Bay Books   **Open Shop**
1964 Oak Bay Avenue V8R 1E2   (250) 592-2933

Collection: General stock of paperback and hardcover.
# of Vols: 5,000-8,000
Hours: Mon 11:30-5:30. Tue-Sat 10-5:30.
Travel: At corner of Amphion.
Credit Cards: No
Owner: Patricia St. Denis

Year Estab: 1960's
Comments: A modest collection of paperback and hardcover volumes with little depth in any subject areas. Most of the books appeared to be in good condition.

Penelope's Book Stop
1610 Island Highway V9B 1H8

Open Shop
(250) 391-9529
Fax: (250) 474-4087
E-mail: parden@pinc.com

Collection: General stock of paperback and hardcover.
# of Vols: 25,000
Hours: Mon-Sat 9:30-5.
Services: Search service, accepts want lists, mail order.
Travel: From Victoria: Colwood exit off Hwy 1. Proceed on Colwood for two km. After crossing Parsons Bridge, shop is in a small shopping mall on right. (Island Hwy is Hwy 1A.)
Credit Cards: Yes
Owner: Penelope Arden
Year Estab: 1996
Comments: Stock is approximately 70% paperback.

Poor Richard's Books Ltd.
968 Balmoral Road V8T 1A8
Web page: www.islandnet.com/~poorich

Open Shop
(250) 384-4411
Fax: (250) 384-1938
E-mail: poorich@islandnet.com

Collection: General stock.
# of Vols: 20,000
Specialties: Illustrated; early children's; history; travel.
Hours: Mon-Sat 10-5.
Services: Search service, catalog, accepts want lists.
Travel: From Hwy 1 (Blanshard St South), turn left at Fisgard which becomes Balmoral. Shop is at the corner of Vancouver in a residence. On site parking is available.
Credit Cards: Yes
Owner: Joanna & Barney Hagar
Year Estab: 1978
Comments: No serious bookperson visiting Victoria should miss a stop at this establishment. Located in a portion of a private residence; one might think they were visiting the library of one of the late robber barons. The books on display here are without exception in the finest condition one could expect of scarce collectible and antiquarian volumes in almost any subject one could imagine. There are some newer volumes as well for the shop ignores nothing of importance. Enjoy the decor and the look, smell and feel of the books.

Quadra Books
805 1147 Quadra Street V8W 2K5
Web page: www.abebooks.com/home/quadrabooks

By Appointment
Tel & Fax: (250) 480-5127
E-mail: anteater@islandnet.com

Collection: General stock.

(Victoria)

# of Vols:	3,000
Specialties:	Canadiana; nautical; biography; autobiography.
Services:	Search service; accepts want lists; mail order.
Credit Cards:	No
Owner:	Ted Siermachesky
Year Estab:	1997

Renaissance Books   **Open Shop**
579 Johnson Street V8W 1M2   (250) 381-6469
                                                E-mail: jiredale@pinc.com

Collection:	General stock of hardcover and paperback.
# of Vols:	30,000
Specialties:	Literature; art; history; books on books; natural history; first editions.
Hours:	Mon-Sat 10-5.
Travel:	Between Government and Store.
Credit Cards:	Yes
Owner:	Peter Gray
Year Estab:	1974
Comments:	One flight up, a nice combination of mostly hardcover volumes in generally good condition. Easy to browse. Reasonably priced. The shop offers enough of a selection in most categories with plenty of unusual titles and is within a block and a half of three other dealers. Note: Only about half of the volumes cited above were on display at the shop at the time of our visit.

Rockland Books   **By Appointment**
1706 Rockland Avenue V8S 1W8   (250) 595-6409
                                                E-mail: rocs@home.com

Collection:	Specialty books and ephemera.
# of Vols:	3,000
Specialties:	Western Canadiana.
Services:	Appraisals, catalog. Also publishes bibliography and price guide to Western Canadiana.
Credit Cards:	No
Owner:	Kim & Sheena Whale
Year Estab:	1987

Royal Oak Books   **Open Shop**
20 1530 Cooper Road V9A 7B3   (250) 361-1282

Collection:	General stock of mostly paperback.
Hours:	Mon-Sat 1-5.

Russell Books   **Open Shop**
734 Fort Street V8W 1H2   (250) 361-4447
Web page: www.bibliofind.com   Fax: (250) 381-3939
                                                E-mail: rusbooks@islandnet.com

Collection:	General stock mostly used hardcover and paperback.

# of Vols:	200,000
Hours:	Mon-Sat 9-5:30.
Services:	Appraisals, book binding, search service, accepts want lists, mail order.
Travel:	Between Douglas and Blanshard.
Credit Cards:	Yes
Owner:	Diana dePol
Year Estab:	1991
Comments:	A large shop with a solid collection of both hardcover and paperback books nicely organized. Just when you think you've wandered through all of the aisles and seen all the books, you learn that one flight up (through a separate side entrance off the street) there's a second level equal in size to the main floor filled with additional books. (This location is also the workshop for the shop's resident book binder/restorer.) If you don't see what you're looking for on either floor, inquire as additional books offered on the Internet may, under special circumstances, also be viewed. In our opinion, a shop well worth visiting.

Smart Book Shop   **Open Shop**
3643 Shelbourne Street V8P 4H1   (250) 721-4200

Collection:	General stock of mostly used paperback and remainders.
# of Vols:	30,000+
Hours:	Mon-Sat 10-6. Sun 12-5.

Snowden's Book Store   **Open Shop**
619 Johnson Street V8W 1M5   (250) 383-8131

Collection:	General stock of mostly paperback and magazines.
# of Vols:	50,000
Hours:	Mon-Sat 10-5.
Travel:	Between Broad and Government.
Credit Cards:	Yes
Year Estab:	1959
Comments:	If you're in the market for paperbacks and/or older magazines, drop in. The store also has a small collection of hardcover volumes, mostly popular titles.

Tell Me A Story Family Book Shop   **Open Shop**
1848 Oak Bay Avenue V8R 1C5   (250) 598-8833

Collection:	General stock of mostly paperback, games and videos.
# of Vols:	15,000-20,000
Hours:	Winter: Mon-Sat 10-5. Sun 12-4. Summer: Mon-Sat 9:30-5:30. Sun 12-4.

Timeless Books   **Open Shop**
100B 2244 Sooke Road V9B 1X1   (250) 474-5200

Collection:	General stock of mostly paperback.
# of Vols:	1,000
Hours:	Tue-Sat 9:30-4:30.

(Victoria)

Bjarne Tokerud–Bookseller **By Appointment**
216 885 Dunsmuir Road V9A 6W6 Tel & Fax: (250) 381-2230
E-mail: bjarne@datanet.ab.ca

Collection:	Specialty books and ephemera.
# of Vols:	2,500
Specialties:	Travel & exploration, Canadiana; Western Canadiana; Arctic; Yukon; fur trade; military.
Services:	Search service, catalog.
Credit Cards:	Yes
Year Estab:	1980
Comments:	Additional stock is on display in an open shop in Edmonton, AB.

Vintage Books **Open Shop**
839 Fort Street V8W 1H6 (250) 382-4414
Web page: www.abebooks.com/home/vintagebooksvictoria
E-mail: vintagebooks@cvnet.net

Collection:	General stock.
# of Vols:	15,000
Specialties:	Canadiana; European history; military; art.
Hours:	Mon-Sat 10-5:30.
Services:	Accepts want lists, mail order.
Travel:	Between Quadra and Blanshard.
Credit Cards:	Yes
Owner:	Kate Bryan
Year Estab:	1982
Comments:	A solid collection with good hardcover volumes of mixed vintage. Most items were in reasonably good condition and were moderately priced. At the time of our visit there were fewer volumes on display than noted above.

Wells Books **Open Shop**
824 Fort Street V8W 1H8 (250) 360-2929
Fax: (250) 361-1812
E-mail: wellsbks@pinc.com

Collection:	General stock of hardcover and paperback and ephemera.
# of Vols:	40,000
Specialties:	Nautical; scholarly; religion; metaphysics; natural history; science; children's; military.
Hours:	Mon-Sat 10-5.
Services:	Appraisals, search service, catalog, accepts want lists.
Credit Cards:	Yes
Owner:	Jeri Bass & Diane Wells
Year Estab:	1988
Comments:	A "not to be missed" bookshop with quality volumes in every category and few if any categories unrepresented. We saw many volumes here not seen elsewhere. Traveling book people will appreciate the spacious, browser friendly layout of the shop.

Neil Williams, Bookseller
2741 Asquith Street   V8R 3Y6
Web page: www.islandnet.com/~neilw

Mail Order
(250) 598-6405
Fax: (250) 598-4385
E-mail: neilw@islandnet.com

Collection:	Specialty
Specialties:	Children's; illustrated; mystery and detective; Canadian literature.
Services:	Search service, catalog, accepts want lists.
Credit Cards:	Yes
Owner:	Neil & Carol Williams
Year Estab:	1994

West Vancouver
(Map 7, page 85)

Amber Bookshop   **Open Shop**
2460A Marin Drive   V7V 1L1   (604) 926-1133
                                                                      Fax: (604) 926-8236

Collection:	General stock of hardcover and paperback and some new.
# of Vols:	5,000-10,000
Hours:	Mon-Sat 9:30-5:30.
Travel:	See The Bookstall in Ambleside below. Continue on Marine Dr to 24th St. The shop is one flight down.
Credit Cards:	Yes
Owner:	Kathleen Nairne
Year Estab:	1979
Comments:	A mix of hardcover and some paperback books plus a selection of small press new books. Most of the books were of mixed vintage. The shop is easy to browse and attractively decorated with non book items, some of which are for sale.

The Bookstall in Ambleside   **Open Shop**
115 1425 Marine Drive   V7T 1B8   (604) 926-2425

Collection:	General stock of mostly hardcover.
# of Vols:	75,000
Hours:	Mon-Sat 10-5:30.
Services:	Accepts want lists.
Travel:	From Vancouver, proceed on Hwy 99 to Lion's Gate Bridge. Follow signs to West Vancouver which leads to Marine Dr. Shop is at 14th St. Alternate approach from Hwy 1: 15th St exit. Proceed south on 15th, then left on Marine.
Credit Cards:	No
Owner:	David A. Moon
Year Estab:	1966
Comments:	At the time of our visit the shop's entrance was crowded with boxes which may have been part of a shipment the owner was getting ready to mail out. However, the rest of the shop was equally crowded, both with boxes and tables filled with books, making it rather difficult to

view all of the shelves. (We were advised that the owner had moved into this smaller location several months prior to our visit.) What we were able to see was an extensive collection, both on the shelves and in labeled boxes above the shelves. The hardcover books, whether of newer vintage or much older volumes, seemed to us to be priced most reasonably. The shelves were clearly labeled and a patient browser has a better chance of finding a long lost gem here than he or she would at the typical friendly "neighborhood bookstore."

The Wayfarer's Bookshop　　　　　　　　　　**By Appointment**
335 Southborough Drive V7S 1L9　　　　　　　　(604) 921-4196
Web page: www.intergate.bc.ca/business/wayfarer　　Fax: (604) 921-4197
　　　　　　　　　　　　　E-mail: wayfarer@intergate.bc.ca
Collection:　Specialty books and ephemera.
# of Vols:　1,000
Specialties:　Travel & exploration; voyages; topography (all pre-1920); some related natural history, archaeology, anthropology and transport.
Services:　Catalog, accepts want lists.
Credit Cards:　Yes
Owner:　Eric R. Waschke
Year Estab:　1996

Westbank
(Map 4, page 44)

Mad Hatter Bookstore　　　　　　　　　　**Open Shop**
5 2483 Main Street V4T 2E8　　　　　　　　　(250) 768-2231
Collection:　General stock of mostly paperback.
# of Vols:　30,000
Hours:　Tue-Sat 9:30-5:30.

White Rock
(Map 5, page 50)

Mozart & Twain Books & Sound　　　　　　**Open Shop**
1235 Johnston Road V4B 3Y8　　　　　　　　(604) 531-6677
　　　　　　　　　　　　　Fax: (604) 535-3583
Collection:　General stock of hardcover and paperback and CDs.
# of Vols:　65,000
Hours:　Mon-Fri 11-5:30. Sat 10:30-5:30. Check before printing
Travel:　From Surrey: Proceed south on King George Hwy (Hwy 99A), then continue south on 152nd St which becomes Johnston Road in White Rock. From USA: Hwy 99 north, then left on 8th Ave and right at the light onto King George Hwy, then left on 16th Ave and left on 152nd St.
Credit Cards:　Yes
Owner:　Liz Rist
Year Estab:　1996

Comments: An attractive shop with a mix of hardcover and paperback books and new CDs. (Note the shops's name.) The hardcover volumes consisted of some identified as antiquarian (some older volumes), a set or two, some older Modern Library editions and some shelves marked "first editions" consisting of many popular writers, e.g., Norman Mailer, Stephen King, etc. The remaining volumes were of fairly recent vintage and represented a broad variety of subjects.

White Rose Bookstore   **Open Shop**
1481 Johnston Road V4B 3Z4   (604) 531-7353

Collection: General stock of hardcover and paperback.
# of Vols: 20,000
Specialties: Art; natural history.
Hours: Mon-Sat 10-5:30.
Travel: See Mozart & Twain above.
Credit Cards: Yes
Owner: Dirk Schouten
Year Estab: 1981
Comments: A good balance of hardcover volumes and paperbacks with a nice section of leather bound books and (for its size) a reasonable number of good books in most subject areas. As this guide goes to press, we are advised that the store may change hands. Thus, it is possible that when you read this, there may also be some changes in the shop's ambience and/or stock. Should this be the case, please advise us so that we can advise future visitors in a later Supplement.

Williams Lake
(Map 4, page 44)

Cariboo Book Bin   **Open Shop**
35A South 1st Avenue V2G 1H4   (250) 392-7079

Collection: General stock of mostly used paperback.
Hours: Mon-Fri 9:30-5:30. Sat 10-5.

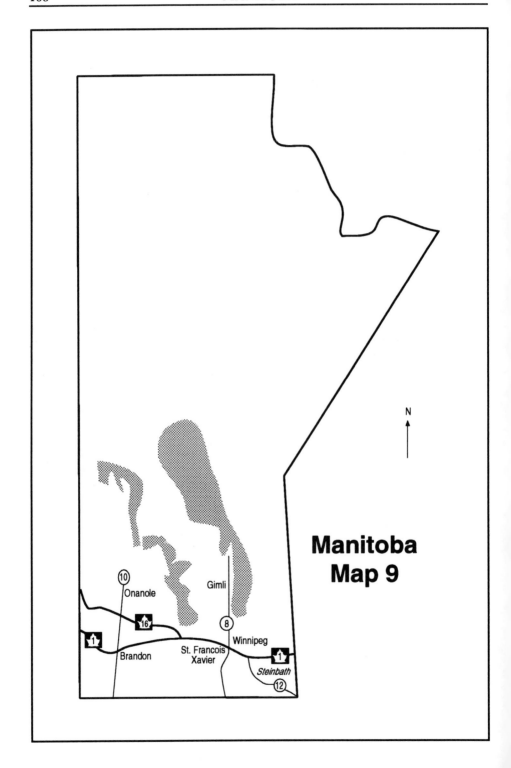

N

**Manitoba
Map 9**

Onanole
Gimli
Brandon
St. Francois
Xavier
Winnipeg
Steinbath

Manitoba

Alphabetical Listing By Dealer

Alphabetical Listing By Location

Altona

Pandora's Books Ltd   **Mail Order**
PO Box 1298 R0G 0B0   (204) 324-8548
Mailing address: PO Box 54 Neche ND (USA) 58265   Fax:(204) 324-1628
Web page: www.pandora.ca/pandora   E-mail: pandora@mts.net

Collection:	Specialty
# of Vols:	120,000
Specialties:	Science fiction; fantasy; horror; crime fiction.
Services:	Accepts want lists.
Credit Cards:	Yes
Owner:	Pam & Tim Friesen & Grant Thiessen
Year Estab:	1977
Comments:	Collection may also be viewed by appointment.

Brandon

George Strange's Book Mart   **Open Shop**
653–10th Street R7A 4G6   (204) 728-2633

Collection:	General stock of paperback and hardcover.
# of Vols:	60,000-80,000
Specialties:	Military; local history.
Hours:	Mon-Sat 10-6.
Services:	Accepts want lists, mail order.
Travel:	18th St exit off Hwy 1. Proceed south on 18th St, east on Victoria, then south on 10th.
Credit Cards:	Yes
Owner:	George Strange
Year Estab:	1984
Comments:	A mix of mostly paperback books with a modest number of hardcover volumes which ran the gamut from recent bestsellers to how-to books and some not so golden oldies.

McGilligan Books   **Open Shop**
841 Rosser Avenue R7A 0L1   (204) 727-0971
                                          E-mail: mcgill@mb.sympatico.ca

Collection:	General stock of paperback and hardcover.
# of Vols:	40,000-50,000
Hours:	Mon-Sat 9-5.
Services:	Search service, accepts want lists, mail order.
Travel:	18th St exit off Hwy 1. Proceed south on 18th St, then left on Rosser. Shop is at corner of Rosser and 9th St.
Credit Cards:	Yes
Owner:	Dr. Decter
Year Estab:	1990
Comments:	In our many travels visiting used book dealers we've come across a number of interesting combination businesses offering books with pizza,

books with flowers, books with pets and books with fishing lures. A stop here offered us the first opportunity to visit a bookstore on the same premises as a post office and an eye doctor (who also owns the bookstore). This by no means should be considered a negative as the shop's two levels (street level and basement) offer a respectable selection of hardcover books in mixed condition, along with a large number of paperbacks. Some of the books appeared to be either new or remainders; others most definitely older volumes. The books were generally reasonably priced. The shop also carries magazines. A sharp eyed scout could well hit it lucky here.

Neverending Stories — **Open Shop**
3 1847 Queens Avenue R7B 3V4 — (204) 571-0701

Collection:	General stock of mostly paperback.
# of Vols:	25,000+
Hours:	Mon-Sat 9:30-6.

Gimli

Page's Book Exchange — **Open Shop**
33 Centre Street — (204) 642-9509
Mailing address: PO Box 1152 Gimli R0C 1B0   E-mail: gpage@mb.sympatico.ca

Collection:	General stock of mostly paperback.
# of Vols:	10,000
Hours:	Tue-Sat 10-5.

Shelemy's Sewing Notions & Book Nook — **Open Shop**
107–7th Avenue — (204) 642-8330
Mailing address: Box 1678 Gimli MB R0C 1B0

Collection:	General stock of mostly paperback.
# of Vols:	10,000
Hours:	Mon-Sat 10-5:30. Summer: Also, Sun 12-3.

Onanole

Poor Michael's Bookshop — **Open Shop**
Hwy 10 — Home: (204) 726-9626
Mailing address: 416–11th Street Brandon MB R7A 4K1

Collection:	General stock of hardcover and paperback.
# of Vols:	9,000
Specialties:	Canadiana; literature.
Hours:	Jul & Aug: Daily 11-8. May, Jun, Sept & Oct: Fri-Sun 11-8.
Services:	Search service, accepts want lists.
Travel:	On Hwy 10, two km south of Riding Mountain National Park.
Credit Cards:	Yes
Owner:	Murray D. Evans
Year Estab:	1992

St. Francois Xavier

Nunnery Book Nook in the Olde Nunnery						Open Shop
1033 PTH 26 R0H 1J0										(204) 864-2389

Collection:	General stock of hardcover and paperback.
# of Vols:	20,000
Specialties:	Canadiana; children's.
Hours:	Mon & Tue 11-4. Wed-Sun 11-7. Jan & Feb: Wed-Fri 11-4. Sat & Sun 11-6.
Services:	Accepts want lists, mail order.
Travel:	Ten minutes west of Winnipeg. From Hwy 1, turn north on Hwy 26 (look for a statue of a white horse). The shop is located in the former convent, in the same complex as the Tin Lizzie Car Barn.
Credit Cards:	Yes
Owner:	Terry-Lynn Champagne
Year Estab:	1998
Comments:	Stock is approximately 75% hardcover.

Steinbath

Comic World										By Appointment
Box 21986 R5G 1B5									(204) 346-3674
											Fax: (204) 326-5871

Collection:	General stock of paperback and hardcover, comics and records.
# of Vols:	300,000
Specialties:	Science fiction; mystery; comic related; television; westerns; magazines.
Services:	Appraisals, accepts want lists, mail order.
Credit Cards:	Yes
Owner:	Doug Sulipa
Year Estab:	1971
Comments:	Stock includes approximately 50,000 hardcover titles.

Winnipeg
(Map 10, page 114)

Blacks' Vintage Books & Antiques						Open Shop
2059 Portage Avenue R3J 0K9								(204) 889-0610

Collection:	General stock of hardcover and paperback, ephemera and records.
# of Vols:	40,000
Specialties:	Canadiana; new age; philosophy; history; sports; literary criticism.
Hours:	Daily, except closed Wed, 11:30-6. (Nov-Mar open till 5:30.)
Services:	Accepts want lists, mail order.
Travel:	On western end of Winnipeg. Hwy 1 becomes Portage Ave (Hwy 85). Shop is opposite Assiniboine Park.
Credit Cards:	Yes

Owner: Margaret & Daniel Black
Year Estab: 1979
Comments: A good balance of books covering a wide range of subject areas, most
                 in quite good condition. Some older volumes. Plenty of paperbacks and
                 a healthy selection of vintage titles. Easy to browse. Reasonably priced.

Book Ends   **Open Shop**
220 St. Mary's Road R2H 1J3   (204) 237-4388

Collection: General stock of mostly paperback.
# of Vols: 12,000-15,000
Hours: Tue & Wed 10-5. Thu 11-7. Fri 10-4. Sat 10-5.

Book Fair Winnipeg   **Open Shop**
366 Portage Avenue R3C 0C5   (204) 944-1630

Collection: General stock of mostly paperback.
# of Vols: 10,000-15,000
Hours: Mon-Fri 10-6. Sat 10-5.

The Bookcase   **Open Shop**
382 Donald Street R3B 2J2   (204) 947-5931

Collection: General stock of mostly paperback.
# of Vols: 10,000
Hours: Mon 12-5:30. Tue-Fri 10-5:30. Sat 10-5.

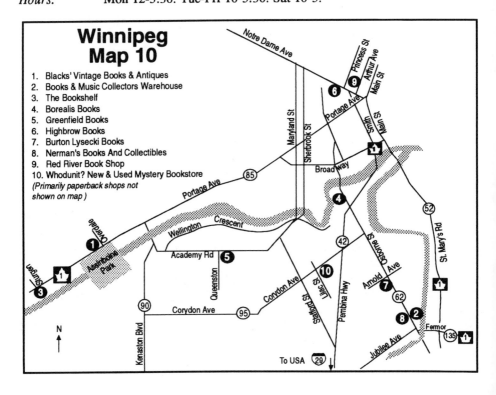

Winnipeg Map 10

1. Blacks' Vintage Books & Antiques
2. Books & Music Collectors Warehouse
3. The Bookshelf
4. Borealis Books
5. Greenfield Books
6. Highbrow Books
7. Burton Lysecki Books
8. Nerman's Books And Collectibles
9. Red River Book Shop
10. Whodunit? New & Used Mystery Bookstore
(Primarily paperback shops not shown on map)

Books & Music Collectors Warehouse   **Open Shop**
736 Osborne Street R3L 2C2 *   (204) 475-2665
                                                   E-mail: mbooks@sprint.ca
Collection: General stock of mostly used hardcover and paperback and records.
# of Vols: 15,000
Specialties: Marilyn Monroe; socialism; T.S. Eliot; poetry; first editions; sports;
                   art; women's studies; Hollywood (books and ephemera).
Hours: Tue-Sat 11-5. Sat 11-6. Sun 12-4. Reduced hours during Jan & Feb.
Services: Appraisals, search service, mail order.
Travel: See Burton Lysecki Books below.
Credit Cards: No
Owner: Morris J. Bay
Year Estab: 1995
Comments: Another "collectibles" shop with a heavy selection of LPs, CDs, comic
                   books and a nice assortment of hardcover volumes if you're into vin-
                   tage and nostalgia. Worth a visit.

                   * The owner will be relocating in Winnipeg in late 1999, early 2000.

The Bookshelf   **Open Shop**
3050 Portage Avenue R3K 0Y1   (204) 889-6270
Collection: General stock of paperback and hardcover, comics and CDs.
# of Vols: 25,000+
Hours: May-Dec: Mon-Fri 10-8. Sat 10-6. Sun 12-5. Jan-Apr: Mon 10-7. Tue
                   11-7. Wed 10-7:30. Thu & Fri 10-8. Sat 10-6. Sun 12-5.
Services: Search service, accepts want lists.
Travel: On western end of Winnipeg. Hwy 1 becomes Portage Ave (Hwy 85).
                   Shop is just east of Hwy 100 (Perimeter Hwy).
Credit Cards: Yes
Owner: Tony Hazzard
Comments: The shop is heavily paperback with a very large collection of comics, both
                   new and vintage. Some hardcover volumes, but not a substantial number.

Borealis Books   **Open Shop**
107½ Osborne Street R3L 1Y4   (204) 475-4669
                                                  E-mail: borealis@escape.ca
Collection: General stock of hardcover and paperback.
# of Vols: 40,000
Specialties: Scholarly; anthropology; science; performing arts; Canadiana.
Hours: Mon-Fri 10-6. Sat 10:30-5.
Services: Search service, accepts want lists, mail order.
Travel: See Burton Lysecki Books below. Shop is between River and Stradbrook.
Credit Cards: Yes
Owner: Richard Orlandini & Rick McNair
Year Estab: 1996
Comments: Located one flight up, this shop is divided into seven separate rooms,
                   each devoted to a particular genre, that surround a much larger room.
                   The shop offers a healthy collection of books and is particularly strong

(Winnipeg)

in the arts and sciences as well as philosophy and history. If your tastes are into more serious subjects (don't look for much in the way of humor or mysteries here although that's not to say that you might not find some) you should find this shop well worth visiting.

Browse & Buy Books   **Open Shop**
964 St. Mary's Road R2M 3R8   (204) 255-2980

Collection: General stock of mostly paperback.
# of Vols: 10,000
Hours: Mon-Sat 10-5, except Tue & Thu till 7. Sun 12-4.

Family Book Exchange   **Open Shop**
567 St. Mary's Road R2M 3L6   (204) 237-4949

Collection: General stock of mostly paperback.
Hours: Tue-Fri 10:30-7, except Wed till 5:30. Sat 10-5.

Flipped Pages Book Exchange   **Open Shop**
398B Edison Avenue R2G 0L8   (204) 338-0647

Collection: General stock of mostly paperback.
# of Vols: 15,000
Hours: Tue & Wed 10:30-5:30. Thu 10:30-7. Fri 10:30-5:30. Sat 11-4.

Greenfield Books   **Open Shop**
438 Academy Road R3N 0C4   (204) 488-2023
Web page: www.escape.ca/~greenfld   Fax: (204) 488-3508
                                                      E-mail: greenfld@escape.ca

Collection: General stock.
# of Vols: 15,000
Specialties: Fine bindings; magic; occult; medicine; law; true crime; Arctic; nautical.
Hours: Mon-Sat 10-6.
Services: Appraisals, search service, mail order, book repairs.
Travel: From Hwy 1 eastbound: Continue on Portage Ave, then turn south on
                 Hwy 90 (Kenaston Blvd) and left on Academy Rd. Shop is between
                 Brock and Queenston.
Credit Cards: Yes
Owner: Michael Park
Year Estab: 1994
Comments: A nice selection of books, primarily hardcover, most in good to excel-
                 lent condition. The books are attractively shelved and the shop is easy
                 to browse. Some more "delicate" items behind glass. Reasonably priced.

Highbrow Books   **Open Shop**
304 Notre Dame R3B 1P4   (204) 943-5668
Web page: www.abebooks.com   E-mail: highbrow@pangea.ca

Collection: General stock of hardcover and paperback.
# of Vols: 10,000
Hours: Mon, Wed-Fri 11-5. Sat 10-5. Sun 12-4.

Services: Appraisals, accepts want lists, mail order.
Travel: From Broadway (Hwy 1 in downtown area), turn north on Smith and
                 left on Notre Dame. Shop is on left, between Princess and Hargrave.
Credit Cards: No
Owner: Les Mundwiler
Year Estab: 1984
Comments: While not large in size, the shop does come by its name honestly. Its
                 shelves are heavily laden with a fine cross section of the world's great
                 literature. Volumes covering non fiction categories (science, history,
                 biography, etc.) are also represented although not in great depth. The
                 books that we saw (mostly hardcover but also a nice selection of
                 paperback titles) were in mixed to good condition. If you're a serious
                 reader and want to discover books you should have read years ago, this
                 is a place where you can catch up on that reading.

Burton Lysecki Books   **Open Shop**
527 Osborne Street R3L 2B2   (204) 284-4546
Web page: www.abebooks.com/home/lysecki   Fax: (204) 284-4547
                                                        E-mail: lysecki@mts.net
Collection: General stock of mostly hardcover.
# of Vols: 65,000
Specialties: Military; history; Western Canadiana; Canadian literature; art; fiction.
Hours: Mon-Sat 11-6.
Services: Mail order.
Travel: Westbound on Hwy 1: Hwy 1 becomes Fermor Rd (Hwy 135). At end
                 of Fermor, turn right and continue north on Hwy 62 which becomes
                 Osborne. Eastbound on Hwy 1: Hwy 1 becomes Portage Ave (Hwy 85)
                 in Winnipeg. Continue east on Portage, then right on Memorial and
                 right (south) on Osborne.
Credit Cards: Yes
Year Estab: 1971
Comments: One has to only speak to the owner of this shop for a few moments to
                 realize that he is in love with books. But even if we did not have that
                 opportunity, walking around his shop would reveal that secret. The
                 shop is a joy to visit. Books of every category are displayed in suffi-
                 cient quantity to keep one's eyes peeled to the shelves that hold the
                 particular subject areas that might be of interest. Strong in Canadiana
                 as well as history, but we had problems finding any areas that were not
                 attractively represented. We have observed many stores over the years
                 that displayed complete sets of the writings of distinguished authors;
                 none in our memory carried quite as many sets as are on display here.

Nerman's Books And Collectibles   **Open Shop**
721 Osborne Street R3L 2C1   (204) 475-1050
Web page: www.abebooks.com/home/nerman   Fax: (204) 947-0753
                                                        E-mail: nerman@escape.ca
Collection: General stock of mostly hardcover and ephemera.
# of Vols: 40,000

(Winnipeg)

Specialties:	Children's; film; nostalgia; vintage paperbacks.
Hours:	Daily 10-5.
Services:	Appraisals, mail order.
Travel:	See Burton Lysecki above.
Credit Cards:	Yes
Owner:	Gary Nerman & Mary Ann Huen
Year Estab:	1992
Comments:	Over the years, we've visited lots of shops that refer to themselves as specialists in "collectibles"; this one fits the bill perfectly, particularly for those interested in children's books and children's series titles. In addition to its collection of vintage paperbacks, the shop carries pulp magazines, Big Little Books, comic books and a respectable section of hardcover volumes, both on the main level and one flight down. More desirable titles are located behind the front counter. If you want to examine the way thousands of children's books were published and illustrated around the turn of the century and in the early part of this century, you're sure to get a taste of that here. As it's name implies, the shop also carries some non book collectibles

Pembina Book Exchange   **Open Shop**
1187 Pembina Highway R3T 2A5   (204) 452-3628

Collection:	General stock of mostly paperback.
Hours:	Mon-Sat 10-5, except Thu till 7:30.

PhilosoTea Book and Tea Room   **Open Shop**
284 Tache Avenue R2H 2A2   (204) 233-5048

Collection:	General stock of mostly paperback.
# of Vols:	5,000-10,000
Hours:	Tue-Sat 11-5.

Red River Book Shop   **Open Shop**
92 Arthur Street R3B 1H3   (204) 943-9788

Collection:	General stock of paperback and hardcover, comics and videos.
# of Vols:	50,000
Hours:	Mon-Fri 10-8. Sat & Sun 10-7.
Travel:	See Highbrow Books Ave. Shop is between McDermott & Bannatyne.
Credit Cards:	Yes
Year Estab:	1970's
Comments:	Located in a large stone building (a former warehouse), the ground level might be described as "sprawling" in terms of its size and opportunity for browsing. Lot and lots of space. Plenty of books. The shop seems to cater to modern and older comic book tastes with a large selection in both categories. It also offers a large selection of videos along with paperbacks, magazines, hardcover titles (mostly reading copies) and a few rarer items behind the counter.

Selkirk Book Exchange   **Open Shop**
442 McGregor Street R2W 4X8   (204) 586-5127

Collection: General stock of mostly paperback.
# of Vols: 40,000
Hours: Tue, Wed, Fri, Sat 10-3. Thu 1-7.

Whodunit? New & Used Mystery Bookstore   **Open Shop**
165 Lilac Street R3M 2S1   (204) 284-9100
Web page: whodunitcanada.com   Fax: (204) 453-5351
                                                E-mail: whodunit@escape.ca

Collection: Specialty new and used.
# of Vols: 10,000
Specialties: Mystery, with emphasis on Canadian and British mysteries and mys-
                  tery reference.
Hours: Mon-Fri 10-6. Sat 10-5. Sun 12-4.
Services: Search service, accepts want lists, mail order.
Travel: See Burton Lysecki Books above. From Osborne, turn west on Corydon
                  and north on Lilac.
Credit Cards: Yes
Owner: Gaylene Chesnut & Henrietta Wilde
Year Estab: 1993
Comments: Stock is evenly divided between used and new books. Used stock is
                  approximately 75% paperback.

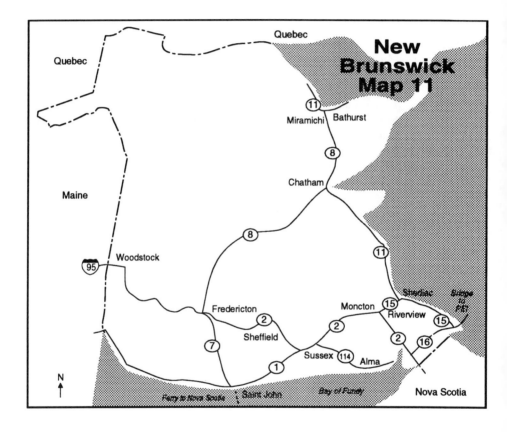

New Brunswick

Alphabetical Listing By Dealer

Alphabetical Listing By Location

Alma

Cleveland Place Books **Open Shop**
8580 Main Street (506) 887-2213
Mailing address: PO Box 76 Alma NB E0A 1B0

Collection:	General stock of mostly new and some used hardcover.
# of Vols:	5,000
Hours:	Daily 7-7.
Travel:	Located on Rte 114, at east gate to Fundy National Park.
Credit Cards:	Yes
Owner:	Wallace West
Year Estab:	1950's
Comments:	Stock is approximately 20% used hardcover.

Bathurst

Rising Sun Book Shop **Open Shop**
1180 St. Peter Avenue E2A 2Z9 (506) 546-2243

Collection:	General stock of mostly paperback.
# of Vols:	5,000
Hours:	Mon-Fri 10-7. Sat 10-5. Later hours in summer.

Chatham

Gateway Esoteric Shop **Open Shop**
104 Duke Street E1N 1H2 (506) 773-9994

Collection:	General of mostly used paperback.
# of Vols:	10,000 (used)
Hours:	Mon-Sat 10-6.

Fredericton

Augustine Funnell Books **By Appointment**
179 Main Street E3A 1E1 (506) 472-2053
Web page: www.medianet.ca/atlantic/augustin/augustin.htm

E-mail: gobruins@nbnet.nb.ca

Collection:	General stock of hardcover and paperback.
# of Vols:	5,000+
Specialties:	Science fiction; mystery; vintage paperbacks.
Services:	Search service, accepts want lists, mail order.
Credit Cards:	Yes
Owner:	Gus Funnell
Year Estab:	1993

Harry E. Bagley Books   **Mail Order**
PO Box 691 E3B 5B4   (506) 459-3034
Web page: www.bagbooks.nb.ca   Fax: (617) 531- 2094
                                                 E-mail: bagbooks@nbnet.nb.ca

Collection: Specialty books and ephemera.
Specialties: Canadiana (pre-1900); travel; angling.
Services: Appraisals, search service, accepts want lists.
Credit Cards: Yes
Year Estab: 1965

FitzPatrick Books   **Mail Order**
80 Spencer Street   E3A 7S2   (506) 444-8989
                                          E-mail: pfitzpat@nb.sympatico.ca

Collection: General stock.
# of Vols: 85,000-90,000
Specialties: Canadiana
Services: Appraisals, search service, catalog, accepts want lists.
Credit Cards: No
Owner: Patrick, Geraldine & J.W. J. FitzPatrick
Year Estab: 1976

Lapsilla IV   **Open Shop**
390 Queen Street E3B 1B2   (506) 455-2455

Collection: Specialty
# of Vols: 1,000
Specialties: New age; art; music; French language books.
Hours: See Owl's Nest Bookstore below.
Travel: Located on the second floor of the Owl's Nest Bookstore.
Owner: Julie Bernier & John Butters
Year Estab: 1995

Owl's Nest Bookstore   **Open Shop**
390 Queen Street E3B 1B2   (506) 458-5509

Collection: General stock of paperback and hardcover.
# of Vols: 100,000
Hours: Mon-Fri 9-5:30 (Apr-Jun till 8 and Jul & Aug till 9). Sat 9-5. Sun 12-5.
Travel: Northbound on Hwy 2: Regent St exit. Continue on Regent, then left
                   on Queen. Park in city lot.
Credit Cards: Yes
Year Estab: 1993
Comments: A large collection, that while heavy in paperbacks, also has a respect-
                   able number of hardcover volumes in a series of nooks and crannies
                   and a small room called the "Collector's Closet." This is the kind of
                   shop that a less than patient visitor might dismiss quickly as having too
                   many common items that are not all in the best condition and, in the
                   process, inadvertently skip over a hidden prize or two. Don't miss the
                   separate shop located on the second floor. (See Lapsilla IV above.)

Reading Corner   **Open Shop**
230 Main Street E3A 1C9   (506) 458-9680

Collection: General stock of mostly paperback.
# of Vols: 15,000
Hours: Mon-Thu 10-5. Fri 10-8. Sat 10-5.

United Book Stores   **Open Shop**
349 King Street E3B 1E4   (506) 454-5333

Collection: General stock of mostly paperback.
# of Vols: 10,000
Hours: Sun-Wed 9-9. Thu-Sat 9am-10pm.

Miramichi

John's Used Books   **Open Shop**
87 Henry Street   (506) 622-7914
Mailing address: PO Box 31 Miramichi NB E1V 3M2

Collection: General stock of hardcover and paperback.
# of Vols: 30,000+
Specialties: Canadian literature (early and current).
Hours: Daily 1-6. Longer hours in summer.
Services: Accepts want lists, mail order.
Travel: From Moncton, proceed north on Hwy 11 to Miramichi, then west on
                  King George Hwy and left on Newcastle Blvd. Continue down the hill
                  and turn right on Henry. Shop is located near City Hall in the souvenir
                  shop, Lobster Creations.
Credit Cards: No
Owner: John Bethell
Year Estab: 1985
Comments: If you're into ecology you'll be happy to learn that a nearby factory
                  that processes lobsters makes the shells of these crustaceans available
                  to the owner of this establishment who in turn turns them into a variety
                  of figurines painted to represent all kinds of God's creatures, from
                  brides and grooms to Santa Claus and Elvis Presley. On the other hand,
                  if you're looking for rare or unusual books, expect to find a shop
                  loaded with paperback titles, magazines and comics, some displayed
                  on open shelves and, at the time of our visit, many more packed away
                  in boxes, and a modest number of hardcover volumes, mostly recent
                  best sellers. The owner advised us that occasionally he does buy and
                  sell what he describes as a "rare book." He also advised us that once he
                  was set up in his new location (the address noted above) he hoped to
                  display more of the stock we saw packed away in boxes.

Moncton

Attic Owl Bookshop   **Open Shop**
885 Main Street E1C 1G5   (506) 855-4913
Web page: www.abebooks.com/home/atticbooks
                                                    E-mail: eepond@nb.sympatico.ca

Collection:	General stock of hardcover and paperback.
# of Vols:	35,000
Specialties:	New Brunswick, Acadia; philosophy; modern first editions.
Hours:	Mon-Sat 10-6. Winter: Mon-Sat 11-5.
Services:	Appraisals, search service.
Travel:	Eastbound on Hwy 2: Exit 504. Continue west on Hwy 15, then Botsford exit off Hwy 15. Left on Botsford, then right on Main. Westbound on Hwy 2, turn left on Hwy 15, left on Botsford and right on Main.
Credit Cards:	Yes
Owner:	Edward Lemond
Year Estab:	1993
Comments:	We visited this bi-level shop on our first full day in Canada (after a 12 hour drive from home the previous day) and are pleased to report that the shop offers the traveling book lover all the attributes of a used book store that one could want. The shop carries a nice mix of mostly hardcover books in generally good condition and representing a wide range of topics. We found the books to be attractively priced and the store easy to browse.

Laurie Landry-Used & Antiquarian Book Dealer   **By Appointment**
PO Box 571 E1C 8L9   (506) 855-8860
                                                             E-mail: landryl@fox.nstn.ca

Collection:	Specialty (French and English)
# of Vols:	2,000+
Specialties:	Maritime; Acadia.
Services:	Mail order.
Credit Cards:	No
Year Estab:	1991

United Book Stores   **Open Shop**
347 Mountain Road E1C 2M7   (506) 857-8582
                                                                     Fax: (506) 857-1705
                                                    E-mail: ubsmctn@nbnet.nb.ca

Collection:	General stock of mostly paperback and comics.
# of Vols:	15,000
Hours:	Daily 9am-10pm.

Riverview

Parlour
720 Coverdale Road E1B 3L8

Open Shop
(506) 387-8020

Collection: General stock of mostly paperback.
Hours: Mon-Fri 9:30-9. Sat 9:30-6.

Spectrum Books
704 Coverdale Road E1B 3L1

Open Shop
(506) 387-3108

Collection: General stock of mostly paperback.
# of Vols: 15,000-20,000
Hours: Mon-Tue 10-6. Wed-Fri 10-9. Sat 10-5. Sun 12-5.

Saint John

Book Broker Used Books
196 Union Street E2L 1B1

Open Shop
(506) 657-6310
E-mail: joe_beebe@hotmail.com

Collection: General stock of mostly paperback.
# of Vols: 22,000
Hours: Mon-Sat 9:30-5:30.

The Book Trellis
15 Canterbury Street E2L 2D3

Open Shop
(506) 633-7584

Collection: General stock of paperback and hardcover.
# of Vols: 5,000
Hours: Mon-Sat 10:30-5.
Travel: Downtown, just off King St, across from Brunswick Square shopping center.
Credit Cards: No
Owner: Ardell Wills
Year Estab: 1995
Comments: A nice mix of both paperback and hardcover volumes, shelved both together and separately. Most of the volumes we saw were in good to better condition and were reasonably priced.

Loyalist City Coins & Collectibles
160 Union Street E2L 1A8

Open Shop
(506) 642-3143

Collection: General stock of paperback and hardcover, LPs and ephemera.
# of Vols: 10,000
Hours: Mon-Fri 10-4, except Fri till 8. Sat 11-4.
Travel: Located in downtown.
Credit Cards: Yes
Owner: Ross Harris
Year Estab: 1979

Comments: An interesting shop that offers, in addition to its books (mostly paper-
                back), an assortment of comics, magazines, old coins and nostalgia
                items. The hardcover books were of mixed vintage and covered most
                subject areas. While the books were not all in the best condition, there
                were some volumes that could be of interest to collectors.

Paper Treasures   **Open Shop**
40 Coburg Street E2L 3J5   (506) 648-9828
                                             E-mail: tkeleher@nb.net.nb.ca

Collection: General stock.
# of Vols: 4,000
Specialties: Primarily older books.
Hours: Apr-Nov: Mon-Fri 10-5. Dec-Mar: by appointment only.
Credit Cards: No
Travel: Just off Union St.
Owner: Terry Keleher
Year Estab: 1981

The Scholar's Den   **Open Shop**
105 Prince Edward Street   (506) 657-2665
Mailing address: 36 Richmond Street Saint John NB E2L 3B2
                                             E-mail: sden@nbnet.nb.ca

Collection: General stock of hardcover and paperback and records.
# of Vols: 2,500
Specialties: Primarily non fiction with some first editions of popular novels.
Hours: Mon-Sat 11-5.
Services: Accepts want lists.
Travel: Wall St exit off Hwy 1. Proceed south toward City Centre. Take left
                fork onto Paddock St and continue to Waterloo. Left on Waterloo, then
                right on Richmond. Shop is at end of street.
Credit Cards: No
Owner: Bill & Cony Brienza
Year Estab: 1997
Comments: Most of the hardcover volumes were of fairly recent vintage, some
                book club editions and a few older volumes. The books were in gener-
                ally mixed condition and quite reasonably priced.

United Book Stores   **Open Shop**
25 Charlotte Street E2L 2H3   (506) 693-4835

Collection: General stock of mostly paperback.
# of Vols: 10,000
Hours: Daily 8:30am-9pm.

United Book Stores   **Open Shop**
168 Rothesay Avenue E2J 2B5   (506) 642-5500

Collection: General stock mostly paperback.
# of Vols: 10,000
Hours: Mon-Sat 9am-10pm.

Shediac

Page à Page   **Open Shop**
334 Main Street E0A 3G0   (506) 532-4664

Collection:	General stock of paperback and hardcover.
# of Vols:	4,500
Hours:	May-Jun: Mon-Wed 9-5. Thu & Fri 9-9. Sat 9-5. Sun (starting May 15) 12-5. Jul & Aug: Daily 8am-10pm. Sept-Apr: Mon-Sat 9-5.
Travel:	Downtown.
Owner:	Edward Lemond
Year Estab:	1999
Comments:	Stock is approximately 60% French. The shop is located inside a coffee shop. The owner's main location is in Moncton. See Attic Owl Bookshop above.

Sheffield

Crawford's Used Books   **Open Shop**
2031 Route 2 Highway E3A 8H8   (506) 357-3820

Collection:	General stock of mostly hardcover.
# of Vols:	100,000
Hours:	Generally, from early May-mid Oct: Mon-Sat 9-9. Best to call ahead.
Travel:	On Hwy 2, between Fredericton and Jemseg.
Credit Cards:	No
Owner:	Ralph E. Crawford
Year Estab:	1972

Sussex

Main Street Books   **Open Shop**
577 Main Street E0E 1P1   (506) 432-6246

Collection:	General stock of mostly paperback.
# of Vols:	6,000+
Hours:	Mon-Sat 9:30-5:30, except Fri till 7:30.

Woodstock

Cover to Cover Book Store   **Open Shop**
553 Main Street E7M 2B9   (506) 328-8806

Collection:	General stock of mostly paperback.
# of Vols:	9,000+
Hours:	Mon-Thu 9-5. Fri 9-8. Sat 9-2.

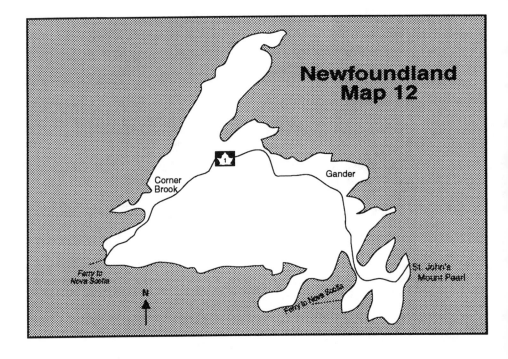

Newfoundland

Alphabetical Listing By Dealer

Alphabetical Listing By Location

Corner Brook

The Book Grotto **Open Shop**
44A Main Street A2H 1C3 (709) 639-7750
Fax: (709) 639-1402

Collection: General stock of mostly paperback.
Hours: Mon, Tue, Sat 9-5:30. Wed, Thu, Fri 9-9. Sun 12-4.

The Book Hollow **Open Shop**
Millbrook Mall (709) 639-1949
2 Herald Avenue A2H 4B5

Collection: General stock of mostly paperback.
# of Vols: 5,000
Hours: Mon & Tue 9:30-5:30. Wed-Fri 9:30-9. Sat 9:30-5:30. Sun 12-5.

Paul's Books & Souvenirs **Open Shop**
93 West Street A2H 2Y6 (709) 634-5955

Collection: General stock of mostly paperback.
# of Vols: 5,000
Hours: Mon-Sat 10-6.

Gander

The Book Worm **Open Shop**
Gander Mall Tel & Fax: (709) 651-2777
132 Bennett Drive E-mail: the book_worm@hotmail.com
Mailing address: PO Box 287 Gander NF A1V 1W6

Collection: General stock of mostly paperback.
Hours: Daily 9:30-9.

Mount Pearl

The Book Closet **Open Shop**
7 Commonwealth Avenue (709) 368-7323
Mailing address: PO Box 694 Mount Pearl A1N 2X1

Collection: General stock of mostly paperback.
# of Vols: 15,000+
Hours: Mon-Fri 10-6, except Thu & Fri till 9. Sat 10-5:30.

St. John's

Afterwords Book Store **Open Shop**
245 Duckworth Street A1C 1G8 (709) 753-4690

Collection: General stock of paperback and hardcover.
Hours: Mon-Sat 10-5:30, except Fri till 9. Sun 12-5. Best to confirm.
Travel: Downtown, one block off Water St.
Comments: Stock is approximately 70% paperback.

Newfoundland and Labrador Bookfinder   **By Appointment**
123 Waterford Bridge Road A1E 1C7   Tel & Fax: (709) 722-8310
Web page: bookfinder.nf.ca   E-mail: skanes@bookfinder.nf.ca

Collection:	General stock of hardcover and paperback and ephemera.
# of Vols:	2,000
Specialties:	Newfoundland; Labrador.
Services:	Appraisals, search service, catalog, accepts want lists.
Credit Cards:	Yes
Owner:	Graham Skanes
Year Estab:	1997

The Olde London Market   **Open Shop**
179 Water Street A1C 1B1   (709) 579-7355

Collection:	General stock.
# of Vols:	600-1000
Hours:	Wed-Sat 11-4. Other days by chance or appointment.
Services:	Mail order.
Travel:	Across from the courthouse.
Comments:	Also sells antiques and collectibles.

Gerald Penney Rare Books and Maps   **By Appointment**
29 Smith Avenue   Tel & Fax: (709) 739-7227
Mailing address: PO Box 428 St. John's NF A1C 5K4   E-mail: gpaltd@nlnet.nf.ca

Collection:	Specialty used and new.
Specialties:	Newfoundland; Labrador.
Services:	Appraisals, search service, catalog, accepts want lists.
Credit Cards:	Yes
Year Estab:	1994
Comments:	Stock is approximately 75% used. Books are in English and French.

Second Page Bookstore & Poster Shop   **Open Shop**
363 Water Street A1C 1C2   (709) 722-1742

Collection:	General stock of mostly paperback.
# of Vols:	5,000-10,000
Hours:	Mon-Sat 10-5:30, except Thu & Fri till 9. Sun 12-5.

Second Page Bookstore & Poster Shop   **Open Shop**
38 Pearson Street A1A 3R1   (709) 722-3638

Collection:	General stock of mostly paperback.
# of Vols:	5,000-10,000
Hours:	Mon-Sat 10-5:30, except Thu & Fri till 9. Sun 12-5.

Second Page Bookstore & Poster Shop   **Open Shop**
655 Topsail Road A1E 2E3   (709) 364-8154

Collection:	General stock of mostly paperback.
# of Vols:	5,000-10,000
Hours:	Mon-Sat 10-5:30, except Thu & Fri till 9. Sun 12-5.

Wordplay   **Open Shop**
221 Duckworth Street A1C 1G7   (800) 563- 9100   (709) 726-9193
Web page: www.wordplay.com   Fax: (709) 726-9190
                                              E-mail: jbaird@wordplay.com

Collection:	General stock of hardcover and paperback.
# of Vols:	50,000
Specialties:	Newfoundland; fiction; history.
Hours:	Mon-Sat 10-6, except Thu & Fri till 9. Sun 12-5.
Services:	Appraisals, search service, accepts want lists, mail order.
Travel:	Duckworth is the major street in downtown.
Credit Cards:	Yes
Owner:	Jim Baird
Year Estab:	1989
Comments:	Stock is approximately 60% hardcover. The shop also has a coffee bar and art gallery.

Nothing replaces a good book.

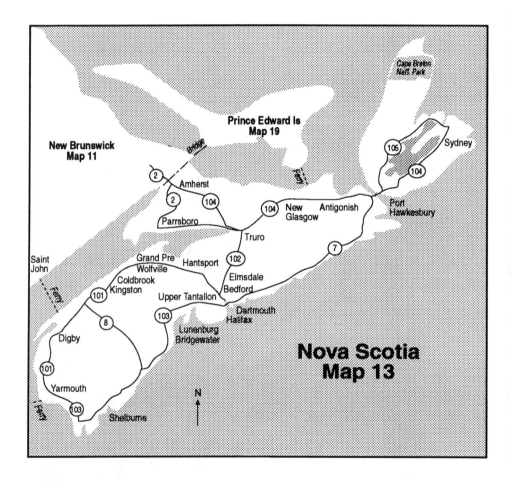

New Brunswick
Map 11

Prince Edward Is
Map 19

Cape Breton
Nat'l Park

Sydney

105

104

2

Amherst

2

104

104 New Antigonish
Glasgow

Port
Hawkesbury

Parrsboro

Truro

7

Saint
John

Grand Pre Hantsport
Wolfville

102

Coldbrook
Kingston

Elmsdale
Bedford

101

Upper Tantallon

Digby

8

103

Dartmouth
Halifax

Lunenburg
Bridgewater

Nova Scotia
Map 13

101

Yarmouth

N

103

Shelburne

Nova Scotia

Alphabetical Listing By Dealer

Alphabetical Listing By Location

Amherst

Amy's Used Books   **Open Shop**
4 Robert Angus Drive, Centennial Plaza   (902) 667-7927
Mailing address: 13 Fletcher Drive Amherst NS B4H 4M4

Collection:	General stock of hardcover and paperback.
# of Vols:	200,000
Specialties:	Science fiction; mystery; maritime.
Hours:	Mon-Thu 10-6. Fri 10-9. Sat 10-5.
Services:	Accepts want lists, mail order.
Travel:	Exit 4 off Hwy 104. At exit, turn towards Amherst and go approximately one half km. Turn right at first light, then left into small strip shopping area.
Credit Cards:	Yes
Owner:	Doug Patrquin
Year Estab:	1993
Comments:	There's no question but that this shop does offer in excess of 200,000 volumes, the vast majority of which are paperback. At the time of our visit (see note below) we have to report that the aisles were exceedingly narrow, that books were shelved from floor to ceiling, piled in the aisles and even on the support beams between the aisles. Walking down the aisles, my worst fear was that the earth might tremble and I'd be buried in books. (Not a bad fate I suppose for someone who loves books but not one that I relish at this time of my life.) While one could admire the owner of this shop for his apparent desire to fill every square inch of his shop with books, the downside of such industry is that it is exceedingly difficult to read the titles of a good many of the volumes on hand, thus detracting from the size of the stock. While aisles are labeled and a diligent and patient browser can find the section/s that have the greatest appeal, the real challenge begins when one tries to identify specific titles as so many of the books are shelved horizontally with their spines hidden from view.

Note: Shortly after our visit we were advised, in a phone conversation with the owner, that should he be successful in his efforts to acquire additional space adjoining his shop, future visitors may find the shop less crowded than the one we describe above.

Antigonish

Bookends   **Open Shop**
342 Main Street B2G 2C3   (902) 863-6922

Collection:	General stock of mostly paperback.
Hours:	Mon-Sat 10-5, except Fri till 9.

Bedford

Mulberry Books   **Open Shop**
1475 Bedford Highway B4A 3Z5   (902) 832-3477
                                                                 Fax: (902) 832-3499

Collection:	General stock of hardcover and paperback.
# of Vols:	10,000
Hours:	Mon-Wed 10-6. Thu & Fri 10-9. Sat 10-5:30. May-Oct: Also Sun 12-5.
Travel:	From Halifax, proceed north on Hwy 2 (Bedford Hwy). Shop is on right, in Canada Trust Court shopping center, just after the Fish Hatchery Park.
Credit Cards:	Yes
Owner:	Maureen Kirk & Debbie Bauld
Year Estab:	1998
Comments:	This shop best fits the description of a "friendly neighborhood establishment" in that the books (both hardcover and paperback) are primarily of recent vintage and are of "popular" interest although we did spot some older books and a fair share of classics. There's a delightful children's section to the rear of the store which should hold the attention of younger visitors while making it easier for the grown ups to browse the store's other offerings.

Bridgewater

Carousel Bookstore   **Open Shop**
527 King Street B4V 1B3   (902) 543-1434

Collection:	General stock of mostly paperback.
Hours:	Mon-Sat 10-5 except Fri till 8.

Coldbrook

Books Galore   **Open Shop**
2591 Highway 1 B4R 1B6   (902) 679-9816

Collection:	General stock of paperback and hardcover.
# of Vols:	25,000
Hours:	Mon-Fri 10-9. Sat 10-5:30. Sun 12-5.
Travel:	Exit 14 off Hwy 101. Head west on Hwy 1. Shop is in Coldbrook Centre.
Comments:	Several aisles of paperbacks interspersed with some hardcover volumes, most of which were older and not in the best condition. There was, however, a small corner devoted exclusively to more recent hardcover volumes, the majority of which sported dust jackets and which were offered at moderate prices. The owner operates similar shops in Elmsdale and Upper Tantallon.

Dartmouth

Quality Used Books   **Open Shop**
211 Pleasant Street B2Y 3R5   (902) 463-1475
                                          E-mail: fmason@ns.sympatico.ca

Collection:	General stock of mostly paperback.
# of Vols:	35,000
Hours:	Mon-Fri 9-9. Sat 9-6.
Travel:	Hwy 111 south toward Cole Harbour. At end of Rte 322, turn right. Shop is about 1.5 km ahead in the Woodside Mall.

Digby

New To You Music & Books   **Open Shop**
100 Montague Row B0V 1A0   (902) 245-4707
Web page: www3.ns.sympatico.ca/newtoyou   E-mail: newtoyou@ns.sympatico.ca

Collection:	General stock of paperback and hardcover, comics, cassettes and CDs.
# of Vols:	10,000
Hours:	Mon-Sat 10-5 (except closed 12-1 for lunch).
Travel:	Exit 26 off Hwy 101. Proceed north on Hwy 303 to Digby. Continue straight through the lights, down the hill, and then left at end of street. Shop is across from the museum.
Credit Cards:	Yes
Owner:	Phil Robertson
Year Estab:	1997
Comments:	A relatively small shop with far more paperbacks than hardcover volumes. If you're a hockey fan, you might find an item of interest here.

Elmsdale

Books Galore & More   **Open Shop**
Highway 102   (902) 883-1335

Collection:	General stock of paperback and hardcover.
# of Vols:	10,000
Hours:	Mon-Fri 9:30-9. Sat 9:30-5. Sun 1-5.
Travel:	Exit 8 off Hwy 102. Shop is just off exit in Sobeys Mall.
Comments:	Stock is approximately 75% paperback.

Grand-Pré

marchandise   **Open Shop**
11491 Highway 1   (902) 542-4419
Mailing address: PO Box 51 Grand-Pré NS B0P 1M0

                                          E-mail: marchand@glinx.com

Collection:	General stock of new and used books and ephemera.
# of Vols:	1,000
Specialties:	Acadia; Nova Scotia; Canadiana; gardening; natural history.
Hours:	Most days, 12-6.

Services:	Search service, accepts want lists, mail order.
Travel:	Exit 10 off Hwy 101. Shop is two miles east of Wolfville.
Credit Cards:	No
Owner:	Jocelyne Marchand
Year Estab:	1998
Comments:	Stock is approximately 70% new. The owner's Evangeline collection is on display at the store.

Halifax

Attic Owl Bookshop   **Open Shop**
5802 South Street B3H 1S5   (902) 422-2433
                                          E-mail: aj348@chebucto.ns.ca

Collection:	General stock of paperback and hardcover.
# of Vols:	15,000
Specialties:	Buddhism
Hours:	Mon-Sat 10:30-6. Sun 12-5.
Travel:	Between Wellington St and Tower Rd.
Owner:	Jan Watson
Year Estab:	1993
Comments:	If you're looking for a simple shop with lots of paperbacks (some old, most newer) and a few hardcover volumes, you'll have found it here. On the other hand, if you're looking for a rare volume, your chances of finding it at this shop are less likely.

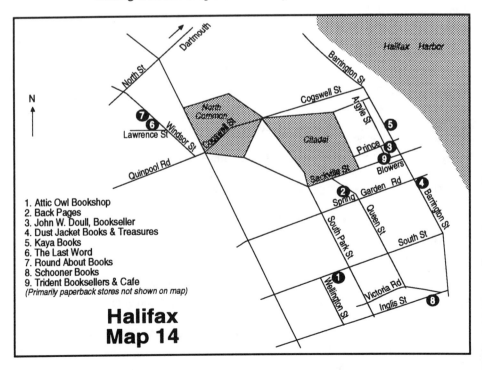

1. Attic Owl Bookshop
2. Back Pages
3. John W. Doull, Bookseller
4. Dust Jacket Books & Treasures
5. Kaya Books
6. The Last Word
7. Round About Books
8. Schooner Books
9. Trident Booksellers & Cafe
(Primarily paperback stores not shown on map)

**Halifax
Map 14**

Back Pages   **Open Shop**
1526 Queen Street B3J 2H8   (902) 423-4750
                                                    E-mail: backpage@istar.ca

Collection: General stock of hardcover and paperback.
# of Vols: 20,000
Hours: Mon-Sat 9:30-5:30. Sun 12-5. Extended hours in summer and fall.
Travel: Between Spring Garden Rd and Sackville St.
Credit Cards: Yes
Owner: Michael Norris
Year Estab: 1979
Comments: Quite a nice shop with an excellent collection, well balanced in terms of
                  vintage, nicely organized and reasonably priced. The vast majority of
                  the books we saw were in good condition. Several unusual titles and, if
                  you're a serious collector, you might be fortunate enough to be invited
                  to the second floor where some of shop's better books are on display.

Books R Us   **Open Shop**
6050 Almon Street B3K 1T8   (902) 455-7832

Collection: General stock of mostly paperback.
Hours: Mon-Fri 9-5. Sat 12-5.

Buy The Book And More   **Open Shop**
1 Flamingo Drive B3M 1S4   (902) 445-5003

Collection: General stock of mostly paperback.
# of Vols: 10,000
Hours: Mon-Sat 10-7, except Fri till 9. Sun 12-6.

John W. Doull, Bookseller   **Open Shop**
1684 Barrington Street B3J 2A2   (902) 429-1652
Web page: www.doullbooks.com   E-mail: jwdoull@ns.sympatico.ca

Collection: General stock of hardcover and paperback.
# of Vols: 100,000
Specialties: Nautical; Newfoundland; Labrador; Nova Scotia; modern first editions.
Hours: Jun-Sept: Mon-Fri 9:30-9. Sat 10-9. Remainder of year: Mon-Tue
                  9:30-6. Wed-Fri 9:30-9. Sat 10-9.
Services: Appraisals, catalog, accepts want lists.
Travel: Downtown, at corner of Prince St.
Credit Cards: Yes
Year Estab: 1987
Comments: A large collection of both hardcover and paperback books in generally
                  good condition and meticulously organized both by subject and, in the
                  case of fiction, by author. In addition to the books located on the first
                  and second levels of the shop, there's a separate room on the second
                  floor devoted exclusively to nautical titles. This is the kind of shop
                  that an experienced traveling book lover will want to spend a bit more
                  time visiting.

(Halifax)

Dust Jacket Books & Treasures   **Open Shop**
1505 Barrington Street B3J 3K5   (902) 492-0666
                                            E-mail: dustjacket@ns.sympatico.ca

Collection:	General stock of hardcover and paperback.
# of Vols:	30,000
Specialties:	Nautical; gardening; Maritime provinces; Canadiana; home repair; crafts.
Hours:	Mon-Fri 10-4.
Services:	Downtown, at foot of Spring Garden Rd. Shop is in the Maritime Centre on level B2.
Credit Cards:	No
Owner:	Chris Cooper
Year Estab:	1997
Comments:	Don't be fooled by the "popular" appearance of this shop, possibly necessitated by its location on the lower level of an indoor shopping mall located within a larger office building. From the shop's windows, one sees lots of colorful titles and a heavy concentration of paperbacks in addition to used magazines. A careful and experienced browser, however, is also likely to spot some hard-to-find and unusual titles (both American and Canadian) at reasonable prices. This is an easy shop to browse and, if your tastes are in any of the less scholarly areas, a place where you may find several books to your liking.

Kaya Books   **Open Shop**
1903 Barrington Street B3J 3L7   (902) 422-8182
                                            E-mail: kayabooks@ns.sympatico.ca

Collection:	General stock of hardcover and paperback, ephemera and magazines.
# of Vols:	25,000
Hours:	Mon-Sat 9:30-6, except Thu & Fri till 9.
Services:	Appraisals, accepts want lists, mail order.
Travel:	On lower level of Barrington Place Shops. Entrance is from Barrington or Granville Streets.
Credit Cards:	Yes
Owner:	Neil E. Eamon
Year Estab:	1992
Comments:	Located in an indoor shopping mall in the heart of downtown Halifax, this shop displays lots of nostalgia related posters, sheet music and other memorabilia in its windows and along the walls. The books, both hardcover and paperback, covered many subject areas, including, at the time of our visit, a strong collection of vintage hardcover mysteries. While the shop has some tight corners, for the most part, it's generally accessible for most browsers.

The Last Word   **Open Shop**
2160 Windsor Street B3K 5B6   (902) 423-2932

Collection:	General stock of paperback and hardcover.
# of Vols:	15,000

Specialties:	Literature
Hours:	Mon-Sat 10-6.
Travel:	Between Lawrence & Duncan.
Credit Cards:	No
Owner:	Wayne Greene
Year Estab:	1996
Comments:	A modest sized shop with a mix of paperback and hardcover volumes, most in good condition, of fairly recent vintage and with an emphasis on popular titles.

Round About Books   **Open Shop**
2166 Windsor Street B3K 5B6   (902) 429-7685
                                   E-mail: pat.webster@ns.sympatico.ca

Collection:	General stock of hardcover and paperback.
# of Vols:	4,000
Specialties:	Non fiction only.
Hours:	Tue-Sat 11-5.
Services:	Accepts want lists, mail order.
Credit Cards:	No
Owner:	Pat Webster
Year Estab:	1999
Comments:	Unfortunately this recently opened shop, next door to another used bookstore, was closed at the time of our visit. (The owner was courteous enough to leave a note on her door advising visitors that she would not be open during her normal hours that day.) A glance through the shop window suggests a cozy atmosphere. The stock is evenly divided between hardcover and paperback.

Schooner Books   **Open Shop**
5378 Inglis Street B3H 1J5   Tel & Fax: (902) 423-8419
                                   E-mail: SchoonerBooks@ns.sympatico.ca

Collection:	General stock of mostly hardcover.
# of Vols:	50,000
Specialties:	Canadiana; illustrated.
Hours:	Mon-Fri 9:30-6. Sat 9:30-5:30.
Services:	Appraisals, catalog
Travel:	Just west of Barrington.
Credit Cards:	Yes
Owner:	John D. Townsend & Mary Lee MacDonald
Year Estab:	1975
Comments:	A "must see" shop for any serious book person. In addition to its "run of the mill" titles, this shop has shelf after shelf of hard-to-find and unique titles. Don't miss the second floor and bring something to wipe the drool from your mouth as you note the titles displayed behind glass. The owners are knowledgeable, the books are worth taking home, and the location of the store (away from the busy downtown area where parking can be a hassle) makes a stop here a worthwhile investment of your time.

(Halifax)

Seaside Book & Stamp
5670 Spring Garden Road B3J 1H6
Web page: http://fox.nstn.ca/~gtucker/

Open Shop
(902) 423-8254
Fax: (902) 423-6731
E-mail: gtucker@fox.nstn.ca

Collection:	General stock of mostly paperback.
Hours:	Daily 11-6, except Fri till 9.

Trident Booksellers & Cafe
1570 Argyle Street B3H 1S1

Open Shop
Tel & Fax: (902) 423-7100

Collection:	General stock of used and new.
# of Vols:	25,000
Hours:	Mon 9-6. Tue-Sat 9-9. Sun 10-6.
Travel:	Downtown, between Sackville and Blowers.
Credit Cards:	Yes
Owner:	Hudson Shotwell
Year Estab:	1992
Comments:	The coffee shop was doing a brisk business at the time of our early arrival (just before 9am). The books, which occupy the entire right half of the shop, consist of a combination of mostly newer hardcover volumes (remainders) and paperbacks. The vast majority of the hardcover volumes sported dust jackets and were in good to excellent condition. Few if any vintage items.

United Book Stores
1669 Barrington Street B3J 1Z9

Open Shop
(902) 423-6980

Collection:	General stock of mostly paperback.
# of Vols:	10,000
Hours:	Mon-Fri 8:30-9. Sat 10-9. Sun 10-6.

Hantsport

Time Regained Books
17 Avon Street B0P 1P0

Open Shop
(902) 684-3904
E-mail: time.regained@ns.sympatico.ca

Collection:	General stock.
# of Vols:	40,000
Specialties:	Music; classics; religion.
Hours:	May-Dec: Mon-Sat 9-6. Remainder of year by appointment or chance.
Services:	Search service, accepts want lists, mail order.
Travel:	From Halifax: Exit 8 off Hwy 101. Follow signs to Hantsport. Left at "T" intersection, right on Main, right on Tannery and right on Avon. Eastbound on Hwy 101 (from Digby): Exit 8A (flashing light). Proceed to Main St in Hantsport, then left at Tannery Rd and right on Avon.
Credit Cards:	Yes
Owner:	John Tickner
Year Estab:	1996

Comments: Located in a stand alone building behind the owner's home, this primarily hardcover collection offers the visitor a wide selection of books in most subject areas. The shelves are meticulously organized and while the aisles are slightly narrow most browsers, even those of moderate girth, should have little trouble viewing the titles. We saw more than the average share of hard-to-find and unusual titles and certainly believe that a visit here could be gratifying.

Kingston

Ruth's Book and Comic Exchange   **Open Shop**
575 Highway 1   (902) 765-4356
Mailing address: PO Box 238 Kingston NS B0P 1RO   E-mail: noah@glinx.com

Collection:	General stock of paperback and hardcover and comics.
# of Vols:	15,000
Hours:	Mon-Sat 9-5, except Fri till 8. Sun 10:30-5.
Travel:	Exit 17 off Hwy 101. At stop sign, turn south on Maple St and proceed to bottom of road. At next stop sign, turn west onto Hwy 1.
Credit Cards:	Yes
Owner:	John & Ruth Fuller
Year Estab:	1985
Comments:	Stock is approximately 70% paperback.

Lunenburg

Attic Owl Book Shop   **Open Shop**
134 Montague Street   (902) 634-8149
Mailing address: PO Box 1171 Lunenburg NS B0J 2C0

Collection:	General stock of hardcover and paperback.
# of Vols:	15,000
Specialties:	Nautical
Hours:	Oct-Mar: Mon-Sat 11-5. Apr-Sep: Mon-Sat 9-7. Sun 12-5.
Services:	Accepts want lists, mail order.
Travel:	First street up from the harbor.
Credit Cards:	Yes
Owner:	Elizabeth Brown
Year Estab:	1993
Comments:	If you're planning to do any vacation reading, you should have no trouble selecting from one of the paperbacks or hardcover books, most of fairly recent vintage, that are on hand in this shop. The shop also carries some new books, most of which deal with local history.

Mahone Bay

J.C. Bell, Books & Ephemera   **Mail Order**
Box 212 B0J 2E0   (902) 624-0393
Web page: www.abebooks.com/home/ROCKBOUND
         E-mail: bell.rogers@ns.sympatico.ca

Collection:	General collection of hardcover and paperback and ephemera.
# of Vols:	10,000
Specialties:	Maritime provinces; Canadian literature; vintage paperbacks; modern first editions; science fiction; fantasy; social radicalism.
Services:	Search service, accepts want lists.
Credit Cards:	No
Owner:	John Bell
Year Estab:	1998

New Glasgow

Garretts by the Bridge   **Open Shop**
124 Kempt Street B2H 4L8   (902) 752-7161

Collection:	General stock of mostly hardcover.
# of Vols:	5,000
Specialties:	Maritime Provinces.
Hours:	Mon-Sat 10:30-5.
Travel:	Exit 23 off Hwy 104. Follow signs for New Glasgow. Right at bridge, then first left after crossing bridge.
Credit Cards:	Yes
Owner:	Edward MacArthur
Year Estab:	1959
Comments:	If you're looking for books dealing with this shop's specialty, the Maritime Provinces, by all means either call or visit. The shop's other books (some on the first level and a few more one flight up) are of a more general nature and are less distinctive. The shop also carries an assortment of used furniture, bric a brac and maritime related collectibles.

Parrsboro

DeLouchery's Antiques & Old Books   **Open Shop**
RR #1 B0M 1S0   (902) 254-3404

Collection:	General stock of mostly hardcover.
# of Vols:	5,000+
Hours:	May 15-Sept 15: Usually 10-6.
Travel:	From Amherst, proceed south on Hwy 2 through Parrsboro. Continue on Hwy 2 towards Truro. Shop is on Hwy 2, about five km outside of Parrsboro. Look for two yellow barns.
Credit Cards:	No
Owner:	Ada DeLouchery
Year Estab:	1969
Comments:	Shop also sells antiques.

Port Hawkesbury

Worth The Wait Consignments   **Open Shop**
405 Granville Street B0E 2V0   (902) 625-0548

Collection:	General stock of mostly paperback.
Hours:	Mon-Sat 10-5, except Thu till 7. Extended summer hours.

Shelburne

The Whirligig   **Open Shop**
135 Water Street B0T 1W0   (902) 875-1117

Collection: General stock of mostly paperback.
# of Vols: 10,000
Hours: Tue-Sat 9-5, except Fri till 6. Summer: Also open Mon and Fri till 8.

Sydney

Hal's Used Books & Things   **Open Shop**
418 Charlotte Street B1P 1E2   (902) 562-4600

Collection: General stock of mostly paperback.
Hours: Mon-Sat 1-5.

Reynolds Book Store   **Open Shop**
369 Charlotte Street B1R 1R3   (902) 564-2665
                                       E-mail: reynoldsbooks@hotmail.com

Collection: General stock of paperback and hardcover.
# of Vols: 20,000
Hours: Mon-Fri 10-5, except Thu till 8. Sat 10-4.
Services: Search service, catalog, accepts want lists.
Travel: Hwy 104 to downtown. Right on Wentworth. Shop is one block ahead
                   at corner of Wentworth and Charlotte.
Credit Cards: Yes
Owner: Carol Reynolds
Year Estab: 1996

Truro

The Book Merchants   **Open Shop**
904 Prince Street B2N 1H5   (902) 893-8008

Collection: General stock of mostly paperback.
# of Vols: 30,000
Hours: Mon-Thu 10-5:30. Fri 10-9. Sat 10-5.

The Book Nook   **Open Shop**
10 Dominion Street B2N 3N8   (902) 893-7766

Collection: General stock of used and new.
Hours: Mon-Fri 9:30-5. Sat 9-4:30. (Mid-May to mid-Sep: Sat 9-12:30).
Travel: Downtown, two blocks from Tourist Bureau.
Comments: Stock is approximately 60% used.

Upper Tantallon

Books Galore & More   **Open Shop**
5209 St. Margaret's Bay Rd, Ste 102A B3Z 1E3   (902) 826-1565

Collection: General stock of paperback and hardcover.

# of Vols:	15,000
Hours:	Mon-Fri 10-8. Sat 10-5. Sun 12-5.
Travel:	Exit 5 off Hwy 103. Proceed south on Hammonds Plains Rd (towards Peggy's Cove). Shop is in shopping center at end of road.
Comments:	Stock is approximately 65% paperback.

Wolfville

Authors' Inn/The Bookshop   **Open Shop**
232 Main Street B0P 1X0   (902) 542-4423

Collection:	General stock of mostly paperback.
# of Vols:	10,000
Hours:	Mon-Thu 9:35-5:30. Fri 9:35-8. Sat 9:36-5. Sun 12:30-5.

The Odd Book   **Open Shop**
8 Front Street   (902) 542-9491
Mailing address: PO Box 863 Wolfville NS B0P 1X0
Web page: www3.ns.sympatico.ca/theoddbook

                                        E-mail: theoddbook@ns.sympatico.ca

Collection:	General stock of hardcover and paperback.
# of Vols:	10,000-15,000
Specialties:	Technology; agriculture; archaeology.
Hours:	Mon-Sat 9:30-5:30. Open evenings from mid Jun-mid Sept.
Services:	Appraisals, search service, accepts want lists, mail order.
Travel:	Exit 11 off Hwy 101. Follow signs to Wolfville. Right at stop sign onto Main St, left at first light onto Elm then right on Front.
Credit Cards:	Yes
Owner:	Jim Tillotson
Year Estab:	1977
Comments:	Without reflecting on the tastes of those who might find greater favor with shops that carry a preponderance of paperbacks, our visit to this establishment seemed like a breath of fresh air. Don't get us wrong. This shop stocks an ample supply of paperbacks also. But its hardcover collection was strong, the volumes we saw were varied and often unusual in nature. Alas, if only we had more room on our shelves back home, we would have left this shop with many additional titles to add to our own collection.

Yarmouth

Lam's Used Book Store   **Open Shop**
28 John Street B5A 3H2   (902) 742-2149

Collection:	General stock of paperback and hardcover and magazines.
# of Vols:	10,000+
Hours:	Mon-Sat 9-5.
Travel:	From Hwy 103, proceed east on Starrs Road, then left on Main St and left again on John.
Credit Cards:	No

Owner: Sung Cao
Year Estab: 1994
Comments: The vast majority of the books in this shop are paperback and the few hardcover items we saw appeared to be of recent vintage, e.g., bestsellers. The shop also carries a large assortment of vintage comics, jigsaw puzzles and popular magazines. While you're not likely to find a rare book in the store, if you're traveling with children, they might enjoy a stop here.

Running out of space for your books?
Think about converting a door.

Ontario

Alphabetical Listing By Dealer

Alphabetical Listing By Location

ONTARIO

(Unless otherwise noted, all cities can be found on Map 15, page 166)

Ajax

Gnu Books   **Open Shop**
200 Harwood Avenue South L1S 2H6   (905) 427-8070

Collection:	General stock of used and new paperback and hardcover and comics.
Hours:	Mon-Wed 10-7. Thu & Fri 10-8. Sat 10-6. Sun 11-5.
Comments:	Stock is approximately 50% used, 75% of which is paperback.

O & I Books   **Mail Order**
15 Willows Lane   L1S 6E7   (905) 686-6295
Web page: www.oibooks.com   Fax: (905) 427-4278
                                              E-mail: sales@oibooks.com

Collection:	Specialty. Mostly used and some new.
# of Vols:	2,500
Specialties:	History; fiction; poetry; books in Spanish.
Services:	Search service, accept want lists.
Credit Cards:	Yes
Year Estab:	1990

Alexandria

Second Time Around Books   **Open Shop**
58 Main Street South   (613) 525-9940
Mailing address: PO Box 1443 Alexandria ON K0C 1A0 E-mail: gale@glen-net.ca

Collection:	General stock of mostly paperback.
Hours:	Tue-Fri 10-5. Sat 10-3.

Allenford

The Sharon Shop   **Open Shop**
Highway 21   (519) 934-2173
Mailing address: PO Box 4 Allenford ON N0H 1A0

Collection:	General stock mostly hardcover.
# of Vols:	15,000
Hours:	Daily 10-6.
Services:	Mail order.
Travel:	In downtown.
Owner:	Gerald Wright
Year Estab:	1989
Comments:	Shop also sells antiques.

Alliston

A Novel Idea   **Open Shop**
103B Victoria West   (705) 435-5917
Mailing address: 100 Boyne Cres. Alliston ON L9R 1K3 E-mail: mck@interhop.net

Collection:	General stock of mostly paperback.

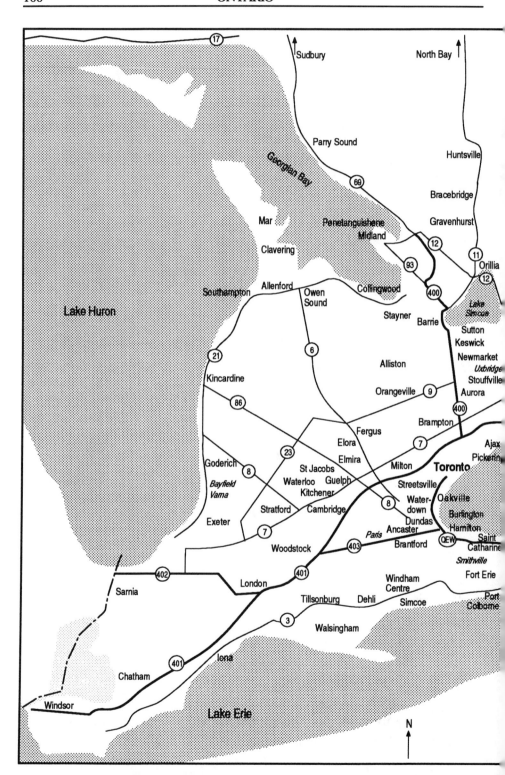

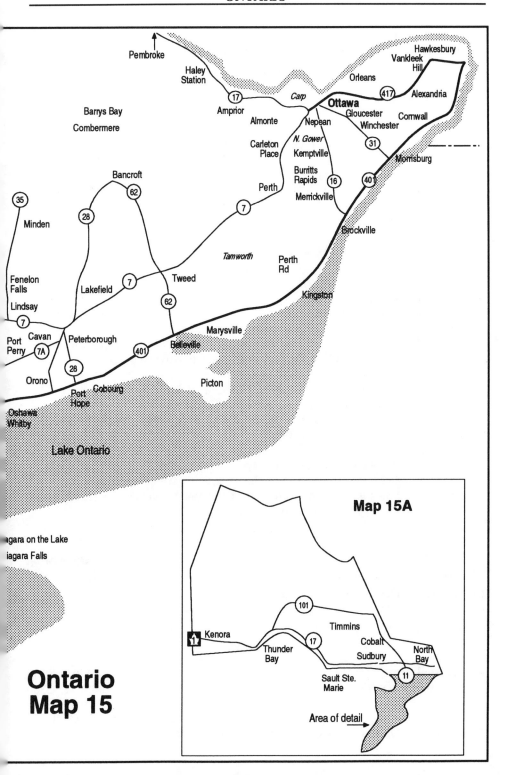

Pembroke

Haley
Station

Barrys Bay

Combermere

Amprior

Almonte

Carleton
Place

Carp

Orleans

Ottawa

Gloucester

Nepean

N. Gower

Kemptville

Burritts
Rapids

Merrickville

Hawkesbury
Vankleek
Hill

Alexandria

Cornwall

Winchester

Morrisburg

Perth

Bancroft

Minden

Fenelon
Falls

Lindsay

Port
Perry

Cavan

Peterborough

Orono

Port
Hope

Cobourg

Oshawa
Whitby

Lakefield

Tweed

Tamworth

Marysville

Belleville

Picton

Perth
Rd

Kingston

Brockville

Lake Ontario

agara on the Lake

iagara Falls

Map 15A

Kenora

Thunder
Bay

Timmins

Cobalt

Sudbury

North
Bay

Sault Ste.
Marie

Area of detail

Ontario
Map 15

# of Vols:	18,000
Hours:	Mon-Fri 10-5:30. Sat 10-5. Sun afternoon by chance in summer.

Almonte

Ottawa Valley Books   **Open Shop**
63 Mill Street K0A 1A0   (613) 256-3796
                                                     E-mail: ovbooks@storm.ca

Collection:	General stock of hardcover and paperback.
# of Vols:	6,000+
Hours:	Tue-Sat 9-5. Sun 1-4 (summer only).
Travel:	Cty Rd 29 exit off Hwy 7. Proceed north on Cty Rd 29 to Almonte, then right on Perth St and left on Mill.
Owner:	John Fife
Year Estab:	1989
Comments:	Stock is evenly divided between hardcover and paperback.

Ancaster

The Book Shop   **Open Shop**
73 Wilson Street West L9G 1N1   Tel & Fax: (905) 648-8579
Web page: www.abebooks.com/home/thebookshopancaster
                                                     E-mail: chenierl@idirect.ca

Collection:	General stock of remainders and mostly paperback used.
# of Vols:	20,000 (used)
Hours:	Mon-Wed 10-5. Thu & Fri 10-8. Sat 10-5.
Services:	Search service, accepts want lists.
Travel:	Fiddler's Green exit off Hwy 403. Proceed southwest on Fiddler's Green then left on Wilson.
Credit Cards:	Yes
Owner:	Rosemary & Lou Chenier
Year Estab:	1995
Comments:	Stock is evenly divided between remainders and used books. Approximately 80% of used stock is paperback.

Arnprior

McNab's Kin   **Open Shop**
107 John Street North K7S 2N5   (613) 623-9487

Collection:	General stock of mostly paperback.
# of Vols:	5,000
Hours:	Mon-Sat 10-5.

Aurora

R & R Book Bar   **Open Shop**
14800 Yonge Street L4G 1N3   (905) 727-3300
                                                            Fax: (905) 727-2620
                                                     E-mail: RWall9999@aol.com

Collection:	General stock of used and new paperback and hardcover.

# of Vols:	50,000
Hours:	Mon-Wed 10-6. Thu & Fri 10-9. Sat 9-6. Sun 12-5.
Travel:	King Sideroad exit off Hwy 400. Proceed east to Yonge, then north on Yonge for eight km.
Credit Cards:	Yes
Owner:	Ron Wallace & Rosemary Schumaker
Year Estab:	1985
Comments:	Stock is approximately 50% used, 80% of which is paperback.

Deanna Ramsay, Bookseller   **Mail Order**
14083 Leslie Street   L4G 7C5   (888) 447-6769   (905) 841-1187
Web page: www.ramsaybooks.com   E-mail: deanna@ramsaybooks.com

Collection:	General stock of mostly hardcover.
# of Vols:	15,000
Specialties:	Aviation; horses; history.
Services:	Accepts want lists. Owner of the BooksCanada mailing list.
Credit Cards:	Yes
Year Estab:	1987

Bancroft

Ashlie's Books   **Open Shop**
105 Hastings Street North   K0L 1C0   (613) 332-2946
                               E-mail: ashlies@bancom.net

Collection:	General stock of used and new hardcover and paperback.
# of Vols:	10,000
Hours:	Mon-Sat 9:30-4:30.
Services:	Search service, accepts want lists, mail order.
Travel:	From Hwy 401, proceed north on Hwy 62. Hastings St is Hwy 62.
Credit Cards:	Yes
Owner:	John & Pamela Taylor
Year Estab:	1993
Comments:	Stock is approximately 65% used, 60% of which is hardcover.

Barrie

Good Old Books   **By Appointment**
274 Bradford Street   L4N 3B8   (705) 735-1951
                          E-mail: marmayt@cois.on.ca

Collection:	General stock.
# of Vols:	5,000-10,000
Specialties:	Modern first editions.
Services:	Search service, accepts want lists, mail order.
Credit Cards:	No
Owner:	Shirley Smith
Year Estab:	1992

Holmes Bookstore & Self-Help Centre   **Open Shop**
79 Dunlop Street West L4N 1A5   (877) 737-5671   (705) 737-5671
Web page: www3.sympatico.ca/link.2.holmes   Fax: (705) 737-4204
                                            E-mail: link.2.holmes@sympatico.ca
Collection: General stock of mostly paperback.
Hours: Mon-Sat 9:30-5:30, except Fri till 8.

Kerry's Book Store   **Open Shop**
25 Dunlop Street West L4N 1A1   (705) 737-0312
Collection: General stock of paperback and hardcover.
# of Vols: 55,000
Hours: Mon-Sat 9-6, except Fri till 9. Sun 12-4.
Travel: Hwy 90 (Dunlop St) exit off Hwy 400. Proceed east on Dunlop.
Year Estab: 1973
Comments: Paperbacks galore of almost every type on the first floor with a signifi-
                   cant number of hardcover books one floor below. The hardcover vol-
                   umes are almost exclusively of quite recent vintage and in generally
                   good condition.

The Old Forester Bookshop   **Open Shop**
153 Dunlop Street East L4M 1B2   Tel & Fax: (705) 722-5267
Collection: General stock of paperback and hardcover.
# of Vols: 20,000
Hours: Mon-Sat 9-5.
Travel: See Kerry's Book Store above.
Year Estab: 1985
Comments: The hardcover items we saw consisted of both recent titles and vintage
                   oldies. This is not necessarily a place where one might expect to find a
                   rare first, but in the book world where new stock shows up every day,
                   one never knows.

Barrys Bay

The Vintage Shoppe   **Open Shop**
20 Opeongo Line East K0J 1B0   (613) 756-1832
Collection: General stock of mostly used paperback and hardcover.
# of Vols: 3,000
Hours: Winter: Tue-Sat 9:30-5:30. Summer: Daily 9:30-5:30.
Travel: On Hwy 16.
Year Estab: 1993
Comments: Used stock is approximately 75% paperback.

Bayfield

Theodore Long's Collectable & Rare Books & Antique Maps   **By Appointment**
RR #1 N0M 1G0   (519) 482-9810
Collection: General stock.
# of Vols: 3,000

Specialties: Travel & exploration; North American Indians; Canadiana; maps.
Credit Cards: No
Year Estab: 1984

Belleville

The Book Store   **Open Shop**
243 North Front Street K8P 3C3   (613) 966-8227

Collection: General stock of mostly paperback.
# of Vols: 15,000-20,000
Hours: Mon-Sat 10-5:30.

Titles Book Shop   **Open Shop**
213 Front Street K8N 2Z4   (613) 967-1773

Collection: General stock of hardcover and paperback.
# of Vols: 40,000
Hours: Mon-Fri 9:30-5:30, except Fri till 8. Sat 9:30-5.
Services: Appraisals, accepts want lists, mail order.
Travel: Exit 543A (Hwy 62) off Hwy 401. Proceed south on Hwy 62 which
                 becomes Front St.
Credit Cards: Yes
Owner: John C. & Susan West
Year Estab: 1987
Comments: A rather pleasant surprise finding this shop. While not necessarily a
                 haven for the rare book specialist, the scope of its collection was such
                 as to make us feel quite at home in terms of being able to identify section
                 after section of good books (including many new faces we were quite
                 unfamiliar with). Whether you're looking for an old favorite or want to
                 discover a new and unusual title, a stop here could prove fortuitous.

Bracebridge

My Bookstore   **Open Shop**
166 Manitoba   (705) 645-5874
Mailing address: 26 Kimberly Avenue Bracebridge ON P1L 2A3

Collection: General stock of paperback and hardcover.
# of Vols: 10,000
Hours: Mon-Thu 11-6. Fri & Sat 10:30-6. Later hours in summer.
Credit Cards: Yes
Year Estab: 1985
Comments: A mostly paperback shop that also sells CDs and comics. There are
                 several shelves of newer hardcover volumes selling for one half the
                 new list price and several more shelves of used hardcover books that
                 have seen better days.

The Owl Pen   **Open Shop**
58 Manitoba Street P1L 1S1   (705) 645-1966

Collection: General stock of hardcover and paperback.

# of Vols:	10,000
Specialties:	Muskoka related; local history; Canadiana.
Hours:	Mon-Sat 9-5:30. Sun (summer only) 9-5:30.
Services:	Accepts want lists, mail order.
Travel:	Northbound on Hwy 11: Muskoka District Rd exit. Proceed west, then right at first light onto Ecclestone Dr which becomes Manitoba St. Southbound: Taylor Rd exit. Proceed west on Taylor to end. Shop is at the "T" intersection.
Credit Cards:	No
Owner:	Jim & Wenda Cumberland
Year Estab:	1992
Comments:	A moderate sized bi-level shop. The books ran the gamut from those in quite good condition to reading copies and from recent publications to vintage and older volumes. The shop also has its share of paperbacks. While you may not find that special esoteric want of yours here, we enjoyed our visit and believe that most book hunters will do the same.

Brampton

Book Haven   **Open Shop**
Brampton Mall
160 Main Street South, #15 L6W 2E1   (905) 796-0678

Collection:	General stock of mostly paperback.
# of Vols:	5,000
Hours:	Mon-Wed 10-6. Thu 12-8. Fri 10-8. Sat 10-5.

Fleming MGB Books   **Mail Order**
76 Lord Simcoe Drive   L6S 5G6   (905) 453-8513
Web page: http://members.aol.com/goldeneye/   Fax: (905) 453-0339
                                                      E-mail: goldeneye@aol.com

Collection:	Specialty
Specialties:	James Bond; Ian Fleming; other 1960's spy genre.
Credit Cards:	No
Owner:	David A. Reinhardt
Year Estab:	1980

Brantford

The Book Barn   **Open Shop**
128 Nelson Street N3S 4B6   (519) 753-4311

Collection:	General stock of mostly used paperback.
Hours:	Mon-Wed & Fri 10-7. Thu & Sat 10-5.

Brantford Bookworm   **Open Shop**
331 Brant Avenue N3T 3J8   (519) 759-6921

Collection:	General stock of mostly paperback.
# of Vols:	20,000
Hours:	Mon-Fri 10-7. Sat 10-5.

Brockville

Walkabout   **Open Shop**
93 King Street West K6V 3R1   (613) 345-0127

Collection:	General stock of mostly paperback.
# of Vols:	20,000
Hours:	Mon-Thu 9:5:30. Fri 9-9. Sat 9-5. Sun. Seasonal.
Travel:	Hwy 29 exit off Hwy 401. Proceed south on Hwy 29, then right on King.
Credit Cards:	Yes
Owner:	Matt Chatelain
Year Estab:	1989
Comments:	Planning a trip to the Thousand Islands? Forgot to bring your favorite paperback mystery or romance novel? Have no fear. You can always visit this shop which is heavily paperback. The shop also carries computer games, videos, an assortment of novelty items and, oh yes, a couple of hundred hardcover volumes.

Burlington

Appleby Book Ranch   **Open Shop**
2201 Brant L7P 3N8   (905) 332-1209
                                                 E-mail: GSTAP27@aol.com

Collection:	General stock of mostly paperback.
Hours:	Mon-Fri 9:30-9. Sat 9:30-6.

Appleby Book Ranch   **Open Shop**
5111 New Street L7R 3X4   (905) 637-5751

Collection:	General stock of mostly paperback.
Hours:	Mon-Fri 9:30-9. Sat 9:30-6.

Lakeview Books   **Open Shop**
5295 Lakeshore Road L7L 1C7   (905) 639-4622

Collection:	General stock of mostly paperback.
# of Vols:	25,000
Hours:	Mon 12-6. Tue-Thu 10-6. Fri & Sat 10-6. Sun 12-4.

Terry Nudds   **By Appointment**
707 King Road L7T 3K5   (905) 632-9291
Web page: www/abebooks.com/home/LOSTLIBRARY
                                                 E-mail: tnudds@cgocable.net

Collection:	General stock of paperback and hardcover and ephemera.
# of Vols:	14,000
Specialties:	Science fiction; fantasy; pulps.
Services:	Search service, accepts want lists, mail order.
Credit Cards:	No
Owner:	Terry Nudds & Shirley Nicks
Year Estab:	1997
Comments:	Stock is approximately 65% paperback.

Lewis Sherman Books & Art   **Mail Order**
865 Danforth Place   L7T 1S1   (905) 522-9082
                                                 Fax: (905) 522-4563
                                        E-mail: lewbooks@networx.on.ca

Collection: Specialty
# of Vols: 7,000
Specialties: Travel and exploration; cookbooks; first editions.
Services: Accepts want lists.
Credit Cards: No
Year Estab: 1986

W. Fraser Sandercombe   **Mail Order**
1293 Headon Road   L7M 1S3   (905) 332-0050
Web page: www.abebooks.com/home/yarrow   E-mail: yarrow@idirect.com

Collection: General stock of mostly hardcover and ephemera.
Specialties: Fantasy; science fiction; horror; mystery.
Services: Appraisals, search service, accepts want lists.
Credit Cards: No
Year Estab: 1997

Burritts Rapids

The Village Bookshop   **Open Shop**
5 Grenville Street   Tel & Fax: (613) 269-2331
Mailing address: PO Box 531 Merrickville on K0G 1N0
Web page: www.abebooks.com/home/villagebookshop   E-mail: vbooks@magma.ca

Collection: General stock, maps and prints.
# of Vols: 9,000
Specialties: Literature (19th century).
Hours: Sat & Sun. Best to call ahead.
Travel: From Hwy 43, turn north on Hill/Grenville Rd. From Cty Rd 2, turn
                   south on Dwyer Hill Rd.
Credit Cards: Yes
Owner: Carole & Bill Roberts
Year Estab: 1985
Comments: We had the privilege of viewing this collection a couple of months
                   before the owners moved to their current location. The collection is
                   modest in size but not in quality. The vast majority of the books were
                   in good to excellent condition, represented scholarly subjects and were
                   most reasonable in terms of price.

Cambridge

Cambridge Book Nook   **Open Shop**
107 Westminster Drive North N3H 1S1   (519) 653-5884
Collection: General stock of paperback and hardcover.
# of Vols: 43,000

Hours:	May 24-Labor Day: Mon-Wed 9-5. Thu & Fri 10-8. Sat 10-4. Remainder of year: Mon-Fri 9-5. Sat 10-4.
Travel:	Hwy 8 exit off Hwy 401. Proceed south on Hwy 8, then left on Westminster.
Credit Cards:	No
Owner:	John Hauck
Year Estab:	1996
Comments:	Stock is 65% paperback.

Paperbacks Unlimited   **Open Shop**
36 Dickson Street N1R 1T4   (519) 740-7880
Web page: www.golden.net/~paperbacks   Fax: (519) 740-7882
                                                     E-mail: paperbacks@golden.net

Collection:	General stock of mostly paperback.
# of Vols:	22,000
Hours:	Mon-Wed 9:30-6. Thu & Fri 9:30-8. Sat 9:30-5.

Carleton Place

Book Gallery   **Open Shop**
18 Allan Street K7C 1T2   (613) 257-2373

Collection:	General stock of mostly used paperback and hardcover and remainders.
# of Vols:	80,000 (used)
Hours:	Mon-Fri 9:30-5:30, except Fri till 8. Sat 9:30-6. Sun 12-5.
Travel:	Carleton Place exit off Hwy 7. Proceed northwest on Bridge St, then left on Allan.
Credit Cards:	No
Year Estab:	1991
Comments:	Used stock is approximately 75% paperback.

Carp

The Old Book Cellar   **By Appointment**
2962 Carp Road K0A 1L0   (613) 831-3173
Web page: http://magi.com/~oldbook   Fax: (613) 831-2748
                                                        E-mail: oldbook@magi.com

Collection:	General stock of mostly hardcover.
# of Vols:	10,000+
Specialties:	Charles Dickens; modern first editions.
Services:	Accepts want lists, mail order.
Credit Cards:	Yes
Owner:	Robert Hargrave
Year Estab:	1995
Comments:	Located in a 150 year old stone house that also serves as a bed and breakfast (Kirkstone House).

Cavan

The Little Barn Antiques   **Open Shop**
893 Highway 7A L0A 1C0   (705) 944-5653

Collection:	General stock of mostly hardcover.
# of Vols:	5,000
Specialties:	Canadiana
Hours:	Daily, except closed Thu, 10-5.
Services:	Mail order.
Travel:	Cavan exit off Hwy 115. Continue north to Hwy 7A, then left on Hwy 7A. Shop is just ahead on left.
Credit Cards:	Yes
Owner:	Wes Eardley
Comments:	A new shop scheduled to open in the summer of 1999. The owner was formerly associated with a bookshop in Peterborough.

Chatham

Clem's Book Exchange   **Open Shop**
15 King Street East N7M 3M6   (519) 352-8290

Collection:	General stock of mostly paperback.
# of Vols:	200,000
Hours:	Mon-Thu 8-5:30. Fri 8am-8:30pm. Sat 9-5. Sun by chance.
Services:	Search service, accepts want lists.
Travel:	Westbound on Hwy 401: Hwy 40 exit. Proceed north on Hwy 40 which becomes Park Ave. After first light, turn right on Queen. Keep to the right and continue on William St. At third light, turn right onto King St. Eastbound on Hwy 401. Exit 81. Proceed north on Bloomfield, right on Park, left on Queen and right on King.
Credit Cards:	Yes
Owner:	Norman & David Clements
Year Estab:	1978
Comments:	If you're a paperback collector searching for books you haven't been able to find elsewhere and you have lots and lots of patience, a visit here will afford you the opportunity to browse several rooms filled from floor to ceiling with paperbacks of every variety imaginable. The shop also carries a modest number of hardcover volumes, mostly reading copies, as well as some magazines and other non book collectibles.

Clavering

The Clavering Book shop   **Open Shop**
On Highway 6   (519) 935-2638
Mailing address: RR 1 Wiarton ON N0H 2T0

Collection:	General stock of used and new hardcover and paperback.
Hours:	Late May-Jun: Weekends only, 11-4:30. Jul-Oct: Usually daily 11-4:30.
Owner:	Albert Rollison

Comments: Stock is approximately 65% used and is evenly divided between hard-
                cover and paperback.

Cobalt
(Map 15A, page 166)

Highway Book Shop   **Open Shop**
RR #1 P0J 1C0   (705) 679-8375
                                                      Fax: (705) 679-8511
                                              E-mail: bookshop@nt.net
Collection: General stock of mostly used hardcover.
# of Vols: 300,000
Specialties: Canadiana; native studies; cookbooks; diet; military.
Services: Search service, accepts want lists, mail order.
Travel: On Highway 11, approximately 130 km north of North Bay.
Credit Cards: Yes
Owner: Dr. Douglas C. Pollard
Year Estab: 1957

Cobourg

The Clothes Horse Thrift Shop   **Open Shop**
11 King Street East K9A 1K6   (905) 372-8451
Collection: General stock of mostly paperback.
# of Vols: 500+
Hours: Mon-Sat 10-4:30
Comments: Non profit shop run by volunteers for the local Humane Society.

Cobourg Bookroom & Antiques   **Open Shop**
150 King Street West K9A 2M5   (905) 373-8868
                                              E-mail: cbra@sympatico.ca
Collection: General stock of hardcover and paperback.
# of Vols: 3,000-5,000
Specialties: Art; Canadiana.
Hours: Mon-Fri 9-5. Sat 10-5. Sun 12-5.
Travel: Exit 472 (Burnham St) off Hwy 401. Proceed south on Burnham, then
                left on William and left on King.
Credit Cards: Yes
Year Estab: 1992
Comments: A modest sized collection spread over four small rooms. The books are
                a mix of hardcover volumes, including a fair number of vintage and
                even antiquarian items, and a generous display of paperbacks.

Collingwood

Cover To Cover   **Open Shop**
11 Ontario Street N0C 1C0   (877) 815-6315   (705)446-0513
                                              E-mail: cover2@bconnex.net
Collection: General stock of paperback and hardcover, comics and CDs.

Hours:	Mon-Fri 9:30-5:30. Sat 10-4.
Services:	Search service, accepts want lists.
Travel:	Hwy 26 exit off Hwy 400. Proceed west on Hwy 26 to Collingwood. Left on Hurontario, then left on Ontario.
Credit Cards:	Yes
Owner:	Scott & Margaret Harrison
Year Estab:	1996
Comments:	Stock is approximately 75% paperback.

Combermere

Madonna House Bookshop   **Open Shop**
Highway 517 K0J 1L0   (613) 756-3149

Collection:	General stock hardcover and paperback.
# of Vols:	5,000+
Specialties:	Spirituality
Hours:	Jun-Aug: Thu-Sat 2-5. Call for other hours. Remainder of year: phone and mail order only.
Travel:	Hwy 517 exit off Hwy 62. Shop is just ahead.
Comments:	Stock is approximately 75% hardcover. All books are donated. Operated by Madonna House. Proceeds help support the group's mission.

Cornwall

Hooked On Books   **Open Shop**
220 Pitt Street K6J 3P6   (613) 936-2230

Collection:	General stock of mostly paperback.
# of Vols:	10,000
Hours:	Mon-Fri 10-5. Sat 10-4:30.

The Old Book Store   **Open Shop**
168 Montreal Rd K6H 1B3   (613) 933-7323
Fax: (613) 525-4484
E-mail: rothgeb@glen-net.ca

Collection:	General stock of mostly paperback.
# of Vols:	21,000
Hours:	Mon-Sat 10-5. Sun 1-5.

Delhi

Fernlea Ivix Non-Profit Books   **Open Shop**
RR #3 N4B 2W6

Collection:	General stock of hardcover and paperback.
# of Vols:	25,000
Hours:	Daily 2-5.
Travel:	On Hwy 3, six km west of Delhi and 10 km east of Tillsonburg.
Credit Cards:	No
Year Estab:	1990
Comments:	All books are donated.

Dundas

Chapman Books   **Open Shop**
11 Cross Street L9H 2R3   (905) 627-5007

Collection:	General stock of new and used hardcover and paperback.
# of Vols:	15,000
Hours:	Mon-Sat 10-6.
Travel:	Main St west exit off Hwy 403. Continue west on Main St, then right on Cootes Dr. Continue on Cootes into downtown where it becomes King St, then right on Cross.
Comments:	Stock is approximately 35% used and evenly divided between hardcover and paperback.

Filedelphia Purveyors of the Written Word   **Open Shop**
60 King Street West L9H 1T8   (905) 627-8960

Collection:	General stock of new and used hardcover and paperback.
Hours:	Mon-Sat 8:30-5:30, except Fri till 8.
Travel:	Between Main and Sydenham.
Credit Cards:	Yes
Year Estab:	1995
Comments:	Stock is evenly divided between new and used, hardcover and paperback.

John C. Stirling   **By Appointment****
212 Hatt Street L9H 2G8   (905) 627-5008

Collection:	General stock and original prints.
# of Vols:	5,000
Specialties:	Artist biographies; illustrated; children's (pre-1940); portrait-miniature related; literature (20th century); Canadiana; transportation; medical journals; Edith Osbert; Sacheverell Sitwell; Gertrude Stein.
Hours:**	Sat & Sun 10-6 (please call ahead). Other times by appointment.
Services:	Appraisals, accepts want lists, mail order.
Credit Cards:	Yes
Year Estab:	1984

Elmira

Rising Trout Sporting Books   **Open Shop**
At Fyfield Manor, 14 Hampton Street   (519) 669-1303
Mailing address: PO Box 338 Elmira ON N3B 2Z7   Fax: (519) 669-8671
                                                         E-mail: moldy@golden.net

Collection:	Specialty books and ephemera.
# of Vols:	4,000
Specialties:	Angling, fly fishing, fly tying.
Hours:	Daily 9-5.
Services:	Appraisals, search service, catalog, accepts want lists.
Travel:	Hwy 8 exit off Hwy 401. Proceed north on Hwy 8. Follow signs, taking Hwy 86 north. Shop is five minutes north of Waterloo.
Credit Cards:	Yes

Owner:	John A. Moldenhauer
Year Estab:	1973
Comments:	Shop also sells antique fishing tackle and offers B&B accommodations.

Elora

The Elora Antique Warehouse   **Antique Mall**
6484 Wellington Road, #7 N0B 1S0   (800) 393-8715

Hours:	Daily 10-6.
Travel:	Wellington Rd, #7 exit off Hwy 6. Continue on Wellington to Elora.

Exeter

Exeter Automotive Collectibles   **Open Shop**
20 Nelson Street N0M 1S2   (519) 235-1088

Collection:	Specialty
Specialties:	Automobile related (mostly magazines); also some other magazines.
Hours:	Tue-Sat 9-6.
Travel:	Nelson St exit off Hwy 4. Turn towards the water tower and continue on Nelson to town.
Credit Cards:	Yes
Year Estab:	1995

Fenelon Falls

The Bookfinder   **Open Shop**
32 Colborne Street K0M 1N0   Tel & Fax: (705) 887-5052
Web page: www.abebooks.com/home/dcarpntr E-mail: dcarpntr@lindsaycomp.on.ca

Collection:	General stock of hardcover and paperback.
# of Vols:	8,000-10,000
Specialties:	Canadiana
Hours:	Mid May-Sept: Mon-Sat 10-5. Sun 12-4. Oct-May: Thu-Sat 10-5.
Services:	Appraisals, catalog, search service, accept want lists.
Travel:	Located on Hwy 122.
Credit Cards:	Yes
Owner:	Doreen E. Carpenter
Year Estab:	1993
Comments:	An unassuming shop that initially gives one the impression of selling primarily paperback books but which does have a respectable selection of hardcover volumes of mixed vintage and enough titles of interest, particularly in Canadian literature, to appeal to traveling book hunters. Prices are reasonable.

Fergus

Quality Used Books   **Open Shop**
285 Beatty Line N1M 2W7   (519) 843-3722

Collection:	General stock mostly paperback.

# of Vols:	10,000
Hours:	Mon-Fri 9-5.
Travel:	Located inside Fergus Machine Shop.

Fort Erie

William Matthews Books   **Open Shop**
16 Jarvis Street L2A 2S1   (905) 871-8484
Web page: www.vaxxine.com/matthews   E-mail: matthews@vaxxine.com

Collection:	General stock of hardcover and paperback and ephemera.
# of Vols:	100,000
Specialties:	Older fiction; sensational fiction; science fiction.
Hours:	Mon-Sat 10-5:30.
Services:	Appraisals, search service, catalog.
Travel:	Central Ave exit off QEW. Proceed north on Central, then east on Jarvis.
Credit Cards:	Yes
Owner:	William Matthews & Annie Hall
Year Estab:	1976
Comments:	You'll love it or you'll hate it. If your interests are strictly scholarly titles and/or you're looking for books only in pristine condition, this shop probably will not appeal to you. On the other hand, if you're the patient sort and don't mind spending several hours eyeballing shelf after shelf on the main level and in the basement, you could leave this shop after making several pleasant purchases. In one section of the shop (hardcover science fiction), in addition to some of the more common titles found almost everywhere else, we spotted a number of vintage fantasy titles that catalog dealers would be asking big bucks for. While the store has a somewhat cluttered appearance, patience can clearly pay off.

Gloucester

Book Bank   **Open Shop**
4000 Bridle Path Drive K1T 2C4   (613) 248-3634
Web page: booksnstuff.com   Fax: (613) 739-7353
                                              E-mail: rbhart@cyberus.ca

Collection:	General stock of mostly paperback.
# of Vols:	5,000
Hours:	Mon-Fri 12-7. Sat 12-6. Sun 12-4.

Goderich

Michelle's Reading Room   **Open Shop**
114 Courthouse Square N7A 1M8   (519) 524-4080
                                                 Fax: (519) 524-9705
                                        E-mail: mrotteau@odyssey.on.ca

Collection:	General stock of used and new hardcover and paperback.
# of Vols:	4,000

Specialties:	Women's studies; religion; local history.
Hours:	Mon-Wed 10-6. Thu & Fri 10-8. Sat 10-5. Sun 12-3 (Winter) or 11-5 (Jun-Sept).
Services:	Search service, accepts want lists, mail order.
Travel:	From all highways running through Goderich, follow signs to "The Square."
Credit Cards:	Yes
Owner:	Michelle Rotteau
Year Estab:	1998
Comments:	Shares space with an art gallery. Stock is approximately 70% used, 65% of which is hardcover.

The Used Book Peddler   **Open Shop**
34 West Street N7A 2K3   (519) 524-5224

Collection:	General stock of mostly paperback.
# of Vols:	17,000
Hours:	Mon-Fri 10-6. Sat 10-5.

Gravenhurst

Book Store   **Open Shop**
120 Muskoka Road South P1P 1V2   (705)687-0555

Collection:	General stock of mostly new and some used hardcover and paperback.
# of Vols:	500 (used)
Hours:	Mon-Sat 9:30-5:30.
Comments:	Used stock is evenly divided between hardcover and paperback.

Desu Books of Muskoka   **Open Shop**
225 Muskoka Road North   (705) 687-8686
Mailing address: Box 179, Station Main Gravenhurst ON P1P 1T6
                                       E-mail: desubooks@canada.com

Collection:	General stock of mostly paperback.
Hours:	Jul & Aug: Mon-Sat 10-5. Sept-Jun: Thu-Sat 10-5 and other times by appointment.

Guelph

Ali Baba Bookshop   **Open Shop**
9 Douglas Street N1H 2S7   (519) 766-4829

Collection:	General stock of paperback and hardcover.
# of Vols:	5,000-8,000
Hours:	Mon-Wed 11-6. Thu & Fri 11-7:30. Sat 11-5.
Comments:	Stock is approximately 75% paperback.

Macondo Books   **Open Shop**
18 Wilson Street N1H 4G5   (519) 836-0430
                                       E-mail: macondo@kw.igs.net

Collection:	General stock of hardcover and paperback.

# of Vols:	30,000
Hours:	Mon-Wed 10-6. Thu & Fri 10-9. Sat 9-6. Sun 12-5.
Travel:	Brock Rd exit off Hwy 401. Proceed north on Brock to Guelph, then right on MacDonnell and right on Wilson.
Credit Cards:	Yes
Owner:	Nancy Giovanelli
Year Estab:	1978
Comments:	A nice shop with a good balance of hardcover and paperback titles. Most of the hardcover items appeared to be of fairly recent origin although we did spot a number of older volumes on the shelves. The books we saw were in quite good condition and reasonably priced.

Nostalgia Books   **Antique Mall**
PO Box 1443, Main Station N1H 6N9   (519) 821-9580
                                              E-mail: broberts@sentex.ca

Collection:	General stock and ephemera.
# of Vols:	4,000
Specialties:	Canadiana; art; antiques; maps.
Hours:	(See Comments)
Services:	Appraisals, search service, accepts want lists, mail order.
Credit Cards:	Yes
Owner:	William Roberts
Year Estab:	1973
Comments:	Collection is displayed at several local antique malls. For details, contact the dealer.

Haley Station

Ye Olde Book Shoppe & Kindred Gifts   **Open Shop**
RR 1, Highway 17 K0J 1Y0   (613) 433-9368
                                              E-mail: psboese@on.aibn.com

Collection:	General stock of mostly paperback.
Hours:	Tue-Sat 10-5:30. Extended hours during summer.

Hamilton

Amity Goodwill Industries   **Open Shop**
225 King William Street L8R 1B1   (905) 526-8481

Collection:	General stock of hardcover and paperback.
# of Vols:	2,000+
Hours:	Mon-Thu 9-5:30. Fri 9-9. Sat 9-5.
Travel:	From Toronto: Hwy 6/York Blvd exit off Hwy 403. Continue on York for about three km, then right on Ferguson. Shop is two blocks ahead on left. From St. Catharines: Burlington St exit off QEW. Continue on Burlington, left on Wellington, right on Cannon, and left on Ferguson. Shop is about three blocks ahead on left.
Comments:	Other Goodwill locations in Hamilton have primarily paperbacks.

(Hamilton)

Philip Byrne Books   **Mail Order**
36 Fairholt Road South   L8M 2T4   (905) 544-7702
                                          E-mail: pbyrne@lara.on.ca

Collection:	General stock of hardcover and paperback.
# of Vols:	7,000
Services:	Appraisals, mail order.
Credit Cards:	No
Year Estab:	1985
Comments:	Stock is approximately 75% hardcover.

Circle "M" Books   **Flea Market**
At Circle "M" Flea Market   (416) 251-2837
Mailing address: 20 Ninth St, #3 Etobicoke ON M8V 3E3

Collection:	General stock and ephemera.
# of Vols:	10,000
Specialties:	Vintage paperbacks; local history.
Hours:	Sun 9-5.
Travel:	On Hwy 5, five km west of Hwy 6 or just north of Hwy 403.
Owner:	Michael Cowan
Year Estab:	1988
Comments:	The owner maintains an open shop in Oakville. See below.

Ibis–The Book Arts   **By Appointment**
50 Sanders Boulevard L8S 3J6   (905) 522-4802
Web page: www.netaccess.on.ca/~ibisbks/   Fax: (905) 522-8814
                                        E-mail: ibisbks@netaccess.on.ca

Collection:	General stock.
# of Vols:	18,000
Specialties:	Judaica; typography; private press; art; books about books; Leonard Baskin.
Services:	Appraisals, search service, catalog, accepts want lists.
Credit Cards:	No
Owner:	Bernard & Marjorie Baskin
Year Estab:	1988

Lion's Book Den   **Mail Order**
Web page: www.abebooks.com/home/ELDERGODS/   (905) 385-8644
                                        E-mail: Lshoup@worldchat.com

Collection:	General stock.
# of Vols:	5,000-7,000
Services:	Appraisals, search service, accepts want lists.
Credit Cards:	No
Owner:	Leonard Shoup
Year Estab:	1992

J. Lovett
PO Box 33552   L8P 1A0
E-mail: peatbog@idirect.ca
Web page: http://webhome.idirect.com/~peatbog

Collection:	General stock and ephemera.
# of Vols:	1,500
Specialties:	*Time* magazines.
Services:	Accepts want lists.
Credit Cards:	No
Year Estab:	1998

Mike's World of Books
150 James Street South   L8P 3A2
(905) 385-2867
Web page: www.nas.net/~mmorison/
(877) 386-0441
E-mail: mmorison@nas.net

Collection:	General stock of paperback and hardcover.
# of Vols:	50,000
Specialties:	Literature; history; biography; mystery; science fiction; westerns; religion; philosophy; modern first editions.
Hours:	Mon-Sat 9:45-5:15.
Services:	Accepts want lists.
Travel:	East Main exit off Hwy 403. Proceed east on Main, then right (south) on James. Shop is 3½ blocks ahead.
Credit Cards:	No
Owner:	Margaret Morison
Year Estab:	1983
Comments:	A pleasant "neighborhood" bookstore with three small rooms of mostly paperbacks and fairly recent hardcover titles. As is frequently the case in such shops, we were able to spot a few unusual titles, but for the most part, the stock here is not in any way out of the ordinary.

Mountain Bookstore
560 Concession Street   L8V 1A9
(905) 385-6082

Collection:	General stock of mostly paperback.
# of Vols:	50,000
Hours:	Mon, Tue, Wed, Sat 9:30-5:30. Thu & Fri 9:30-8.

Allan Petteplace, Bookseller
27 King William Street   L8R 1A1
(905) 521-5535

Collection:	General stock of used hardcover and paperback and some new books.
# of Vols:	5,000-6,000 (used)
Hours:	Tue-Sat 10-5:30.
Travel:	From Toronto: York St exit off Hwy 403. Proceed east on York, then right on James and left on King William. Books are located on the lower level of the Petteplace Gallery.
Credit Cards:	Yes
Year Estab:	1992

Comments: Located one flight down, this shop offers primarily newer stock in both hardcover and paperback. The books we saw were in generally good to excellent condition and priced to sell.

Rerr Books   **Open Shop**
165 John Street South L8N 2C3   (905) 524-3805

Collection: General stock of hardcover and paperback.
# of Vols: 20,000
Hours: Mon-Sat 12-7.
Travel: York Blvd exit off Hwy 403. Proceed east on York, which becomes Cannon, then right on James, left on Augusta and left on John. Shop is at corner of Augusta and John.
Credit Cards: No
Owner: Bill Hughes
Year Estab: 1998
Comments: A rather crowded shop with a mix of older hardcover items as well as paperbacks. Some randomly displayed; some in labeled sections. As we have said many time before, scouts have been known to discover treasures in such locations. Our luck was not quite that good.

John Rush–Books   **By Appointment**
116 Eastbourne Avenue L8M 2M8   (905) 545-0661
                                                                Fax: (905) 545-2477

Collection: Specialty books and ephemera.
# of Vols: 2,000
Specialties: Canadiana
Services: Appraisals, catalog.
Credit Cards: No
Year Estab: 1979

The Westdale Bookworm   **Open Shop**
852 King Street West N3T 4K7   (905) 523-4345

Collection: General stock of mostly paperback.
# of Vols: 12,000
Hours: Tue-Fri 10-6. Sat 10-4.

Hawkesbury

Norm's Book Exchange   **Open Shop**
259 Main Street East K6A 1A1   (613) 632-7421

Collection: General stock of paperback and hardcover.
# of Vols: 20,000
Hours: Mon-Sat 9:30-5:30.
Comments: Stock is approximately 65% paperback.

P & P Books   **Open Shop**
164 Main Street East K6A 1A3   (613) 632-5546

Collection: General stock of paperback and hardcover.
# of Vols: 25,000+

Hours:	Mon-Fri 9:30-5. Sat 9:30-4.
Travel:	Hawkesbury exit off Hwy 417. Proceed east on Hwy 34 through Vankleek Hill and into Hawkesbury where Hwy 34 becomes Main St.
Credit Cards:	No
Owner:	Pat Seguin
Year Estab:	1995
Comments:	Stock is approximately 75% paperback.

Huntsville

Cover To Cover Used Books   **Open Shop**
Novar Square Mall, Highway 11   (705) 788-2322
Mailing address: 18 Peter Street Novar ON P0A 1R0

Collection:	General stock of paperback and hardcover.
# of Vols:	9,000
Hours:	Mon-Sat 9:30-5:30.
Travel:	On Hwy 11, 16 km north of Huntsville.
Credit Cards:	Yes
Year Estab:	1998
Comments:	Stock is approximately 60% paperback.

Yesterday's Books   **Open Shop**
9 Main Street East P1H 2C9   (705) 789-8517

Collection:	General stock of mostly paperback.
# of Vols:	10,000
Hours:	Winter: Tue-Sat 9:30-4. Summer: Mon-Sat 9:30-5.

Iona

Holland House Restaurant   **Open Shop**
R.R. #3 N0L 1P0   (519) 764-2495

Collection:	General stock of mostly hardcover.
# of Vols:	5,000
Hours:	Daily 8am-7pm Daily. Closing time can vary.
Travel:	Exit 157 off Hwy 401. Proceed on Hwy 14 toward Iona. Shop is at intersection of Hwy 14 and Hwy 3.
Credit Cards:	Yes
Owner:	Marty Angenent
Year Estab:	1991
Comments:	Shop also sells antiques and is a full service restaurant.

Kemptville

Book End   **Open Shop**
314 Clothier Street West K0G 1J0   (613) 258-4629

Collection:	General stock of mostly paperback.
# of Vols:	15,000
Hours:	Tue-Fri 10-5. Sat 9-5.

Kenora
(Map 15A, page 166)

Elizabeth Campbell Books   **Open Shop**
129 Main Street South P9N 1T1   (800) 361-3527   (807) 468-5546
                                                      Fax: (807) 468-4032
                                              E-mail: ecbooks@voyageur.ca

Collection:	General stock of new and used paperback and hardcover.
# of Vols:	30,000
Hours:	Winter: Mon-Sat 9-5. Summer: Mon-Sat 9-5:30. Other times by appointment.
Services:	Search service, accepts want lists, mail order.
Travel:	Located on Hwy 17 at corner of Main and Second St S. (Note: Do not take bypass.)
Credit Cards:	Yes
Year Estab:	1991
Comments:	Stock is approximately 30% used, 70% of which is paperback.

Keswick

Book Store   **Open Shop**
Glenswood Mall 443 The Queensway South, Unit 19 L0E 1N0   (905) 476-5696

Collection:	General stock of new and mostly paperback used.
# of Vols:	2,000-5,000 (used)
Hours:	Mon 9-5. Tue 11-6. Wed 1-6. Thu 11-6. Fri 11-6. Sat 10-5:30. Sun 12-4.

Kincardine

Cheers Laundromat & Book Exchange   **Open Shop**
337 Kincardine Avenue   (519) 396-4592
Mailing address: PO Box 537 Lucknow ON N0G 2H0

Collection:	General stock of paperback and hardcover.
# of Vols:	10,000
Hours:	May-Oct Mon-Sat 8-7. Sun (Jul & Aug) 8-7. Remainder of year: Mon-Sat 8-5:30.
Travel:	Kincardine Ave exit off Hwy 21. Proceed west Kincardine Ave.
Comments:	Stock is approximately 75% paperback.

Kingston

Berry and Peterson Booksellers   **Open Shop**
348 King Street East K7L 3B6   (613) 549-6652

Collection:	General stock of mostly hardcover.
# of Vols:	25,000-30,000
Hours:	Mon-Thu 10-5. Fri 10-9. Sat 10-5. Sun 11-4. Longer hours in summer.
Services:	Appraisals, search service, accepts want lists.
Travel:	Division St exit off Hwy 401. Proceed south on Division, then right on Princess and right on King. Shop is between Princess and Brock.
Credit Cards:	Yes

Owner: John Channell Berry & Richard Peterson
Year Estab: 1976
Comments: A nice shop with a good selection of books both on the street level and
                one flight up. The books represent a mix of titles of interest to the
                general public and a fair number of rare and antiquarian items, includ-
                ing some nice sets. We believe you'll enjoy a visit here.

Book Market   Open Shop
647 Princess Street K7L 1E4   (613) 544-5488

Collection: General stock of paperback and hardcover.
# of Vols: 100,000+
Hours: Mon-Thu 9:30-6. Fri 9:30-9. Sat 10-6. Sun 12-5.
Travel: At corner of Victoria and Princess.
Comments: Stock is approximately 60% paperback.

The Book Shop (Loyalisit Book Shop)   Open Shop
122 Princess Street K7L 1A7   (613) 546-0734
                                                            Fax: (613) 542-1151
                                                   E-mail: docpossum@hotmail.com

Collection: General stock of paperback and hardcover.
Specialties: Philosophy; history; literature.
Hours: Mon-Wed & Sat 9:30-7. Thu & Fri 9:30-9:30. Sun 11-5.
Services: Accepts want lists, mail order.
Travel: Shop is located in basement.
Credit Cards: Yes
Owner: Ronald Paulson
Year Estab: 1982
Comments: The owner describes his shop as "university oriented" with a mix of
                80% paperback and 20% hardcover books, including a collection of
                both new and used books in French.

Bruce Marshall (formerly Hortulus)   Mail Order
19 Dickens Drive   K7M 2M5   (613) 536-5312
                                                    E-mail: bruce-m@cgocable.net

Collection: Specialty
# of Vols: 3,000
Specialties: Gardening
Services: Accepts want lists.
Year Estab: 1977

Paper Back's Bookstore   Open Shop
857 Princess Street K7L 1G7   (613) 546-9832

Collection: General stock of paperback and hardcover.
# of Vols: 10,000
Hours: Mon-Wed 9:30-5:30. Thu & Fri 9:30-6. Sat 10-5. Sun 11-4.
Travel: Sir John A. MacDonald Blvd exit off Hwy 401. Proceed south on Sir
                John A. MacDonald, then left on Princess.
Comments: Stock is approximately 75% paperback.

J. Turk & Son   **Open Shop**
281 Princess Street K7L 1B4   (613) 546-5267

Collection:	General stock of paperback and hardcover.
# of Vols:	1,500-2,000
Hours:	Mon-Fri 9:30-5. Sat 10-5.
Comments:	Stock is evenly divided between hardcover and paperback.

Vittorio's Books and Collectibles   **Open Shop**
348 Princess Street K7L 1B6   (613) 542-5551
                                          E-mail: vittoria@q.silver.queensu.ca

Collection:	General stock of hardcover and paperback and ephemera.
# of Vols:	8,000
Specialties:	Sheet music.
Hours:	Mon-Sat 10-5:30. Sun 12-5.
Travel:	Between Clergy and Barrie Streets.
Credit Cards:	Yes
Owner:	Donna Vittorio
Year Estab:	1998
Comments:	Most of what we saw here appeared to be reading copies in subject areas of more popular interest, e.g., fiction, entertainment, etc. Some older volumes, a good share of vintage materials and, if you look carefully, even a few antiquarian items.

Wayfarer Books Bought & Sold   **Open Shop**
85 Princess Street K7L 1A6   (613) 542-8615

Collection:	General stock of hardcover and paperback.
# of Vols:	20,000
Hours:	Mon-Sat 10-6. (Seasonal changes)
Travel:	Between Wellington and King.
Credit Cards:	No
Owner:	Walter Cipin
Year Estab:	1979
Comments:	An interesting collection of mostly hardcover volumes, both recent and vintage. While the selection is not overwhelming in number, we spotted some quality items and more than several titles not seen elsewhere. The shop also sells magazines.

Kitchener

A Second Look Books & Videos   **Open Shop**
33 Queen Street South N2G 1V8   (519) 744-2274

Collection:	General stock of hardcover and paperback.
# of Vols:	50,000+
Specialties:	History; sciences; literature.
Hours:	Mon-Thu 9:30-8. Fri 9:30-9. Sat 9:30-6. Sun 12-5.
Travel:	Hwy 8 exit off Hwy 401. Proceed west on Hwy 8 to Kitchener. Hwy 8 becomes King St in downtown. At Queen St, turn south.

Credit Cards:	Yes
Owner:	John Poag & Rosemary Tait
Year Estab:	1985
Comments:	Quite a nice shop with a most respectable collection of hardcover volumes ranging from older collectibles to modern volumes, most in very good condition. The books are attractively shelved which makes browsing easy. The shop also maintains a healthy selection of paperbacks.

Casablanca Bookshop   Open Shop
146 King Street West N2G 1A3   (519) 576-0026

Collection:	General stock of paperback and hardcover, comics and CDs.
# of Vols:	50,000
Hours:	Mon-Wed 10-7. Thu & Fri 10-9. Sat 10-6. Sun 11-6.
Travel:	See A Second Look Books above. Shop is between Ontario and Yonge.
Credit Cards:	Yes
Owner:	Mark Pettigrew
Year Estab:	1985
Comments:	No shortage of books here, particularly paperbacks. The hardcover volumes that we saw were, for the most part, recent bestsellers in generally good condition. If your fancy happens to be adult videos or magazines, the store can supply that as well.

K W Bookstore & Exchange   Open Shop
308 King Street West N2G 1B7   (519) 742-1261
                                                          Fax: (519) 742-1301

Collection:	General stock of new and used paperback and hardcover.
# of Vols:	150,000
Specialties:	Science fiction.
Hours:	Mon-Sat 9-11pm. Sun 10-6.
Credit Cards:	Yes
Owner:	Lucille de la Chevrotière
Year Estab:	1975
Comments:	How nice to find a shop with as large a selection of books as this one has that is also comfortable to browse, has well organized shelves, books that are neatly stacked and easy to locate by subject, and a fair balance of hardcover to paperback titles. While most of the hardcover items were of more recent vintage, we did spot quite a few older, and in our view, desirable items on the shelves and in a large glass display case. There's also a nice children's section, a fair share of comic related material and (discretely shelved) some of the more popular adult magazines. The folks even allow the weary book traveler the use of their restroom.

Lookin' For Heroes   Open Shop
93 Ontario Street South N2G 1X5   (519) 570-4361   (519) 570-0873
                                                          Fax: (519) 894-0115

Collection:	General stock of new and used paperbacks and comics.
Hours:	Mon & Tue 10-6. Wed & Thu 10-7. Fri 10-9. Sat 10-6. Sun 12-5.
Comments:	Stock is evenly divided between new and used books.

Now & Then Books   **Open Shop**
90 Queen Street South N2G 1V9   (519) 744-5571
Web page: www.sentex.net/~dvanhorn

Collection:	Specialty
Specialties:	Science fiction.
Hours:	Mon-Fri 9-8, except Thu & Fri till 9. Sat 9-6. Sun 12-5.
Travel:	Just off Charles.
Credit Cards:	Yes
Owner:	Harry Kremer
Year Estab:	1972

Lakefield

Lakefield Station Bookshop   **Open Shop**
Stanley Street   (705) 652-6872
Mailing address: PO Box 1551 Lakefield ON K0L 2H0   Fax: (705) 657-3125
                                                E-mail: lkfldbookshop@ptbo.igs.net

Collection:	General stock of hardcover and paperback, prints and ephemera.
# of Vols:	12,000
Specialties:	Natural history; children's; travel & exploration; Canadiana.
Hours:	May-Dec: Most days, 10:30-5.
Services:	Catalog, accepts want lists.
Travel:	From Peterborough, proceed north on Hwy 28 for about 15 minutes. Stanley St branches right off highway just past the village center. Shop is located in a restored railway station.
Credit Cards:	Yes
Owner:	David Glover
Year Estab:	1997
Comments:	Thanks to this most accomodating owner, we were able to visit this shop, located in a former railroad station that the owner himself has meticulously restored, in it's "off season" when its shelves were not fully stocked. What we were able to see was a mixed selection of hardcover volumes containing many vintage titles, some older books, sets, a nice children's section and some unusual reference items. We were advised that the owner's collection of signed firsts and other unique items would be available for browsing once the regular season began. A native Australian, the owner has many books from "down under" which an interested bibliophile may wish to inquire about.

Lindsay

Read-It-Again Book Exchange   **Open Shop**
153 Angeline Street North K9V 4X3   (705) 328-2741
Web page: lindsaycomp.on.ca/bookexchange   E-mail: readit@lindsaycomp.on.ca

Collection:	General stock of mostly paperback.
Hours:	Mon-Fri 9:30-5. Sat 9:30-3. Sun 12-4.

London

Attic Books   **Open Shop**
240 Dundas Street N6A 1H3   (519) 432-7277

Collection:	General stock of hardcover and paperback and ephemera.
# of Vols:	60,000
Hours:	Mon-Sat 10-5:30, except Fri till 9 (from Apr-Dec only).
Services:	Appraisals, search service, catalog, accepts want lists.
Travel:	Wellington Rd exit off Hwy 401. Proceed north on Wellington for nine km to downtown, then left on Dundas. Shop is just ahead.
Credit Cards:	Yes
Owner:	Marvin Post
Year Estab:	1976
Comments:	Something for everybody. This delightful shop carries a wonderful selection of books that should please all but the crankiest bookaholic. Most of the books, particularly those on the main level, are in good to excellent condition, represent a wide range of subject matters as well as a wide range of ages and are moderately priced. The collection is meticulously labeled by category and subcategory and ephemera, also in well labeled boxes, is located in the same section as the books dealing with the same subject matter. One floor below one can find an additional assortment of books, including many reading copies at bargain prices. For the knowledgeable collector of "really old books," don't miss the books behind glass. The shop also has sheet music.

Basically Books   **Open Shop**
1009 Wonderland Road South N6K 3S4   (519) 649-0997

Collection:	General stock of paperback and hardcover.
# of Vols:	35,000
Hours:	Mon-Wed 10-6. Thu & Fri 10-8. Sat 10-5:30. Sun 12-4:30.
Travel:	Wellington Rd exit off Hwy 401. Proceed north on Wellington, then west on Southdale and right on Wonderland.
Credit Cards:	No
Year Estab:	1978
Comments:	Stock is approximately 75% paperback.

Books Abound   **Open Shop**
994 Huron Street N5Y 4K6   (519) 433-1817

Collection:	General stock paperback and hardcover.
# of Vols:	4,000
Hours:	Tue-Fri 9-6. Sat 9-4.
Travel:	Highbury exit off Hwy 401. North on Highbury, then west on Huron.
Comments:	Stock is approximately 75% paperback.

City Lights Bookshop   **Open Shop**
356 Richmond Street N6A 3C3   (519) 679-8420

Collection:	General stock of paperback and hardcover, CDs and videos.

(London)

# of Vols:	30,000-35,000
Hours:	Mon-Sat 10-9. Sun 11-6.
Travel:	See Attic Books above. From Wellington, turn left on York and right on Richmond.
Credit Cards:	Yes
Owner:	Jim Capel & Teresa Tarasewicz
Year Estab:	1975
Comments:	The people in this community must like this shop as it was quite crowded on the day of our visit. What we saw was a mix of mostly paperback books with a moderate number of hardcover items, the majority of which were reading copies of fairly recent origin. The emphasis seemed to be on popular subjects. If you're looking for an esoteric title, your chances of finding it here are not very great.

G & A Book Exchange   **Open Shop**
777 Dundas Street N5W 2Z6   (519) 438-5831

Collection:	General stock of mostly paperback.
# of Vols:	5,000
Hours:	Mon-Sat 9:30-5:30, except Fri till 8.

Mainly Books   **Open Shop**
1824 Dundas Street N5V 1B4   (519) 455-2043
                                                         Fax: (519) 455-6828
                                              E-mail: telfer@multiboard.com

Collection:	General stock of mostly paperback.
# of Vols:	25,000
Hours:	Tue-Fri 10-5. Sat 10-3.

Memory Lane   **Antique Mall**
1175 Hyde Park Road N6H 5K6   (519) 471-2835

Hours:	Mon-Sat 10-6. Sun 11-5.
Travel:	Exeter Rd/Wellington Rd off Hwy 401. Proceed west on Exeter, then right on Wonderland and left on Sarnia. Shop is at corner of Sarnia and Hyde Park.

Odyssey Books   **Mail Order**
PO Box 24028 N6H 5C4   Tel & Fax: (519) 641-7069
                                             E-mail: odysseybooks@home.com

Collection:	General stock.
# of Vols:	5,000
Specialties:	Arctic; maritime.
Services:	Search service, catalog, accepts want lists.
Credit Cards:	Yes
Owner:	Tom Smith
Year Estab:	1994
Comments:	Also displays at Memory Lane (see above).

Portobello Road Bookstore   ***
Web page: www.abebooks.com   (800) 583-9345

Collection:	General stock of paperback and hardcover.
# of Vols:	14,000
Owner:	Simon Goodwin
Year Estab:	1994
Comments:	This shop was in the process of closing down as this guide went to press but we were advised that the owner was looking for a new location in London. As we cannot provide our readers with any additional information, we hope that the phone number and Internet information provided above will help track down the owner's new address.

H. Sommers Books   **Open Shop**
436 Richmond Street N6A 3C9   (519) 660-8806

Collection:	General stock of paperback and hardcover.
# of Vols:	30,000
Hours:	Mon-Sat 10-6, except Fri till 8. Sun 1-6.
Services:	Appraisals, search service, accepts want lists.
Travel:	See Attic Books above. From Wellington, turn west on Queen and south at second light onto Richmond.
Credit Cards:	Yes
Owner:	Hank Sommers
Year Estab:	1994
Comments:	The owner of this shop clearly "thinks books." In addition to the book motif hanging that greets visitors as they enter the shop (one flight down) and wallpaper with a book motif, a sharp eyed visitor should also be able to find some other book related items located throughout the store. As for the books, they're neatly displayed, in generally good condition and the shop is easy to browse. At least half the stock is paperback. While this observer was unable to satisfy his collectible thirsts here, the reader of this book may be more fortunate.

Springbank Books   **Open Shop**
390 Springbank Drive N6J 1G9   (519) 474-0211

Collection:	General stock of paperback and hardcover.
# of Vols:	35,000
Hours:	Mon-Sat 10-5:30.
Travel:	From Wellington, turn left on Horton which becomes Springbank.
Credit Cards:	Yes
Year Estab:	1996
Comments:	Stock is approximately 70% paperback.

Thame Valley Books   **Mail Order**
824 Clearview Avenue   N6H 2N2   (519) 471-0227

Collection:	General stock.
# of Vols:	5,000

Specialties:	Modern first editions.
Services:	Catalog, accepts want lists.
Credit Cards:	No
Owner:	David Falls
Year Estab:	1998

Mar

Third Time Around Books   **Open Shop**
RR 1 N0H 1X0   (519) 534-1382

Collection:	General stock of mostly hardcover.
# of Vols:	2,000
Hours:	Mid May-mid Oct: Wed-Mon 9:30-6.
Travel:	On Hwy 10, about 19 km north of Wiarton. From Hwy 10, turn west on Red Bay Rd and continue to the end. Bear right and bear right again at fork, then first right turn.
Owner:	Norman Todd & Paul Kiely
Year Estab:	1994
Comments:	Shop also sells antiques.

Markham
(Map 17, page 243)

Alfsen House Books   **Open Shop**
154 Main Street North L3P 1Y3   (905) 294-2571
E-mail: alfsen-house-books@on.aibn.com

Collection:	General stock of paperback, hardcover and comics.
# of Vols:	30,000+
Hours:	Mon-Fri 10-9. Sat 9:30-6:30. Sun 12-6.
Travel:	Markham Rd exit off Hwy 401. Proceed north on Markham (Hwy 48) which becomes Main St. Shop is after passing Hwy 7.
Credit Cards:	No
Owner:	Adam & Andrew Alfsen
Year Estab:	1992
Comments:	Stock is approximately 75% paperback.

Mike's Book Store   **Open Shop**
6545 Highway 7 L3P 3B4   (905) 294-4860

Collection:	General stock of mostly paperback.
# of Vols:	20,000
Hours:	Tue-Fri 10-6. Sat 10-5:30.

Marysville

The Watermark of Lonsdale   **Open Shop**
1091 Marysville Road, RR #1 K0K 2N0   (613) 396-3029
E-mail: watermrk@ihorizons.net

Collection:	General stock and ephemera.
# of Vols:	4,000

Hours:	Daily 11-6.
Services:	Appraisals, search service, catalog, accepts want lists.
Travel:	Exit 566 (Marysville Rd) off Hwy 401. Proceed north on Marysville Rd for about five km to "T" junction. Turn right, then first left into Lonsdale.
Credit Cards:	Yes
Owner:	Joan & Bruce McBain
Year Estab:	1989
Comments:	Shop is located in a 19th century limestone building.

Merrickville

Woodshed Books   **Open Shop**
117 West Broadway Avenue   (613) 269-3042
Mailing address: PO Box 432 Merrickville ON K0G 1N0
                                               E-mail: woodshedbooks@sprint.ca

Collection:	General stock of hardcover and paperback.
# of Vols:	2,000-3,000
Hours:	Tue-Sun 10-5.
Travel:	Hwy 43 to Merrickville. Shop is on west side of village. Hwy 43 becomes West Broadway.
Credit Cards:	No
Owner:	Mark & Judy Rannells
Year Estab:	1996
Comments:	One might call this a "family" bookshop in that its collection, a mix of hardcover and paperback books, consists of more popular titles than scholarly material. The books were in generally mixed condition. As always, an astute buyer might spot a rare gem if said buyer knows his books.

Midland

Cottage Books   **Open Shop**
480 Elizabeth Street L4R 1Z8   (705) 526-8875

Collection:	General stock of mostly used paperback.
# of Vols:	10,000 (used)
Hours:	Mon-Sat 10-6.

Odd Copy Bookshop   **Open Shop**
RR #1 L4R 4K3   (705) 538-2281
                                                               Fax: (705) 538-1122

Collection:	General stock.
Specialties:	Transportation; Canadiana.
Hours:	Jun 14-Labor Day: Mon-Sat 10-5. Sun 12-5.
Services:	Appraisals, accepts want lists, mail order.
Travel:	On Hwy 12, 8½ km west of Hwy 93.
Credit Cards:	No
Year Estab:	1969

Milton

Recycled Reading   **Open Shop**
184 Main Street East L9T 1N8   (905) 878-6024

Collection: General stock of mostly paperback.
Hours: Mon-Sat 10-3, except Thu & Fri till 6.

Minden

Novel Ideas Bookstore & Gift Shop   **Open Shop**
126 Main Street K0M 2K0   (705) 286-6477

Collection: General stock of mostly used paperback.
# of Vols: 12,000+ (used)
Hours: Tue-Sat 10-5:30, except Jul & Aug: Mon-Sat 10-5:30.

Mississauga

Kalamos Books   **Mail Order**
725 Vermouth Avenue, #1   L5A 3X5   (905) 272-4841
                                          E-mail: kalamosbks@aol.com

Collection: Specialty books and ephemera.
# of Vols: 4,000
Specialties: Greece, with emphasis on modern Greece. Some books in Greek.
Services: Search service, catalog, accepts want lists.
Credit Cards: No
Owner: June Samaras
Year Estab: 1996

Red Lancer Militaria   **Mail Order**
5942 Mersey Street   L5V 1W1   (905) 814-1668
                                               Fax: (905) 814-1591

Collection: Specialty books (new and used) and related artifacts.
# of Vols: 3,000
Specialties: Military
Services: Appraisals, accept want lists.
Credit Cards: No
Owner: Ed Fedora
Year Estab: 1969

Soft Books   **Mail Order**
1889 Silverberry Crescent L5J 1C8   (905) 822-8178
                                       E-mail: softbooks@sympatico.ca

Collection: Specialty
# of Vols: 5,000
Specialties: Science fiction.
Services: Catalog
Credit Cards: No
Owner: Joe Bell
Year Estab: 1979

Morrisburg

Old Authors Bookshop   **Open Shop**
13 Gibson Lane   (613) 543-3337
Mailing address: PO Box 403 Morrisburg ON K0C 1X0   Fax: (613) 543-2380
Web page: www.abebooks.com/home/oldauthors   E-mail: authors@mor-net.on.ca

Collection:	General stock.
# of Vols:	20,000
Specialties:	Electrical technology, including wireless, telegraphy, radio, electricity.
Hours:	May-Oct: Wed-Sun 10-5. Nov-Mar: By appointment or chance.
Services:	Search service, accepts want lists, mail order.
Travel:	Exit 750 off Hwy 401. Proceed south on Hwy 31 for two km, then right on Gibson Ln. Shop is at end of road.
Credit Cards:	Yes
Owner:	Roger Hart & Carol Doyle
Year Estab:	1936
Comments:	A very nice couple who were kind enough to come in on their day off to allow us to wander in and out of the many cubicles that make up the main building housing this shop's collection. The shelves are meticulously labeled and the books, most in quite good condition, represent an excellent selection for the traveling book person hungry for volumes of value. In addition to the many vintage novels, an entire spectrum of history, science and the arts are represented in reasonable depth. We confess that our chat with the owners was so pleasant that we lost track of time and were unable to browse a second building containing additional volumes. Our loss may be our reader's gain.

Nepean

Book Market   **Open Shop**
1534 Merivale Road K2G 3J7   (613) 226-3672

Collection:	General stock of paperback and hardcover.
# of Vols:	40,000
Hours:	Mon-Wed 9:30-6. Thu & Fri 9:30-9. Sat 10-6. Sun 12-5.
Travel:	Maitland exit off Hwy 417. Proceed south on Maitland which becomes Clive which becomes Merivale.
Comments:	Stock is approximately 70% paperback.

R.R. Knott Bookseller   **By Appointment**
3 Roberta Crescent K2J 1G5   (613) 823-2128
Web page: www.cyberus.ca/~rrknott   E-mail: rrknott@cyberus.ca

Collection:	Specialty
# of Vols:	10,000
Specialties:	Canadiana; Canadian literature; mediaeval studies; military; modern first editions; literature.
Services:	Appraisals, catalog, accepts want lists.
Credit Cards:	Yes

Owner: Rhys Knott
Year Estab: 1979

Newmarket

Bonaparte's Repeat Books   **Open Shop**
47 Main Street South L3Y 3Y3   Tel & Fax: (905) 853-2777
                                       E-mail: bonapartesbooks@hotmail.com
Collection: General stock of paperback and hardcover, gifts and greeting cards.
Hours: Tue, Wed, Fri 10-6. Thu 10-8. Sat 10-5. Sun 11-5. Summer: Tue 10-8.
Services: Search service, accepts want lists.
Travel: Davis exit off Hwy 404. Proceed west on Davis. Just past the railroad
                  tracks, turn left then right at the end of the street. Shop is in the
                  shopping plaza on the right.
Credit Cards: Yes
Owner: Gayle Bonaparte
Year Estab: 1997
Comments: Stock is approximately 70% paperback.

Book Market   **Open Shop**
130 Davis Drive L3Y 2N1   (905) 715-7766
Collection: General stock of paperback and hardcover.
# of Vols: 70,000
Hours: Mon-Sat 9:30-6. Sun 11-5.
Travel: Davis Dr exit off Hwy 404. Proceed west on Davis. Shop is about three
                  km ahead.
Credit Cards: Yes
Year Estab: 1979
Comments: Stock is approximately 65% paperback.

Great Books   **Open Shop**
208 Main Street South L3Y 3Z3   (905) 898-1340
                                                          Fax:(905) 898-3738
Collection: General stock of mostly used hardcover and paperback.
# of Vols: 70,000
Hours: Mon-Sat 10-6. Sun 2-5.
Services: Search service, accepts want lists, mail order.
Travel: Davis exit off Hwy 404. Proceed west on Davis, then south on Main.
Credit Cards: Yes
Owner: Tamara & Peter Bolton
Year Estab: 1977
Comments: A shop which, in our opinion, should be a model for most "neighbor-
                  hood" bookstores. Its hardcover collection is sound and runs the gamut
                  from recent to older volumes. Its paperback collection is modest but
                  adequate. Shelf space is generous enough to provide for lots of brows-
                  ing and the labeling and organization of the shop makes visiting it
                  most pleasant. If you don't see what you're looking for ask, as the
                  owners have additional stock off premises.

Starlight Books   **Open Shop**
16700 Bayview L3X 1W1   (905) 898-7179

Collection:	General stock of hardcover and paperback.
# of Vols:	50,000
Hours:	Mon-Wed 10-6. Thu & Fri 10-8. Sat 10-5. Sun 11-4.
Travel:	Mulock exit off Hwy 404. Proceed west on Mulock. Shop is in a strip mall at southwest corner of Mulock and Bayview.
Credit Cards:	Yes
Owner:	David & Margret Crocombe
Comments:	Typically, a store of this size (room after room after room of used books) would contain a certain amount of less attractive (in terms of condition) items. We're delighted to report that this was not the case at this location. While specialists seeking certain esoteric titles may be disappointed if they visit here, the more typical book enthusiast should be pleased with the opportunity to examine books in almost every subject, neatly displayed and in generally good to excellent condition. Plenty of new titles (possibly remainders) and enough oldies to satisfy most tastes.

Niagara Falls

Olde Country Books   **Open Shop**
4604 Erie Avenue L2E 3N4   (905) 357-0133

Collection:	General stock of mostly used paperback and hardcover.
# of Vols:	7,000-10,000
Hours:	Thu-Sun 10-5.
Travel:	Stanley St exit off QEW. Proceed north on Stanley, then right on Bridge and right on Erie.
Credit Cards:	No
Year Estab:	1970's
Comments:	Stock is approximately 75% paperback.

Page One Books   **Open Shop**
5984 Main Street L2G 5Z8   (905) 354-9761

Collection:	General stock of hardcover and paperback.
# of Vols:	35,000+ (See Comments)
Specialties:	Vintage paperbacks; detective fiction; cookbooks; beverages.
Hours:	Mon-Sat 9:30-4. Till 5 in summer.
Services:	Search service, accepts want lists, mail order.
Travel:	After crossing Rainbow Bridge from USA, follow signs to downtown business district. Turn left on Victoria which becomes Ferry, then left on Main.
Credit Cards:	No
Owner:	Sheila Bolton
Year Estab:	1972
Comments:	The center and left side of this shop displays paperbacks from floor to ceiling while several alcoves on the right side of the shop are filled

with hardcover titles, mostly older books, the vast majority of them being reading copies. We did spot a number of collectibles and suspect that a sharp eyed scout could find some winners among what would appear to be the more common titles. We were advised that the owner has an additional 100,000+ volumes in storage, evenly divided between hardcover and paperback.

Niagara-on-the-Lake

Joan Draper, Bookseller   **Open Shop**
267 Victoria Street, Box 729 L0S 1J0   (905) 468-7885
                                                      Fax: (905) 468-3777

Collection:	General stock.
# of Vols:	3,000-5,000
Specialties:	Bloomsbury group.
Hours:	Tue-Sun 11-6. Mon by appointment.
Services:	Appraisals, accepts want lists.
Travel:	From QEW, exit at St. Catharines where sign points to Niagara-on-the-Lake/Shaw Festival. Continue on Hwy 55 following signs into town (Queen St). Right on Victoria.
Credit Cards:	Yes
Year Estab:	1987
Comments:	Located on a quiet residential street in the front room of a private residence, the stock in this shop is primarily hardcover and eclectic. Most of the volumes we saw were in quite good condition. The shop is small enough to be easy to browse yet interesting enough to deserve the time necessary to peruse the various titles. Prices are moderate.

McGarr Books   **By Appointment**
RR #6 L0S 1J0   (905) 468-2249
                                          E-mail: mcgarrbk@vaxxine.com

Collection:	General stock.
# of Vols:	5,000
Specialties:	Military
Services:	Accepts want lists.
Credit Cards:	Yes
Owner:	Richard McGarr
Year Estab:	191

Old Niagara Bookshop   **Open Shop**
44 Queen Street L0S 1J0   (905) 468-2602

Collection:	General stock of mostly new and some used hardcover.
# of Vols:	400-500 (used)
Specialties:	Canadiana; non fiction.
Hours:	Jan-Apr: Tue-Sun 11-6. May-Dec: Daily 10:30-6.
Travel:	See Joan Draper, Bookseller above.

North Bay
(Map 15A, page 166)

Allison The Bookman   **Open Shop**
342 Main Street East P1B 1B4   (705) 476-1450
Web page: http;//tnt.vianet.on.ca/comm/allison/   E-mail: allisond@vianet.on.ca

Collection:	General stock of paperback and hardcover.
# of Vols:	100,000
Hours:	Winter: Mon-Thu 9-6. Fri & Sat 9-9. Sun 10-6. From late May-late Sept: Mon-Sat 9-9. Sun 10-6.
Services:	Mail order.
Travel:	Fisher St exit off Hwy 11. Proceed on Fisher St to Main St East, then right on Main St. Shop is ahead on right.
Credit Cards:	Yes
Owner:	Esther Johnson
Year Estab:	1973
Comments:	Stock is approximately 80% paperback.

Lakeshore Books   **Open Shop**
54 Lakeshore Drive P1A 2A3   (705) 472-7480
                                                E-mail: fernlaf@onlink.net

Collection:	General stock of mostly paperback.
Hours:	Mon-Sat 10-8, except till 6 in winter. Sun 11-5.

North Gower

David Ewens, Books   **By Appointment**
PO Box 128 K0A 2T0   (613) 489-2222
                                                    Fax: (613) 489-0601

Collection:	Specialty books and ephemera.
# of Vols:	2,000
Specialties:	Canadiana; exploration; maps, prints.
Services:	Appraisals, catalog, accepts want lists.
Credit Cards:	No
Year Estab:	1983

North York

Libra Books   **Mail Order**
40 Godstone Road, #1510 M2J 3C7   (416) 495-0522
                                                    Fax: (416) 663- 0808
                                              E-mail: libraboks@yahoo.com

Collection:	General stock.
# of Vols:	2,000
Specialties:	Mystery; fiction; baseball.
Credit Cards:	No
Owner:	Meyer Korman
Year Estab:	1993

Oakville

Capricorn Books   **Open Shop**
Miller News, 323 Church Street L6J 1P2   (905) 337-9231
Web page: www.abebooks.com/home/capricorn   E-mail: capricorn@globalserve.net

Collection:	General stock and ephemera.
# of Vols:	8,000
Specialties:	Antique reference; art; military.
Hours:	Tue-Sat 10-5. Sun 12-5.
Services:	Search service, accepts want lists, mail order.
Travel:	Trafalgar Rd exit off QEW. Proceed south on Trafalgar to downtown. Left at light on Church. Shop is at intersection with Reynolds St.
Credit Cards:	Yes
Owner:	Catherine & Paul Strong
Year Estab:	1995
Comments:	A few steps down into a shop that while small contains enough quality hardcover books in good condition to make a visit here worth a stop. A discriminating visitor will have no trouble determining which books are worthy of a closer examination.

Circle "M" Books   **Open Shop**
At Square Nail Antiques   (905) 337-2310
370 Kerr Street L6K 3B8

Collection:	General stock of hardcover and paperback and ephemera.
# of Vols:	8,000
Hours:	Mon-Sat 10-6. Sun 12-5.
Services:	Accepts want lists.
Travel:	See Treasure Island Books below.
Credit Cards:	No
Owner:	Michael Cowan
Year Estab:	1999
Comments:	We don't profess to know a great deal about antiques which are plentiful in this bi-level shop. As for the books, (far fewer on display than the number indicated by the owner above), if we were on a tighter schedule, we probably would have not missed a great deal had we not stopped here. The owner also displays at a flea market in Hamilton. (See above.)

Second Editions-Discount Books   **Open Shop**
312 Lakeshore Road East, #1 L6J 1J2   (905) 338-6337

Collection:	General stock of hardcover and paperback.
# of Vols:	20,000
Specialties:	History; Canadiana; military; mystery.
Hours:	Mon-Sat 10-5:30. Sun 12-4:30.
Services:	Accepts want lists.
Travel:	Trafalgar exit off QEW. Proceed south on Trafalgar, then east on Lakeshore. The entrance is around the corner on Reynolds.

Credit Cards:	Yes
Owner:	Sheila & John Dixon
Year Estab:	1993
Comments:	We visited this shop just after it had downsized from two storefronts to one and the owners were still in the process of reshelving their stock. What we were able to see was a fair number of vintage hardcover titles as well as more recent hardcover materials, some paperbacks, CDs and some new books. If you're into vintage material, this store is worth a visit.

Treasure Island Books   **Open Shop**
250 Kerr Street L6K 3B2   (905) 845-8009

Collection:	General stock of hardcover and paperback and ephemera.
# of Vols:	100,000
Specialties:	Golf
Hours:	Mon-Sat 10-5:29. Sun 12-5.
Services:	Appraisals, accepts want lists, mail order.
Travel:	Eastbound on QEW: Dorval exit. Continue east on Speers, then south on Kerr. Westbound on QEW: Kerr St exit.
Credit Cards:	No
Owner:	Bruce Ferrier
Year Estab:	1973
Comments:	A shop that initially may give the visitor the sense that it's collection is primarily paperback. Indeed, while it is heavily paper, the shop also offers some older hardcover volumes, a few of them collectible, and other volumes that fall into the reading copy and nostalgia categories. As only a small portion of the inventory is available for browsing, if you don't see what you're looking for ask as the owner may be able to check a storage area upstairs.

Village Bookshoppe   **Open Shop**
8 Lakeshore Road West L6K 3E5   (905) 845-7060
                                           E-mail: villagebookshoppe@on.aibn.com

Collection:	General stock of mostly paperback.
# of Vols:	16,000
Hours:	Tue-Sat 10-6. Sun 12-5.

Orangeville

Hockley Books   **Open Shop**
RR #5 L9W 2Z2   (905) 729-2083
                                                E-mail: jgunn@simcoe.igs.net

Collection:	General stock of hardcover and paperback.
# of Vols:	5,000
Specialties:	Canadiana
Hours:	Sat & Sun and holiday Mon 11-5.
Services:	Accepts want lists, mail order.
Travel:	Proceeding north on Hwy 10, cross over Hwy 9. At flashing light, turn right onto Hockley Rd. Shop is about five km ahead in village.

Credit Cards: Yes
Year Estab: 1995

Readers' Choice   **Open Shop**
82 Broadway L0N 1M0 (See Comments)   (519) 940-8740
Mailing address: RR 1 Mansfield ON L0N 1M0

Collection: General stock of paperback and hardcover.
# of Vols: 25,000+
Hours: Mon-Wed 11-5. Thu 11-6. Fri 11-7. Sat 11-4:30. Sun 12:30-4:30.
Travel: From Hwy 400 north, turn west on Hwy 9 and continue to Orangeville
                 where road becomes Broadway.
Owner: Sharon Thomas
Year Estab: 1997
Comments: Regrettably, if you're looking for hard-to-find hardcover volumes, based
                 on what we saw during our very brief visit, we would not encourage
                 you to be too optimistic about finding them here. The store does have a
                 generous supply of paperback books. Note: At press time, there was a
                 strong possibility that the store would relocate to 151A Broadway.

Summit Books   **Open Shop**
Mono Plaza, R.R. #4 L9W 2Z1   Tel & Fax: (519) 942-0498
Web page: www.sumbooks.com   E-mail: legs@headwaters.com

Collection: General stock of hardcover and paperback.
# of Vols: 15,000
Hours: Mon-Thu 10-6. Fri 10-8:30. Sat 10-5:30.
Services: Search service, accepts want lists, mail order.
Travel: On Hwy 10, 3½ km north of Hwy 9. Proceeding north, Mono Plaza is
                 on the right, just after the light at Hockley Rd.
Credit Cards: Yes
Owner: Leslie G. Sabo
Year Estab: 1986
Comments: The shop carries a generous selection of paperbacks and mixed vintage
                 hardcover volumes. Some of the books we saw would well fit into the
                 "collectible" category while others would more likely be considered
                 reading copies. The shop also sells comics and magazines.

Orillia

The Book Re-View Of Orillia   **Open Shop**
438 West Street North L3V 5E8   (705) 327-2579

Collection: General stock of mostly paperback.
# of Vols: 8,000
Hours: Sun & Mon 11:30-4:30. Tue-Sat 10-5:30, except Fri till 8.

Mike's Book Store   **Open Shop**
110 Mississauga Street East L3V 1V7   (705) 326-6335

Collection: General stock of mostly paperback.
Hours: Mon-Sat 10-5:30.

Orleans

Book Heaven   **Open Shop**
2297 St. Joseph Boulevard K1C 1E7   (613) 830-3365
                                                                        Fax: (613) 830-8721
Collection: General stock of paperback and hardcover.
# of Vols: 150,000
Hours: Tue-Thu 9:30-5:30. Fri 9:30-8. Sat 9:30-5.
Travel: Hwy 17 exit off Hwy 417. Proceed east on Hwy 17 toward Rockland,
                  then Blvd Jeanne D'Arc South exit off Hwy 17. Turn left (east) at
                  second set of lights onto St. Joseph Blvd. Shop is on left, in a small
                  strip mall.
Credit Cards: Yes
Owner: Margaret & Neil Hyland
Year Estab: 1986
Comments: The shop boasts, quite accurately, 150,000 books, the vast majority of
                  which are paperbacks in good condition, complemented by a modest
                  number of hardcover volumes, most in dust jackets, and a nice assort-
                  ment of inexpensively priced remainders. The books are nicely dis-
                  played with sections well labeled for easy browsing. If you have spe-
                  cial wants in mind, you might check with the owners as other titles are
                  available in a second, off premises, location.

Book Market   **Open Shop**
1675 Tenth Line Road K1E 3P6   (613) 824-3198
Collection: General stock of paperback and hardcover.
Hours: Mon-Sat 9:30-6, except Thu & Fri till 9. Sun 12-5.

Lock, Stock & Barrel   **Mail Order**
841 Acadian Garden K1C 2V7   E-mail: gregor7@hotmail.com
Collection: Specialty
# of Vols: 1,500
Specialties: Canadiana, with emphasis on small town histories.
Services: Accepts want lists.
Owner: Greg & Patty

Tales & Tunes   **Open Shop**
5929 Jeanne d'Arc Boulevard K1C 6V8   (613) 841-7016
Web page: www.chatcan.ca/TandT   Fax: (613) 841-7017
                                                                    E-mail: TandT@chatcan.ca
Collection: General stock of mostly paperback.
Specialties: Vintage paperbacks.
Hours: Mon-Sat 10-9. Sun 10-5.

Webber's Books   **Mail Order**
PO Box 49006, Place d'Orleans K1C 7E4   (613) 830-0695
Web page: www.abebooks.com/home/rwebber   E-mail: regwebber@aol.com

Collection:	General stock of mostly hardcover.
# of Vols:	5,000
Specialties:	Canadian literature; poetry (Canadian).
Services:	Search service, accepts want lists.
Credit Cards:	No
Owner:	Reginald Webber
Year Estab:	1997

Orono

Gabrielle Antiques & Collectables   **Open Shop**
3698 Regional Rd #9, RR #1 L0B 1M0   (905) 983-9588

Collection:	General stock of mostly used.
# of Vols:	800-1,000
Hours:	Wed-Sun 10-6. Mon & Tue by chance (except open holiday Mondays).
Services:	Search service, accepts want lists, mail order.
Travel:	From Hwy 401, proceed north on Hwy 35/115 to Kirby cutoff (Regional Rd #9). Shop is first building on left.
Credit Cards:	Yes
Owner:	Ted Thom
Year Estab:	1991
Comments:	Shop also sells non book collectibles.

Oshawa

Gnu Books   **Open Shop**
250 Taunton Road East L1G 7T1   (905) 434-1463

Collection:	General stock of new and used paperback and hardcover and comics.
Hours:	Mon-Wed 10-7. Thu & Fri 10-8. Sat 10-6. Sun 11-5.
Credit Cards:	Yes
Owner:	Janice Truppe
Year Estab:	1984
Comments:	Stock is approximately 50% used, 75% of which is paperback.

Half Price Books   **Open Shop**
133 Taunton Road West L1G 3T4   (905) 728-9468

Collection:	General stock of new and used paperback and hardcover.
# of Vols:	8,000
Hours:	Mon-Thu 10-6. Fri 10-9. Sat 10-6. Sun 12-5.
Travel:	Simcoe St exit off Hwy 401. North on Simcoe, then left on Taunton.
Comments:	What we saw during our brief visit appeared to be overwhelmingly remainders (both hardcover and paperback) and not a likely site for that illusive title you've been searching for, unless, that is, the book was published during the past two or three years.

Half Price Books   **Open Shop**
501 Ritson Road L1H 5K3   (905) 576-9773

Collection:	General stock of new and used paperback and hardcover.

Hours:	Mon-Thu 10-6. Fri 10-9. Sat 10-6. Sun 12-5.
Travel:	Ritson Rd exit off Hwy 401. Proceed north on Ritson to first light.

Half Price Books   **Open Shop**
1615 Dundas Street East L1N 2L1   (905) 728-2179

Collection:	General stock of new and used paperback and hardcover.
# of Vols:	15,000
Hours:	Mon-Fri 10-9. Sat 10-6. Sun 12-5.
Travel:	Thickson Rd exit off Hwy 401. Proceed north on Thickson Rd to Whitby Mall.

Millennium Books   **Open Shop**
64 King Street West L1H 1A6   (905) 725-2375
                                                E-mail: millbook@eagle.ca

Collection:	General stock of paperback and hardcover.
# of Vols:	15,000+
Specialties:	History; modern first editions.
Hours:	Mon-Sat 10-5.
Services:	Accepts want lists, mail order.
Travel:	Park Rd exit off Hwy 401. Proceed north on Park then east on King. Shop is at corner of King & Centre.
Credit Cards:	Yes
Owner:	Angela & Jack Jeffery
Year Estab:	1997
Comments:	Heavily paperback with some hardcover volumes that ranged from collectibles to far more ordinary titles. If the shop carries a significant number of books in the specialties listed above, we were unfortunately unable to view them. The owners operate a second shop in Port Hope. (See Angela's Books below.)

Morningstar Books   **By Appointment**
36 Fernhill Boulevard L1J 5H9   (905) 432-8428
Web page: www.abebooks.com/home/mstar   E-mail: bgervais@idirect.com

Collection:	General stock.
Services:	Search service, accepts want lists.
Credit Cards:	Yes
Owner:	Blayne Gervais
Year Estab:	1999

Morgan Self   **Open Shop**
84 Simcoe Street South L1H 4G6   (905) 723-7621

Collection:	General stock of hardcover and paperback.
# of Vols:	10,000
Hours:	Tue-Fri 10-5:30. Sat 10-5.
Travel:	Simcoe St exit off Hwy 401. Proceed north on Simcoe for about 2½ km.
Credit Cards:	Yes
Year Estab:	1970

Comments: A modest shop with a mix of hardcover and paperback books. A few
                 interesting titles but not sufficiently unique to draw folks who are not
                 already in the vicinity. At the time of our visit, several Big Little
                 Books, on consignment, were displayed under glass.

Ottawa
(Map 16, page 213)

All Books   **Open Shop**
327 Rideau Street K1N 5Y4   (613) 789-9544

Collection: General stock of mostly used paperback.
# of Vols: 50,000 (used)
Hours: Mon-Sat 12-9. Sun 1-9.

Argosy Books   **Open Shop**
209 Dalhousie Street K1N 7C9   (613) 241-1319
                                                                  Fax: (613) 562-0035
                                                          E-mail: argosy@magi.com

Collection: General stock of hardcover and paperback.
# of Vols: 30,000
Specialties: Military, natural history; sciences; children.
Hours: Mon-Fri 10:30-5:30. Sat 9-5:30. Sun 12-5.
Services: Appraisals, occasional catalog, search service, accepts want lists.
Travel: Nicholas exit off Hwy 417 (The Queensway). Proceed north on Nicho-
                 las. When Nicholas splits, take left fork which becomes Dalhousie.
Credit Cards: Yes
Owner: Alice Hughes
Year Estab: 1984
Comments: Quality, quality, quality. What a pleasant surprise–and relief–after
                 visiting so many "half and half" shops to find a wonderful store heavily
                 laden with quality hardcover books of every kind, size and dimension.
                 Many scholarly but popular titles as well in excellent condition. Don't
                 miss it. As an extra added attraction, a store of equal quality is located
                 next door and another nice shop is located across the street.

Arlington Books   **Open Shop**
21 Arlington Avenue K2P 1C1   (613) 232-6975
Web page: www.arlingtonbooks.on.ca   E-mail: ograser@arlingtonbooks.on.ca

Collection: General stock of hardcover and paperback.
# of Vols: 20,000
Specialties: Modern first editions; nautical; Canadiana; history; biography; occult;
                 true crime; books on books; literary criticism.
Hours: Tue-Sat 11-5ish. Usually closed Jun-Sept.
Travel: Between Bank and Kent.
Credit Cards: Yes
Owner: Otto & Gail Graser
Year Estab: 1992

Comments: A shop that grows on you as you walk further and further into the store, skipping some of the paperback volumes and noting several of the older, often hard-to-find hardcover books. While the subjects listed above as specialties are in evidence, the shop has more of a general collection flavor with books in mixed to better condition. Reasonably priced.

The Astrolabe Gallery   **Open Shop**
71 Sparks Street K1P 5A5   Tel & Fax: (613) 234-2348
                                                    E-mail: colbourn@istar.ca

Collection: Specialty
Specialties: Antique maps and prints; books related to maps.
Hours: Mon-Sat 10-5:30.
Services: Appraisals, framing, restoration (paper).
Travel: Between Elgin and Metcalfe.
Credit Cards: Yes
Owner: Joan Colbourn
Year Estab: 1960's

Benjamin Books   **Open Shop**
122 Osgoode Street K1N 6S2   Tel & Fax: (613) 232-7495
                                                    E-mail: benbooks@cyberus.ca

Collection: General stock of hardcover and paperback.
# of Vols: 100,000
Specialties: Scholarly; philosophy; literature; history; social sciences; fine arts; antiquarian.
Hours: Mon-Sat 10-6.
Services: Appraisals, accepts want lists, mail order.
Travel: Nicholas St exit off Hwy 417. Proceed north on Nicholas, right on Laurier, right on King Edward and left on Osgoode.
Credit Cards: Yes
Owner: M. Bubis
Year Estab: 1982
Comments: A winner. The happy visitor to this bi-level shop will find a series of rooms filled with quality books. If you have deep pockets and antiquarian tastes, ask to visit the rare book room which offers volumes that would be at home in any major national library. This ain't a store for the latest bestseller, romance or grandma's favorite cookbook, although that's not to say that you won't find a rare first edition of one of the above here. A must visit if you're anywhere near Ottawa. The owner maintains a second shop in Ottawa with a smaller but equally high quality stock. See below.

Benjamin Books   **Open Shop**
207 Dalhousie Street K1N 7C9   (613) 241-3200
                                                    E-mail: benbooks@cyberus.ca

Collection: General stock mostly hardcover.
# of Vols: 15,000
Specialties: Philosophy; art; Canadiana.

Hours:	Mon-Sat 10-6.
Services:	Appraisals, accepts want lists, mail order.
Travel:	Between Guiges and St. Andrew.
Credit Cards:	Yes
Owner:	M. Bubis
Comments:	A very fine store with excellent books in excellent condition. Shelf after shelf of scholarly titles as well as fine literature. You can't go wrong visiting this shop as its next door neighbor contains high quality material as well and there's a third used book dealer directly across the street.

Book Bazaar   **Open Shop**
755 Bank Street K1S 3V3   (613) 233-4380
Web page: www.abebooks.com   E-mail: bazaarbk@cyberus.ca

Collection:	General stock of hardcover and paperback.
# of Vols:	100,000
Specialties:	Sheet music.
Hours:	Daily 10-6.
Services:	Appraisals, search service.
Travel:	Eastbound on Hwy 417 (The Queensway): Bronson exit. Right on Bronson, left on Chamberlain and right on Bank. Westbound: Metcalfe exit. Exit will lead into Catherine St. Continue on Catherine, then left on Bank. Shop is between 1st and 2nd Avenue.
Credit Cards:	No
Owner:	Jayne Wyatt
Year Estab:	1973
Comments:	A nice shop that carries a comfortable mix of hardcover and paperbacks. Some interesting titles. Most of the books were in good condition and reasonably priced. The shop has the added advantage of being just about one block away from a quality dealer whose shop definitely deserves a visit.

Book Den   **Open Shop**
263 MacLaren K2P 0M1   (613) 236-3142

Collection:	General stock of hardcover and paperback.
# of Vols:	8,000
Specialties:	Literature; Canadiana; religion (Catholic); children's; cookbooks.
Hours:	Tue-Sat 11:30-5:30.
Services:	Appraisals, accepts want lists, mail order.
Travel:	Between Metcalfe and O'Connor.
Credit Cards:	Yes
Owner:	Thurston & Mary Smith
Year Estab:	1981
Comments:	A relatively small shop with a reasonable balance of hardcover and paperback books in generally mixed condition. Popular titles. It's quite possible that one might find a rare item here although for the most part what we saw were a bit more ordinary in terms of flavor.

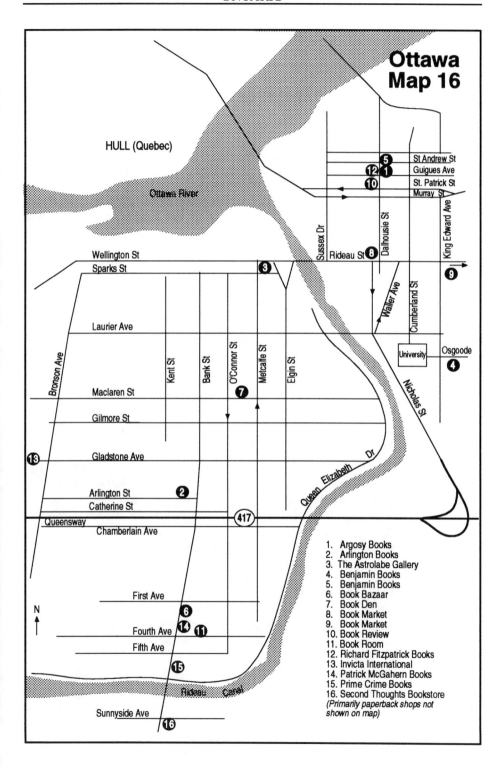

Ottawa Map 16

HULL (Quebec)

Ottawa River

St Andrew St
Guigues Ave
St. Patrick St
Murray St

Wellington St
Sparks St

Rideau St

Sussex Dr
Dalhousie St
King Edward Ave

Laurier Ave

Waller Ave
Cumberland St

University — Osgoode

Bronson Ave
Kent St
Bank St
O'Connor St
Metcalfe St
Elgin St

Maclaren St

Gilmore St

Nicholas St

Gladstone Ave

Arlington St
Catherine St

Queen Elizabeth Dr

Queensway
Chamberlain Ave

417

First Ave

N

Fourth Ave

Fifth Ave

Rideau Canal

Sunnyside Ave

1. Argosy Books
2. Arlington Books
3. The Astrolabe Gallery
4. Benjamin Books
5. Benjamin Books
6. Book Bazaar
7. Book Den
8. Book Market
9. Book Market
10. Book Review
11. Book Room
12. Richard Fitzpatrick Books
13. Invicta International
14. Patrick McGahern Books
15. Prime Crime Books
16. Second Thoughts Bookstore
(Primarily paperback shops not shown on map)

(Ottawa)

Book Market   **Open Shop**
374 Dalhousie Street K1N 7G3   (613) 241-1753

Collection:	General stock of paperback and hardcover.
# of Vols:	120,000+
Hours:	Mon & Tue 9:30-5:30. Wed-Fri 9:30-8:30. Sat 10-6. Sun 12-5.
Travel:	Just north of Rideau.
Comments:	This location is both the headquarters and largest shop of this multi store chain. While we recognize that stock at the other locations clearly represents the used books available in those regions, the following description should serve as a guide for the other stores. Our first reaction upon entering this four story shop was that of books galore. While the preponderance of the stock is paperback, there are plenty of hardcover volumes, most of which are popular titles of fairly recent vintage. If you're looking for self help books, sci fi, romance, movie tie-ins and other similar subjects at fairly inexpensive prices, you can probably find what you're searching for here (or at one of the other Book Market stores). While the shop carries classics, biography and other serious titles, if you're a serious book collector with very specific wants or needs, we suggest you read our entries for some of the others stores in this region.

Book Market   **Open Shop**
580A Montreal Road K1K 0T9   (613) 748-9642

Collection:	General stock of paperback and hardcover.
Hours:	Mon-Wed 9:30-5:30. Thu & Fri 9:30-9. Sat 10-6. Sun 12-5.
Travel:	St. Laurent exit off Queensway. Proceed east on St. Laurent to Montreal Rd, then left on Montreal Road. Shop is in a strip mall.

Book Review   **Open Shop**
236 Dalhousie Street K1N 7E2   Store: (613) 241-9111
Web page: www.abebooks.com/home/BOOKREVIEW   Home: (613) 789-0321
          E-mail: bkreview@ican.net

Collection:	General stock of used hardcover and paperback and some new.
Hours:	Mon-Fri 11:30-4:30. Sat & Sun 11-6. Call for seasonal changes. Other times by appointment.
Credit Cards:	Yes
Owner:	Wendy MacLeod
Year Estab:	1998
Comments:	A mix of hardcover and paperback books, in mixed condition and of a more popular nature. Some new books as well. The shop is close enough to three other used bookstores so that a visit here would not take you far astray. Note: The owner may be relocating within Ottawa.

Book Room   **Open Shop**
101 Fourth Avenue K1S 5H9   Store: (613) 237-4030
          Home: (613) 237-9920

Collection:	General stock hardcover and paperback.

Specialties:	Children's
Hours:	Thu-Sun 1-6.
Services:	Search service, accepts want lists, mail order.
Travel:	East of Bank.
Credit Cards:	No
Owner:	Jacqui Wegren
Year Estab:	1998
Comments:	Stock is 75% hardcover.

Bookmark   **Open Shop**
163 Laurier Avenue East K1N 6N8   (613) 567-0259

Collection:	General stock of mostly paperback.
# of Vols:	40,000
Hours:	Mon-Sat 12-6. Sun 1-6

Neil Cournoyer   **Mail Order**
PO Box 4193, Station E K1S 5B2   Tel & Fax: (613) 237-0500
Web page: www.cyberus.ca/~neilc/   E-mail: neilc@cyberus.ca

Collection:	Specialty
# of Vols:	1,000
Specialties:	19th & 20th century literature.
Services:	Catalog
Credit Cards:	Yes
Year Estab:	1991

Gordon H. Day-Books   **Mail Order**
Web page: www.abebooks.com   (613) 789-0428
                                                   E-mail: gday@cyberus.ca

Collection:	General stock.
Specialties:	Canadiana, with emphasis on Maritime Provinces.
# of Vols:	1,000
Services:	Appraisals
Credit Cards:	No
Year Estab:	1984

Richard Fitzpatrick Books   **Open Shop**
220 Dalhousie Street K1N 7C8   (613) 562-1088
                                                   E-mail: rfitz@cyberus.ca

Collection:	General stock of hardcover and paperback.
# of Vols:	5,000-10,000
Specialties:	Canadiana; Canadian literature; literature.
Hours:	Mon-Sat 12-6. Sun 12-5.
Services:	Catalog, accepts want lists.
Credit Cards:	Yes
Year Estab:	1989
Comments:	We were fortunate to be able to visit this shop just as the owner arrived and found a pleasant mix of titles, including some older (vintage) items as well as a light mix of paperbacks. Definitely worth a visit,

(Ottawa)

particularly as the shop is directly across the street from two other dealers. We left after making a purchase.

Invicta International   **Open Shop**
740 Gladstone K1R 6X5   (613) 232-2263
                                                           Fax: (613) 567-1108

Collection:	Specialty and related items.
# of Vols:	2,000+
Specialties:	Military
Hours:	Tue-Sat 10-5.
Services:	Catalog, accepts want lists.
Travel:	One block west of Bronson.
Credit Cards:	Yes
Owner:	Donald Tresham
Year Estab:	1964

Patrick McGahern Books   **Open Shop**
783 Bank Street K1S 3V5   (613) 230-2275
                                                           Fax: (613) 230-1398
                                          E-mail: mcgahernbooks@cyberus.ca

Collection:	General stock of mostly hardcover.
# of Vols:	20,000
Specialties:	Arctic; Irish; Canadiana; voyages and travel; antiquarian.
Hours:	Mon-Sat 10:30-5:30. Sun 12-5.
Services:	Appraisals, catalog, accepts want lists.
Travel:	See Book Bazaar above.
Credit Cards:	Yes
Year Estab:	1969
Comments:	In addition to the very attractive hardcover books displayed for easy browsing, this shop also offers a large number of truly antiquarian titles, some of which are shelved behind glass. The emphasis here is on the scholarly as well as serious literature. Well worth a visit.

David Poitras, Bookseller   **Mail Order**
773 Hemlock Road   K1K 0K6   (613) 749-9802
Web page: www.resudox.net/~ddvjp   E-mail: ddvjp@resudox.net

Collection:	Specialty
# of Vols:	5,000
Specialties:	Vintage paperbacks.
Services:	Appraisals, search service.
Credit Cards:	No
Year Estab:	1972

Prime Crime Books   **Open Shop**
891 Bank Street K1S 3W4   (613) 238-2583

Collection:	Specialty. Mostly new and some used paperback.
# of Vols:	500 (used)

Specialties:	Mystery
Hours:	Tue-Thu 10-6. Fri 10-7. Sat 9:30-5:30.
Travel:	See Book Bazaar above. Shop is south of Fifth Ave.

Second Thoughts Bookstore   **Open Shop**
280 Sunnyside Avenue K1S 0R8   (613) 730-1142
Web page: www.travel-net.com/~quill   E-mail: quill@travel-net.com

Collection:	General stock of hardcover and paperback.
# of Vols:	30,000
Specialties:	Primarily reading copies of academic subjects.
Hours:	Mon-Thu 12-7:30. Fri 12-9. Sat & Sun 10-6.
Services:	Search service, mail order, accepts want lists.
Travel:	Off Bank St, south of Rideau Canal. Parking is available behind store.
Credit Cards:	Yes
Owner:	Richard Ostrofsky & Carol Motuz
Year Estab:	1995
Comments:	Very much like many used bookstores in the States in terms of its mix of hardcover and paperback volumes and the fact that the hardcover collection is also mixed between newer titles and some "golden old-ies." The store is easy to browse. Prices are reasonable. If you're staying in Ottawa for any length of time, a visit here could result in a pleasant surprise.

Owen Sound

Phoenix Book Store   **Open Shop**
980 2nd Avenue East N4K 2H6   (519) 371-1228
                                                        E-mail: miller@bmts.com

Collection:	General stock of paperback and hardcover.
Hours:	Mon-Sat 9:15-5:30.
Services:	Search service, mail order.
Travel:	Proceeding north on Hwy 6, turn left at third set of lights in Owen Sound. Go down hill then turn left onto 2nd Ave East (Main St). From Hwy 26, turn left at third set of lights, then right at next light and proceed down hill to 2nd Ave East. Turn left.
Credit Cards:	Yes
Owner:	Dave & Bea Miller

Paris

Nelson Ball, Bookseller   **By Appointment**
31 Willow Street N3L 2K7   (519) 442-6113

Collection:	Specialty
# of Vols:	6,000
Specialties:	Canadian literature.
Services:	Appraisals, accepts want lists.
Credit Cards:	No
Year Estab:	1972

Parry Sound

Bearly Used Books   **Open Shop**
45 Seguin Street P2A 1B5   (705) 746-7734
                                                          Fax: (705) 746-6933

Collection: General stock of mostly paperback.
Hours: Mon-Thu 10-5:30. Fri 10-7. Sat 10-5.

Pembroke

Pembroke Book Store   **Open Shop**
467 Pembroke Street West K8A 5P1   (613) 735-7155

Collection: General stock of paperback and hardcover.
Hours: Tue-Sat 9-5.

Penetanguishene

The Reading Room Used Books   **Open Shop**
27 Main Street L9M 1S7   (705) 549-8574

Collection: General stock of paperback and hardcover.
# of Vols: 20,000
Specialties: Canadian history; politics; cookbooks; woodworking; crafts; children's.
Hours: Mon-Sat 10-5:30. Sun 11-4. Later hours in summer.
Travel: Proceed on Hwy 93 to town. Hwy 93 becomes Main St.
Credit Cards: Yes
Owner: Debbie Levy
Year Estab: 1993
Comments: Stock is approximately 70% paperback.

Perth

The Bookworm   **Open Shop**
37-B Foster Street K7H 1R8   (613) 267-1228

Collection: General stock of hardcover and paperback.
# of Vols: 12,000
Specialties: Canadiana; Scotland.
Hours: Tue-Sat 10-5.
Services: Accepts want lists.
Travel: Drummond St exit off Hwy 7. Proceed south on Drummond, then right
                  on Foster for 1/2 block and right into Allen's Lane.
Credit Cards: No
Owner: Anne Murphy
Year Estab: 1987
Comments: A small shop with books compactly shelved. Both the hardcover and
                  paperback books were in mixed condition. Some older volumes but
                  mostly popular titles. Who knows what a sharp eye might discover.
                  Unfortunately, our eyes were rather dull on the day we visited. Note:
                  the shop has been under new ownership for the past two years.

Perth Road

Books in the Woods   **Open Shop**
Box 2014 , RR 1 K0H 2L0   (613) 353-6901

Collection:	General stock of paperback and hardcover.
# of Vols:	6,000
Hours:	Daily 9-9.
Travel:	Division St exit off Hwy 401. Proceed north on Division which becomes Cty Rd 10. Continue for about 25 km to Perth Road. About five minutes north of the village of Perth Road (a cluster of homes), look left for Norman Lane (look for a cluster of signs and two stone posts). Turn into Norman Lane (a dirt road). Shop is about one km ahead.
Credit Cards:	No
Owner:	Grant & Nancy Bourdon
Year Estab:	1991
Comments:	It only required two weeks into our Canadian trip for us to have our first major debate about a shop which David insisted was "off the beaten path" and Susan insisted was "on the way to our next stop and should be visited." So here are two views. David's: A visit to this location will take you far away from any of the major roads, off on a rough side road where you'll be greeted by barking dogs and then have an opportunity to see a modest sized collection that we've been advised is a mix of hardcover and paperback volumes. If you're reading this entry, you'll know we were able to find our way back to the main highway. Susan's: I'm usually a bit more adventuresome than David and, as long as it hadn't rained in a few days, I wasn't put off by the dirt road that was showing the ravages of the spring thaw or the barking dogs who turned out to be most friendly. Once inside the owner's home, I saw far fewer than the number of volumes indicated above (I was advised that the shelves had not yet been restocked for the upcoming spring season) and most of what I saw appeared to be reading copies in mixed condition. Not being the bookperson that David is, I hesitate to say more. The rest is up to you.

Peterborough

The Antique Shop   **Open Shop**
271 George Street North K9J 3G9   (705) 749-2894

Collection:	General stock of hardcover and paperback.
# of Vols:	10,000
Specialties:	Children's
Hours:	Mon-Sat 10-5. Sun 1-4.
Services:	Mail order.
Travel:	From Hwy 115: The Parkway exit. Proceed straight through light onto The Parkway. Right on Landsdowne, left on Aylmer, then right on King and right on George. Shop is between Sherbrooke and King.
Credit Cards:	Yes

(Peterborough)

Owner:	Mike Seeley
Year Estab:	1974
Comments:	Stock is evenly divided between hardcover and paperback.

Books N' Things   **Open Shop**
372 Water Street K9H 3L6   (705) 876-0944

Collection:	General stock of paperback and hardcover.
# of Vols:	10,000
Hours:	Mon-Sat 9-5:30.
Travel:	See Mark Jokinen Books below.
Credit Cards:	Yes
Year Estab:	1992
Comments:	A typical paperback plus shop with its hardcover volumes being mainly reading copies that lack luster.

Dixon's Book Store   **Open Shop**
383 Water Street K9H 3L7   (705) 742-9656

Collection:	General stock of mostly paperback.
# of Vols:	25,000+
Hours:	Mon-Wed 9:30-6. Thu & Fri 9:30-9. Sat 9:30-5:30.

Mark Jokinen Books   **Open Shop**
382 Water Street K9H 3L6   (705) 742-4514

Collection:	General stock.
# of Vols:	17,000
Specialties:	Canadiana; literature; philosophy; history; foreign literature in translation; literary criticism.
Hours:	Mon-Sat 10-5:30.
Services:	Appraisals
Travel:	From Hwy 401, proceed north on Hwy 115 then Parkway exit off Hwy 115. Follow The Parkway to downtown where Clonsilla becomes Charlotte St. Turn left at Water St. Shop is 1½ blocks ahead on right.
Credit Cards:	Yes
Year Estab:	1988
Comments:	A sound collection of mostly hardcover volumes representing the areas identified above as specialties as well as some nice surprises in other areas. What the shop lacks in volume it makes up for in the uniqueness of several of its titles.

Knotanew Book Store   **Open Shop**
261 Charlotte Street K9J 2V3   (705) 876-0190

Collection:	General stock of paperback and hardcover.
# of Vols:	20,000+
Hours:	Mon-Sat 9:30-6.
Travel:	Parkway exit off Hwy 115. Follow Parkway to downtown where Clonsilla becomes Charlotte St.

Credit Cards: No
Year Estab: 1992
Comments: Stock is approximately 75% paperback.

Old Tom Antiques   **Open Shop**
416 George Street North K9H 3R5   (705) 876-6441

Collection: General stock of hardcover and paperback.
# of Vols: 7,000+
Hours: Mon-Sat 10-5.
Travel: From Hwy 115: The Parkway exit. Proceed straight through light onto
                  The Parkway. Right on Landsdowne, left on Aylmer, then right on
                  Brock and left on George. Shop is between Hunter and Brock.
Credit Cards: Yes
Owner: Paul Misener
Year Estab: 1989
Comments: Stock is approximately 75% hardcover.

The Second Story Book Shop   **Open Shop**
203 Simcoe Street, #3 K9H 2H6   (705) 745-5595
Web page: www.kawartha.com/books   Fax: (705) 745-3732
                                              E-mail: books@kawartha.com

Collection: General stock of hardcover and paperback.
# of Vols: 12,000
Specialties: Mysticism and occult; music; science fiction; fantasy; children's; French
                  language novels.
Hours: Mon-Wed 11-7. Thu & Fri 11-8. Sat 11-5:30. Open at 10am in sum-
                  mer. Also other times by appointment.
Services: Appraisals, search service, accepts want lists, mail order.
Travel: See Knotanew Books above. From Charlotte, turn right onto Simcoe.
                  Shop is ahead on right in Charlotte News.
Credit Cards: Yes
Owner: William Barclay & Mike Hearst
Year Estab: 1994
Comments: The owners of this establishment will be the first to remark on how
                  crowded the shop is. Indeed, the door to the shop's restroom doubles as
                  a bookcase (on hinges). If you're agile enough to fit into all the nooks
                  and crannies, you'll find a mix of older volumes (from the turn of the
                  century to the '30's and '40's) as well as some more recent reading
                  copies. The nature of the shop is such that, depending on the time of
                  your visit, on the same shelf as a book you've seen several times
                  elsewhere you may also discover an item you've been searching for for
                  years. Also depending on the time of your visit, you may get to meet
                  the owners' granddaughter who, at 18 months at the time of our visit,
                  was not quite ready to assist us in our perusal of the shop's goods.
                  Note: We were advised during our visit that the owners hope to expand
                  into an adjoining storefront.

Trillium Books   **Mail Order**
1285 Albertus Avenue   K9J 6A4   (705) 749-0461
                                               Fax: (705) 749-2209
                                      E-mail: trillium@pipcom.com

Collection:	Specialty
# of Vols:	500-1,000
Specialties:	Botany; ornithology; natural history; decorative arts.
Services:	Appraisals, catalog, accepts want lists.
Credit Cards:	No
Owner:	William Van Nest
Year Estab:	1998

Pickering

Old Favorites Book Shop Ltd.   **Open Shop**
132 Highway 7   Tel & Fax: (905) 294-3865
Mailing address: RR #1 Locust Hill ON L0H 1J0   E-mail: oldfavs@interlog.com

Collection:	General stock.
# of Vols:	300,000
Specialties:	Military; horses; aviation; children's; Canadiana; poetry.
Hours:	Tue-Sun 11-5.
Services:	Appraisals, search service, accepts want lists, mail order.
Travel:	Hwy 48 (Markham Rd) exit off Hwy 401. Proceed north on Markham, then east on Hwy 7 for eight km. Shop is on Hwy 7, on north side, in hamlet of Green River. (Look for the "Green River" sign.)
Credit Cards:	Yes
Owner:	Ken & Joy Saunders
Year Estab:	1954
Comments:	If you have a lot of time and patience, you could well find some odd or unusual titles in this shop that could be right up your alley. You'll need the time and the patience because, although the shelves are labeled, getting into each aisle, room and assorted nooks and crannies can be slightly challenging. Most of the books we saw were in mixed condition (reading copies) with enough items of interest to satisfy the hearty and adventurous bookperson.

Picton

Travellers' Tales Books   **Open Shop**
1109 County Road 8   (613) 476-1885
Mailing address: PO Box 376 Picton ON K0K 2T0

Collection:	General stock and ephemera.
# of Vols:	20,000
Specialties:	Literature; travel; cookbooks; beverages; children's; Jane Austen; Bloomsbury group.
Hours:	May-Sept: Daily 12-6.
Services:	Search service, accepts want lists, mail order.

Travel:	Eastbound on Hwy 401: Hwy 62 exit. Proceed south on Hwy 62, then east on Hwy 33 to Picton where Hwy 33 becomes Main St. At intersection of Hwy 49, take a sharp right turn on Hwy 33 and continue downhill for two blocks, then right on Cty Rd 8 (Waupoos Rd). Shop is six km ahead. Westbound on Hwy 401: Hwy 49 exit. Proceed south on Hwy 49, then left on Hwy 33.
Credit Cards:	Yes
Owner:	Jill Reville Hill
Year Estab:	1988
Comments:	We regret that this seasonal shop, located in a 19th century farmhouse that offers B&B accommodations, was not yet open at the time of our Ontario travels.

Port Colborne

Alphabet Bookshop   **By Appointment**
145 Main Street West L3K 3V3   Tel & Fax: (905) 834-5323
Web page: www.iaw.com/~alphabet   E-mail: alphabet@iaw.ca

Collection:	Specialty books and ephemera.
# of Vols:	12,000
Specialties:	Modern first editions; illustrated; World War I fiction and poetry; Canadian, American and British literature; mystery; 19th century literature; jazz; beat literature; small general stock.
Services:	Appraisals, catalog, accepts want lists.
Credit Cards:	Yes
Owner:	Richard Shuh & Linda Wooley
Year Estab:	1997

Books In Port   **Open Shop**
218 West Street L3K 4E3   (905) 835-6604
                                            E-mail: feagans@itcanada.com

Collection:	General stock of paperback and hardcover.
# of Vols:	12,000
Specialties:	Canadiana literature; nautical; magazines.
Hours:	Winter: Tue-Sat 10-4. Remainder of year: Tue-Sat 9-5. Sun (summer only) 1-5.
Travel:	From Hwy 3 which becomes Main St, turn south on King, left on Clarence and right (just before the bridge) on West.
Credit Cards:	Yes
Owner:	Nancy Feagan
Year Estab:	1992
Comments:	The shop is heavily paperback and the hardcover books we saw (probably less than 30% of the stock) consisted of books of mixed vintage and what would generally be considered reading copies.

Port Hope

Angela's Books   **Open Shop**
97 Walton Street L1A 1N4   (905) 885-1612
                                                          E-mail: millbook@eagle.ca

Collection:	General stock of paperback and hardcover.
# of Vols:	5,000
Specialties:	Modern first editions; biography; history; military.
Hours:	Mon-Sat 10-5.
Services:	Accepts want lists, mail order.
Travel:	Eastbound on Hwy 401: Hwy 2 exit off Hwy 401. Hwy 2 becomes Ridout St and then Walton St. Westbound: Hwy 28 exit off Hwy 401. Proceed south on Hwy 28 to downtown. Right at "T" intersection.
Credit Cards:	No
Owner:	Angela & John Jeffery
Year Estab:	1995
Comments:	We arrived here before the owner and unfortunately time constraints would not allow us to wait for the shop's normal opening time. Glancing through the front windows we were able to view a shop that was heavily paperback with hardcover books taking up approximately two shelves. To be fair, we would ask any of our readers who visit this shop to share their experiences with us. The owners operate a second shop in Oshawa. See Millennium Books above.

Gryphon Books   **Open Shop**
28 John Street L1A 2Z2   (905) 885-5399

Collection:	General stock of mostly paperback.
# of Vols:	6,000
Hours:	Mon-Thu 9-5. Fri 9-6. Sat 10-5.
Travel:	See Angela's Books above. Right at "T" intersection and first left onto John St.
Credit Cards:	No
Owner:	Lori Henderson
Year Estab:	1995
Comments:	Heavily paperback with another room devoted to comics and sports cards. The several dozen hardcover volumes we spotted were mostly recent bestsellers. Need we say more.

Port Perry

Between Seasons Books   **By Appointment**
268 Cochrane Street L9L 1M5   (905) 985-9527
Web page: www/netacom.ca/~asphilp   E-mail: asphilp@netcom.ca

Collection:	Specialty books and some ephemera.
# of Vols:	1,500
Specialties:	Angling; shooting; gundog.
Services:	Search service, catalog.

Credit Cards: No
Owner: Art Philp
Year Estab: 1998

St. Catharines

Betty's Collectibles   **Open Shop**
114 York Street L2R 6E4   (905) 704-1464

Collection: General stock.
# of Vols: 500
Hours: Mon-Sat 11-4.
Travel: Lake St exit off QEW. Proceed south on Lake, then right on Carlton and left on York.
Credit Cards: Yes
Year Estab: 1996
Comments: Shop also sells antiques.

Blarney Stone Books   **Mail Order**
6 2 Weiden Pines L2M 6W5   (905) 646-8062
Web page: www.tourismniagara.com/blarneystone
                              E-mail: kmccabe@spartan.ac.brocku.ca
Collection: Specialty used and new hardcover and paperback.
# of Vols: 5,000
Specialties: Canadiana (poetry, essays, history); English literature; poetry; literary criticism; Greek and Roman classics; Niagara peninsula (literature and history).
Credit Cards: No
Owner: Kevin McCabe
Year Estab: 1998

The Bookworm   **Open Shop**
10 Summer Street L2R 7P2   (905) 682-3351

Collection: General stock of paperback and hardcover and comics.
# of Vols: 175,000
Hours: Mon-Sat 9-5. Also Sept-Apr: Sun 10-3:30.
Travel: Lake St exit off QEW. Proceed south on Lake, then left on James and right on Summer.
Credit Cards: No
Year Estab: 1992
Comments: Susan wins again. We arrived at this shop a few minutes before the owner and peering through its front windows observed what appeared to be a shop that was overwhelmingly paperback and one that treated its hardcover books in a rather haphazard manner. Once the owner arrived, though, and we were able to inspect the shop more thoroughly, we discovered a substantial number of hardcover volumes, shelved horizontally, properly labeled and most of which were in good condition. We also learned that the reason for the shop's cluttered appearance was the fact that the owner was in the process of opening a third

(St. Catharines)

location in St. Catharines and was getting ready to move a large portion of this store's stock to the new site a few blocks away (see The New Bookroom below). Considering my purchase of a couple of volumes here, I would have egg on my face if I did not admit that my partner's far greater patience should probably be followed more frequently. Don't look for antiquarian titles here. Instead what you'll find is a very nice mix of contemporary material.

Chestnut Lane Books   **Open Shop**
314 Merritt Street L2T 1K2   (905) 227-1622

Collection:	General stock of hardcover and paperback.
# of Vols:	30,000
Specialties:	Local history; automotive; religion; do-it-yourself; literature.
Hours:	Tue-Thu 11-6. Fri 11-7. Sat 12-6.
Services:	Catalog, search service, accepts want lists.
Travel:	Hwy 406 (Glendale) exit off QEW. Proceed east on Glendale, then left on Merritt.
Credit Cards:	No
Owner:	Marilyn & Lowa Katz
Year Estab:	1989
Comments:	The shop was in the process of being renovated at the time of our visit and much of the stock was packed away. Based on our conversation with the owners and a review of one of the store's subject specific catalogs, we suspect that the heavy concentration of paperbacks that we saw at the time of our visit was not indicative of what you may see once the renovations are completed.

D Jay's Bookstore   **Open Shop**
253 Church Street L2R 3E8   (905) 682-6722

Collection:	General stock of mostly paperback.
# of Vols:	10,000
Hours:	Mon-Sat 9-5.

Daltons Collectables   **Open Shop**
361 Merritt Street L2P 1P7   (905) 984-5171
                                         E-mail: sddalton@niagara.com

Collection:	General stock and ephemera.
# of Vols:	1,500
Specialties:	Non fiction; sheet music.
Hours:	Mon-Sat 10-5.
Services:	Accepts want lists, mail order.
Travel:	See Chestnut Lane Books above.
Credit Cards:	Yes
Owner:	Derek & Sandra Dalton
Year Estab:	1989

Comments:	A small shop that sells primarily non book collectibles, sheet music, magazines, LPs, paperbacks and perhaps a 1,000 older hardcover volumes, most of which are reading copies.

Ecce Puer Fine Books   **Mail Order**

PO Box 27020, Lake Port PO L2N 7P8   (905) 938-1851

Mailing address: PO Box 614, 615 Main St. Niagara Falls NY 14302-0614

       E-mail: gerfitz@vaxxine.com

Collection:	General stock.
# of Vols:	20,000
Specialties:	Performing arts; fine bindings.
Credit Cards:	Yes
Owner:	Gerry Fitzgerald
Year Estab:	1994

Hannelore Headley Old & Fine Books   **Open Shop**

71 Queen Street L2R 5G9   (905) 684-6145

Collection:	General stock of hardcover and paperback.
# of Vols:	70,000
Hours:	Mon-Sat 10-5, except Fri 11-6.
Services:	Appraisals, search service, accepts want lists, mail order.
Travel:	Lake St exit off QEW. Proceed south on Lake and left on Queen. Shop is just ahead.
Credit Cards:	Yes
Year Estab:	1972
Comments:	If every community had a bookstore like this one, no one would have to travel far to find books that brought them pleasure. The two floors and several rooms in this shop carry a nice combination of mixed vintage hardcover items and paperback books. You can find a recently published volume in almost pristine condition along with vintage and antiquarian titles. One of the best features of the shop is that its prices are so reasonable.

Huntley's Used Christian Books   **Open Shop**

114 Lake Street L2R 5X8   (905) 988-9223

Collection:	Specialty paperback and hardcover.
# of Vols:	4,000
Specialties:	Religion (Christian, primarily evangelical), including devotionals, concordances, commentaries, hymnals, Christian novels and reference books.
Hours:	Mon & Sat 11-4. Tue-Fri 10-6.
Services:	Accepts want lists.
Travel:	Lake St exit off QEW. Proceed south on Lake toward downtown.
Credit Cards:	No
Owner:	George Huntley
Year Estab:	1994
Comments:	Stock is approximately 60% paperback.

(St. Catharines)

Lens Odds And Ends   **Open Shop**
413 St Paul Street L2R 3N1   (905) 682-6147

Collection: General stock of mostly paperback and comics.
# of Vols: 500+
Hours: Mon-Sat 11-5:30, except Wed 12-7:30 & Fri 11-7:30.

Literacy Pragensis   **By Appointment**
303 Queenston Street L2P 2X5   (905) 704-0873
                                    E-mail: cz.books@literacypragensis.on.ca
Collection: Specialty. Mostly new and some used.
Specialties: Books in Czech language.
Services: Catalog, accepts want lists, mail order.
Credit Cards: No
Owner: Nadia Huhl
Year Estab: 1990

The New Bookroom (See Comments)   **Open Shop**
240 St. Paul East L2R 3M2

# of Vols: 150,000
Hours: Mon-Thu 9-5. Fri 9-9. Sat 9-5. Sun 10-4.
Travel: Lake St exit off QEW. Proceed south on Lake, then left on James and
                   left on St. Paul.
Comments: As this book goes to press, the owner of The Bookroom and D Jay's
                   Bookstore (see above) was in the process of setting up this new, still to
                   be named store, just a few blocks away from The Bookroom. For the
                   latest information, including hours and a telephone number, please call
                   the other store.

The Usual Suspects   **Mail Order**
2 Barbican Gate L2T 3Z7   (905) 227-4897
                                             E-mail: suspect@iaw.on.ca
Collection: General stock.
# of Vols: 3,000
Specialties: Mystery; spy; adventure; Canadian literature; signed. Emphasis is on
                   modern firsts.
Services: Search service, accepts want lists.
Credit Cards: No
Owner: Jeff Coopman
Year Estab: 1998

St. Jacobs

The Bookmill   **Antique Mall**
8 Spring Street, Box 512 N0B 2N0   (519) 664-1195
                                                        Fax: (519) 664-3079
                                                E-mail: bookmill@golden.net

Collection: General stock.

# of Vols:	18,000
Hours:	Mon-Sat 10-6. Sun 12-5:30.
Services:	Search service, accepts want lists, mail order.
Travel:	Hwy 8/Kitchener exit off Hwy 401. Proceed west on Hwy 8, then continue north on Hwy 86 towards Waterloo. Follow signs to "St. Jacob's Country."
Credit Cards:	Yes
Owner:	Tilman Lichter & Ron Hook
Year Estab:	1996
Comments:	If you like to browse antique and craft shops, or shop at a Farmer's Market, you should enjoy a visit to St. Jacob's. As for books, this collection, displayed on the second floor of a multi dealer antique shop, consisted of mixed vintage hardcover volumes in mixed condition (some on open shelves and others behind locked glass cabinets), some paperbacks, ephemera and LPs. At the time of our visit, we would estimate that there were about 3,000-5,000 volumes on display.

Sarnia

Anne's Book Place **Open Shop**
250 Russell Street South N7T 3L8   (877) 643-2663 (519) 336-6570

Collection:	General stock of mostly used paperback.
# of Vols:	75,000
Hours:	Mon-Fri 10-5:30. Sat 10-5.

The Used Book Peddler **Open Shop**
138 Ontario Street N7T 1L1   (519) 383-7922

Collection:	General stock of mostly paperback.
# of Vols:	15,000
Hours:	Mon-Fri 9-5:30. Sat 9-4.

Sault Ste. Marie
(Map 15A, page 166)

Between The Lines Bookstore **Open Shop**
112 East Street P6A 3C6   (705) 254-5863

Collection:	General stock of paperback and hardcover.
# of Vols:	8,000
Specialties:	Vintage paperbacks; first editions; signed.
Hours:	Mon-Sat 10-5. Open evenings in summer.
Services:	Accepts want lists.
Travel:	Proceeding west on Hwy 17 east which becomes Wellington St, turn left on Pim St, and right on Queen St. At first light, turn right on East.
Credit Cards:	No
Owner:	Claire Grondin
Year Estab:	1997
Comments:	Stock is approximately 65% paperback.

Bookworms   **Open Shop**
503 Queen Street East P6A 2A2   (705) 942-0364

Collection: General stock of mostly paperback.
# of Vols: 5,000
Hours: Mon-Sat 11-5.

Friends Of The Library Book Store   **Open Shop**
50 East Street P6A 3C3   (705) 759-5334

Collection: General stock of hardcover and paperback.
Hours: Jul & Aug: Mon 10-5. Tue 1-5. Thu 1-5. Sat 10-4. Sept-Jun: Mon 10-5.
                   Tue 5-8. Thu 1-4. Sat 10-4.
Travel: In lower level of main branch of public library, at corner of East and
                   Bay St.

Garden Room Books   **Open Shop**
503 Queen Street East P6A 2B1   (705) 256-6700

Collection: Specialty new and used.
# of Vols: 1,000+
Specialties: Horticulture; nature; northern outdoors.
Hours: Winter: 11-5 Mon, Thu, Fri, Sat. Remainder of year: Mon, Wed-Sat 11-5.
Travel: After crossing bridge from Michigan, turn left, then right at Albert St.
                   After about six lights, turn right at Spring. Shop is at corner of Spring
                   and Queen, inside the Cornwall Building.
Credit Cards: Yes
Owner: Michaela Keenan
Comments: Stock is evenly divided between new and used. Used stock is mostly
                   hardcover. Owner operates a second shop in Toronto (see below).

Scarborough
(See Map 17, page 243)

Albion Book Shop   **Open Shop**
376 Old Kingston Road M1C 1B6   (416) 284-4801

Collection: General stock of new and mostly paperback used.
# of Vols: 3,000-4,000 (used)
Hours: Mon-Fri 10-6. Sat 10-4.

Birchcliff Books   **By Appointment**
58 Larwood Boulevard M1M 2M5   (416) 266-6771

Collection: Specialty
Specialties: Canadiana, with emphasis on Ontario history; military.
Owner: Alen Clive
Year Estab: 1960's

The Bookshelf-Recycled Reading   **Open Shop**
2981 Kingston Road M1M 1P1   Tel & Fax: (416) 261-7607

Collection: General stock of mostly used paperback.

# of Vols:	10,000
Hours:	Mon-Wed 10-6. Thu & Fri 10-8. Sat 10-5. Sun 11-5.

Simcoe

The Novel Book Exchange   **Open Shop**
154 Norfolk Street South N3Y 2W4   (519) 426-4256
E-mail: jarvis1@execulink.com

Collection:	General stock of mostly paperback.
# of Vols:	16,000
Hours:	Tue & Wed 12-5. Thu & Fri 10-5. Sat 10-3.

Smithville

Art of the Print   **By Appointment**
6391 Sixteen Road, RR #2 L0R 2A0   Tel & Fax: (905) 957-6666
E-mail: artoftheprint@sympatico.ca

Collection:	General stock of books and original art.
# of Vols:	500 (books)
Specialties:	Illustrated books.
Owner:	Greg & Connie Peters

Southampton

Books And Things   **Open Shop**
178 High Street N0H 2L0   (519) 797-1184

Collection:	General stock of hardcover and paperback.
# of Vols:	10,000
Specialties:	First editions; signed.
Hours:	Mon-Fri 10-5:30. Sat 10-4. Summer: Mon-Thu 9-5:30. Fri & Sat 9-8. Sun 12:30-3:30.
Services:	Accepts want lists.
Travel:	Hwy 21 to Southampton. High St is the main street. Turn toward the water.
Credit Cards:	Yes
Owner:	John L. Gervasi
Year Estab:	1997

Stayner

Read It Again   **Open Shop**
236 William Street, #1 L0M 1S0   (705) 428-3288

Collection:	General stock of paperback and hardcover.
# of Vols:	10,000
Hours:	Mon-Fri 10-6. Sat 11-5. Sun 12-4.
Travel:	On Hwy 26, across from the post office. Shop is in Village Square (located behind bank building).
Year Estab:	1998
Comments:	Stock is approximately 75% paperback.

Stouffville

John Lord's Books   **Open Shop**
6356 Main Street   (905) 640-3579
Mailing address: PO Box 453 Stouffville ON L4A 7Z7
Web page: www.abebooks.com/home/johnlordsbooks   E-mail: jlbooks@attcanada.net

Collection:	General stock.
# of Vols:	60,000
Specialties:	Canadiana; horses; railroads; military; Oceaniana.
Hours:	Tue-Thu 9-5:30. Fri 9-7:30. Sat 9-5. Sun 10-4. Other times by appt.
Services:	Appraisals, search service, catalog, accepts want lists.
Travel:	Stouffville exit off Hwy 404. Proceed east on Stouffville Rd which becomes Main St.
Credit Cards:	Yes
Year Estab:	1974
Comments:	What can one say about a shop where one has made several purchases? Clearly, this shop appealed to us and we can only hope it will do the same for our readers. The owner maintains a neat collection of mixed vintage titles with enough material in the classics to satisfy the strongest literary tastes. Other subject areas are also represented, including a neat section on magic. A small section of paperbacks is also on hand as are a modest number of antiquarian items. One could label this a "general" shop in the most positive terms.

Stratford

Book Stage   **Open Shop**
126 Waterloo Street South N5A 4B4   (519) 272-0937
                                                           Fax: (519) 272-0927
                                                    E-mail: bookstage@cyg.net

Collection:	General stock of mostly hardcover.
# of Vols:	15,000-20,000
Specialties:	Performing arts; theater; music; art; literature; first editions; book illustration; German books; children's.
Hours:	May-Oct: Tue-Sat 10-8. Sun 11-2. Nov-Dec: Tue-Sat 10-6. Jan-Apr: Usually Thu-Sat 10-6, but best to call ahead.
Services:	Appraisals, search service, accepts want lists, mail order.
Travel:	Hwy 7/8 exit off Hwy 401. Follow signs to Stratford Festival/Avon Theatre. Shop is at the back of the theatre at corner of Waterloo and George Street East.
Credit Cards:	Yes
Owner:	Manfred Meurer
Year Estab:	1976
Comments:	A modest sized shop with an interesting collection of mixed vintage books in generally good condition. Strong in literature and in the subjects identified above as specialties. The shop also sells new CDs and, at least at the time of our visit, interesting illustrations of various book plates. Reasonably priced.

Canadiana House   **By Appointment**
311 Ontario Street N5A 3H6   (800) 661-6128   (519) 273-5242
Web page: www.canadiana-house.on.ca   E-mail: dnoxon@canadiana-house.on.ca

Collection: Specialty
# of Vols: 25,000
Specialties: Canadiana; early North America (fiction and non fiction).
Services: Appraisals, catalog.
Credit Cards: No
Owner: David B. Noxon
Year Estab: 1960

Yesterdays Things & Books   **Open Shop**
351 Ontario Street N5A 3H7   (519) 271-5180
                                                          E-mail: dmuligan@orc.ca

Collection: General stock of hardcover and paperback and ephemera.
# of Vols: 10,000
Specialties: Theatre; literature; children's; mystery.
Hours: Mon-Sat 10-5. Sun 10-2.
Services: Search service, accepts want lists, mail order.
Travel: Exit 278 off Hwy 401. Proceed west on Hwy 8 which becomes Ontario
                    Street in Stratford.
Credit Cards: Yes
Owner: Dee Mulligan
Year Estab: 1972
Comments: The shop consists of several rooms almost all of which are filled with
                    older hardcover items, some common, some unusual, some collectible,
                    some inscrutable. Condition is mixed. Prices are reasonable. The shop
                    also has some non book collectibles.

Streetsville

Apologia Words & Music   **Open Shop**
63 Queen Street South L5M 1K5   (905) 826-2515
                                                          E-mail: davida@myna.com

Collection: General stock of hardcover and paperback.
# of Vols: 25,000
Specialties: Religion; history.
Hours: Wed & Thu 2-7. Sat 1-5. Other times by appointment.
Travel: Mississauga Rd exit off Hwy 401. Proceed south on Mississauga which
                    becomes Queen Street.
Credit Cards: No
Owner: Vivian Aspinall
Year Estab: 1988
Comments: Unfortunately, the store was closed when we were in the area. We were
                    advised by phone that the stock is evenly divided between hardcover
                    and paperback.

Professor Bookies   **Open Shop**
201 Queen Street South L5M 1L4   (905) 542-9844

Collection: General stock of paperback and hardcover.
# of Vols: 8,000
Hours: Tue-Thu 11-6. Fri 11-7. Sat 10-5. Sun 11-4.
Credit Cards: No
Year Estab: 1992
Comments: Stock is approximately 75% paperback.

Sudbury
(Map 15A, page 166)

Bay Used Books   **Open Shop**
664 LaSalle Boulevard P3A 1X4   (705) 566-9211

Collection: General stock of mostly paperback.
Hours: Daily 9:30-9.
Comments: This is the main store in the chain.

Bay Used Books   **Open Shop**
124 Elm Street P3C 1T6   (705) 673-9311

Collection: General stock of mostly paperback.
# of Vols: 250,000
Hours: Mon-Fri 9:30-8:30. Sat 9:30-5.30. Sun 12-5:30.

Bay Used Books   **Open Shop**
1543 Paris P3E 3B7   (705) 523-4011

Collection: General stock of mostly paperback.
Hours: Mon-Fri 9:30-9. Sat 9:30-5. Sun 12-5.

Books: Rare and Collectible   **By Appointment**
352 Ester Street P3E 5C4   (705) 523-1940
Web page: http:w3.tyenet.com/traulsen/default.htm   E-mail: traulsen@tyenet.com

Collection: General stock.
# of Vols: 800+
Specialties: Canadiana; Ace Doubles; Collins White Cirlce paperbacks; science
                    fiction.
Services: Appraisals, search service, catalog.
Credit Cards: No
Owner: Peter & Judith Traulsen
Year Estab: 1995

Page After Page   **Open Shop**
1643 LaSalle Boulevard P3A 1Z8   (705) 521-1206

Collection: General stock of paperback and hardcover.
# of Vols: 30,000
Hours: Tue & Wed 9:30-5:30. Thu & Fri 9:30-7. Sat 10-5. Sun 12-4.
Credit Cards: No
Year Estab: 1996
Comments: Stock is approximately 60% paperback.

Sutton

Sutton General Store   **Open Shop**
128 High Street   (905) 722-6303
Mailing address: PO Box 1466 Sutton ON L0E 1R0

Collection:	General stock of hardcover and paperback.
# of Vols:	500+
Hours:	Mon-Sat 9-6. Sun 10-3.
Travel:	Sutton exit off Hwy 48. Proceed northwest on High St.

Tamworth

Robert Wright Books   **By Appointment**
PO Box 45 K0K 3G0   (613) 379-2882
Web page: www.netcom.ca/~rwright   E-mail: rwright@netcom.ca

Collection:	Specialty
# of Vols:	10,000
Specialties:	19th & 20th century literary first editions; pre-Raphaelites; William Morris; John Ruskin; Canadian literature; film; hockey; signed books (within these fields). Also photography; books on books; children's; illustrated; some general antiquarian.
Services:	Appraisals, catalog, accepts want lists.
Credit Cards:	Yes
Year Estab:	1987

Thornhill
(Map 17, page 243)

Almark & Co   **By Appointment**
P0 Box 7 L3T 3N1   (905) 764-2665
Web page: www.almarkco.com   Fax: (905) 764-5571
                                          E-mail: almarkco@shaw.wave.ca

Collection:	Specialty
# of Vols:	125,000
Specialties:	Fiction in all genres; Kennedy assassination; Civil War; presidential biographies; true crime; World War I & II. All first editions.
Services:	Appraisals, search service, accepts want lists, mail order.
Credit Cards:	Yes
Owner:	Al Navis
Year Estab:	1977

Thunder Bay
(Map 15A, page 166)

The Bookshelf   **Open Shop**
548–12th Avenue P7B 6C4   (807) 345-1159
Web page: www.thunderbay.com   E-mail: books@baynet.net

Collection:	General stock of mostly paperback.

# of Vols:	30,000
Hours:	Mon-Fri 9-6. Sat 9-5. Sun & holidays 12-4.

Cronos Bookstore Cafe   **Open Shop**
433 South Syndicate Avenue P7E 1E4   (807) 622-9700
                                                          Fax: (807) 628-0982
                                                   E-mail: ctonos@tbaytel.net

Collection:	General stock of paperback and hardcover.
# of Vols:	25,000
Hours:	Mon-Wed 10-6. Thu 10am-11pm. Fri 10am-midnight. Sat 12-12.
Services:	Search service, accepts want lists.
Travel:	Downtown, two blocks south of Hwy 17 (Arthur St).
Credit Cards:	Yes
Owner:	Tom Theodoropoulos
Year Estab:	1995
Comments:	Shop is also a full service restaurant.

Paper Chase Antiques   **By Appointment**
1110 Lakeshore Drive P7B 5E4   (807) 983-2890
                                                 E-mail: paperant@tbaytel.net

Collection:	General stock and ephemera.
# of Vols:	2,000+
Specialties:	Heritage editions; magazines.
Services:	Appraisals, search service, accepts want lists, mail order.
Credit Cards:	Yes
Owner:	Wayne Pettit
Year Estab:	1994

Thunder Bay Used Book Market   **Open Shop**
132 May Street North P7C 3P2   (807) 623-3811

Collection:	General stock of mostly paperback.
# of Vols:	5,000-10,000
Hours:	Mon-Fri 11-6. Sat 10-5. Earlier closing in summer.

Tillsonburg

Odyssey Book Emporium   **Open Shop**
148 Broadway N4G 3P8   (519) 842-7872

Collection:	General stock of mostly paperback.
# of Vols:	4,000
Hours:	Mon-Sat 10-4:30.

Timmins
(Map 15A, page 166)

The Book Bin   **Open Shop**
70 Balsam Street P4N 2C8   (705) 268-7199

Collection:	General stock of mostly paperback.
# of Vols:	40,000
Hours:	Mon-Thu 10-5:30, except Fri till 8. Sat 10-5.

Toronto
(Map 17, page 243 & Map 18, page 247)

A Likely Story   **Open Shop**
1182 Queen Street East M4M 1L4   (416) 405-8668
                                                           Fax: (416) 651-0262
                                                    E-mail: marllet@interlog.com

Collection:	General stock of mostly used paperback and hardcover.
# of Vols:	2,000-3,000
Hours:	Tue & Wed 11-6. Thu & Fri 11-7. Sat 10-6. Sun 12-6. Hours vary seasonally.
Services:	Search service, accepts want lists.
Travel:	Eastbound on Gardiner Expy (Hwy 2): Leslie exit. Proceed north on Leslie, then left on Queen. See Map 17.
Credit Cards:	Yes
Owner:	Marc Ouellet
Year Estab:	1998
Comments:	A small neighborhood shop with primarily paperbacks, some new magazines and a small number of recent hardcover volumes.

ABC Book Store   **Open Shop**
662 Yonge Street M4Y 2A6   (416) 967-7654

Collection:	General stock of paperback and hardcover.
# of Vols:	20,000+
Specialties:	Magazines
Hours:	Mon-Sat 10-10. Sun 12-10.
Travel:	Between Bloor and Wellesley. See Map 18.
Credit Cards:	Yes
Year Estab:	1964
Comments:	Lots of books here, most of which are paperback. However, there are some hardcover volumes along the side walls. The shop also carries *National Geographics*, adults magazines and an assortment of other popular magazines. Not vastly different from similar stores of this nature which provide popular reading but are less likely to be the source of more esoteric finds.

Abelard Books   **Open Shop**
519 Queen Street West M5V 2B4   (416) 504-2665

Collection:	General stock of hardcover and paperback.
# of Vols:	40,000
Specialties:	Philosophy; religion; mediaeval studies; archaeology.
Hours:	Mon-Sat 11-6. Sun 12-5.
Travel:	Between Spadina and Bathurst. See Map 18.
Credit Cards:	Yes
Owner:	Paul Lockwood
Year Estab:	1977
Comments:	A good sized shop with a nice balance of hard-to-find titles, newer

(Toronto)

publications and almost everything in between. You'll certainly find
collectible material here as well as a small section of paperbacks. The
shop is close enough to other dealers to make this shop well worth
visiting.

About Books   **Open Shop**
83 Harbord Street M5S 1G4   Tel & Fax: (416) 975-2668
Web page: http://booknet-international.com/ca/about.books
                                           E-mail: aboutbks@inforamp.net

Collection:	General stock.
# of Vols:	15,000
Specialties:	Natural history; gardening; history; literature.
Hours:	Mon-Fri 10-7. Sat 10-6. Sun 11-5. Holidays: 12-5.
Services:	Appraisals, accepts want lists, mail order.
Travel:	Spadina Ave exit off Gardiner Expy. Continue north on Spadina for about 2½ km, then left on Harbord. Shop is just ahead on south side. Parking available in rear. See Map 18.
Credit Cards:	Yes
Owner:	Antonia Greenwood
Year Estab:	1955
Comments:	A shop that takes its books seriously, as reflected in both the condition and quality of the titles we viewed. The arts, literature and science are all well represented as are history, geography and yes, even gastronomy. Books are displayed on two levels and the shop is within a half block of two other used book dealers.

Acadia Art & Rare Books   **Open Shop**
232 Queen Street East M5A 1S3   (416) 364-7638
                                                       Fax: (416) 364-1446
                                                  E-mail: acadiart@netcom.ca

Collection:	Specialty
# of Vols:	15,000
Specialties:	Visual arts, including, painting; photography; architecture; sculpture; *livres d'artiste*, monographs and Canadian art.
Hours:	Mon-Fri 11-6. Sat 11-5.
Services:	Appraisals, search service, mail order.
Travel:	Just east of Sherbourne St. See Map 18.
Credit Cards:	Yes
Owner:	Carlos Galdamez
Year Estab:	1931

Martin Ahvenus   **Flea Market**
St. Lawrence North Market, Front and Jarvis Streets   (416) 955-9594
Mailing address: 394 Avenue Road, #308 Toronto ON M5A 1S5
Web page: www.abebooks.com   E-mail: mahvenus@interlog.com

Collection:	Specialty
# of Vols:	2,000-3,000

Specialties:	Canadian art; decorative arts; children's; illustrated; folklore.
Hours:	Sundays 5am-5pm. (Indoors)
Credit Cards:	No
Comments:	Additional stock can be viewed by appointment or is available online.

Alexandre Antique Prints, Maps & Books   **Open Shop**
104 Queen Street East M5C 1S6   Tel & Fax: (416) 364-2376
                                     E-mail: alexandremapsbooks@home.com

Collection:	Specialty
# of Vols:	500
Specialties:	Antiquarian
Hours:	Mon-Fri 11-6. Sat 11-5.
Services:	Appraisals, occasional catalog.
Travel:	Between Church and Jarvis Streets. See Map 18.
Credit Cards:	Yes
Owner:	Alexandre Arjomand
Year Estab:	1974

Annex Books   **Open Shop**
1083 Bathurst Street M5R 3G8   (416) 537-1852
Web page: www.abebooks.com/home/annex_books   E-mail: annexbks@inforamp.net

Collection:	General stock of hardcover and paperback.
# of Vols:	15,000
Specialties:	Literature; Canadian literature.
Hours:	Mon-Fri 11-6. Sat 10-6.
Services:	Appraisals, catalog, accepts want lists.
Travel:	North of Bloor St. See Map 18.
Credit Cards:	Yes
Owner:	Janet Inksetter
Year Estab:	1983
Comments:	A neat shop with a nice collection of mostly hardcover volumes of mixed vintage. The majority of the books we saw were in good to excellent condition and most reasonably priced. The shop is located immediately adjacent to another used book dealer, thus giving the visitor "two for the price of one."

Hugh Anson-Cartwright Books, Maps & Prints   **Open Shop**
229 College Street M5T 1R4   Tel & Fax: (416) 979-2441
Web page: http://www.interlog.com/~hac/   E-mail: hac@interlog.com

Collection:	General stock.
# of Vols:	5,000+
Specialties:	Fine bindings; Canadiana; literature.
Hours:	Mon-Fri 10-5:30. Other times by appointment.
Services:	Appraisals, catalog, accepts want lists.
Travel:	Spadina exit off QEW. Proceed north on Spadina, then east on College for about two blocks. See Map 18.
Credit Cards:	Yes
Year Estab:	1966

(Toronto)

Comments: Located in a multi tenant two story building (including a kindergarten at the time of our visit), this distinguished shop carries rare, hard-to-find and antiquarian volumes ranging from the popular P.G. Wodehouse to Charles Dickens, poetry, reference and art. The books we saw were not all overly expensive but all were of fine quality.

Arthur's Book Store   **Open Shop**
762 St Clair Avenue West M6C 1B5   (416) 658-7887

Collection: General stock of paperback and hardcover.
Specialties: History; religion; philosophy; art; women's studies; children's.
Hours: Daily 12-9.
Services: Accepts want lists.
Travel: Dufferin St exit off Hwy 401. Proceed south on Dufferin, then east on St. Clair. See Map 17.
Credit Cards: Yes
Owner: Thomas Khan
Year Estab: 1997
Comments: Stock is approximately 70% paperback.

Atticus Books   **Open Shop**
84 Harbord Street M5S 1G5   (416) 922-6045
Web page: atticus-books.com   Fax: (416) 926-9686
                                                    E-mail: attbooks@interlog.com

Collection: General stock of hardcover and paperback.
# of Vols: 40,000
Specialties: Scholarly
Hours: Mon-Fri 11:30-6. Sat 11:30-5:30. Sun 12-5.
Services: Appraisals, online catalog.
Travel: Just west of Spadina. See Map 18.
Credit Cards: Yes
Owner: Michael Freedman
Year Estab: 1978
Comments: The vast array of scholarly titles here, all in almost universally good to excellent condition, suggests a shop that should attract undergraduates, graduate students and their professors. In addition to the books on the first floor, there's an additional large selection of volumes one floor below, including a room specializing in art books. Hardly a shop for someone looking for yesterday's mystery.

Ayerego Books   **Open Shop**
928 Queen Street West M6J 1G6   (416) 536-6880
Web page: www.abebooks.com/home/ayerego   E-mail: ayerego@passport.ca

Collection: General stock.
# of Vols: 20,000
Specialties: Biography; literature; first editions; art; entertainment; music; film; Canadiana; North Americana; military; terrorism.

Hours:	Usually from 2pm till late at night, or by appointment. Best to call ahead.
Services:	Accepts want lists.
Travel:	Just east of Ossington. See Map 18.
Credit Cards:	Yes
Owner:	George Ayerego
Year Estab:	1995
Comments:	A modest sized shop that carries an interesting selection of volumes in the specialties listed above, although not necessarily in great depth. When we visited here, we were impressed by the owner's deserved pride in the stock that he showed us.

Bakka SF Bookstore   **Open Shop**
598 Yonge Street M4Y 1Z3   (416) 963-9993
E-mail: jdrose@total.net

Collection:	Specialty new and used.
Specialties:	Science fiction; horror; fantasy.
Hours:	Mon-Wed 11-7. Thu 11-8. Fri 11-9. Sat 11-7. Sun and holidays 12:30-6. Closing times may vary.
Travel:	Just north of Wellesley. See Map 18.
Credit Cards:	Yes
Owner:	John Rose
Year Estab:	1972
Comments:	Primarily a "new" bookstore with two bookcases of used material, the majority of which are paperback.

Balfour Books   **Open Shop**
601 College Street M6G 1B5   (416) 531-9911
Fax: (416) 531-5019
E-mail: balfour@netcom.ca

Collection:	General stock of mostly used books.
# of Vols:	15,000-20,000
Specialties:	Art; photography; dogs; scholarly.
Hours:	Daily noon-10pm.
Travel:	Between Palmerston and Ossington. See Map 18.
Credit Cards:	Yes
Owner:	Joyce Blair
Year Estab:	1995
Comments:	A nice collection of hardcover volumes in generally good to excellent condition. In addition to the obvious strengths in the specialties listed above, the shop had a good children's section. The books were reasonably priced and shop was easy to browse.

Batta Book Store   **Open Shop**
710 The Queensway M8Y 1L3   (416) 259-2618

Collection:	General stock of hardcover and paperback.
# of Vols:	90,000
Specialties:	Fiction

(Toronto)

Hours:	Mon-Sat 2-7.
Travel:	Islington Ave exit off QEW. Proceed north on Islington, then right on Queensway. Shop is just east of Royal York Rd. See Map 17.
Credit Cards:	No
Owner:	Mr. & Mrs. Bela Batta
Year Estab:	1965
Comments:	Stock is approximately 65% hardcover.

The Beguiling   **Open Shop**
601 Markham Street M6G 2L7   (416) 533-9168

Collection:	General stock mostly paperback and comics.
# of Vols:	5,000
Hours:	Mon-Thu 11-7. Fri 11-9. Sat 11-7. Sun 12-6.

BMV Books   **Open Shop**
10 Edward Street M5G 1C9   (416) 977-3087
                                                                    Fax: (416) 972-0720

Collection:	General stock of mostly used hardcover and paperback and some re-mainders.
# of Vols:	20,000
Specialties:	Science fiction; literature; philosophy; magazines.
Hours:	Mon-Sat 10-11pm. Sun 12-7.
Services:	Search service.
Travel:	Between Yonge and Bay. See Map 18.
Credit Cards:	Yes
Owner:	Patrick Hempelmann
Year Estab:	1996
Comments:	A large shop with mostly newer hardcover volumes and paperbacks in addition to magazines and a section of adult materials. While your chances of finding a truly rare item here are not extensive, if you're in the neighborhood, drop in. The owner operates a second shop under the same name (see below) which offers a similar stock, although with a larger selection of hardcover volumes.

BMV Books   **Open Shop**
2289 Yonge Street   (416) 482-6002

Collection:	General stock of mostly used hardcover and paperback and some re-mainders.
# of Vols:	30,000
Specialties:	Science fiction; literature; philosophy; magazines.
Hours:	Mon-Sat 10-11pm. Sun 12-7.
Services:	Search service.
Travel:	Between Eglinton and Lawrence. See Map 17.
Credit Cards:	Yes
Comments:	Stock is approximately 70% hardcover. See BMV Books above.

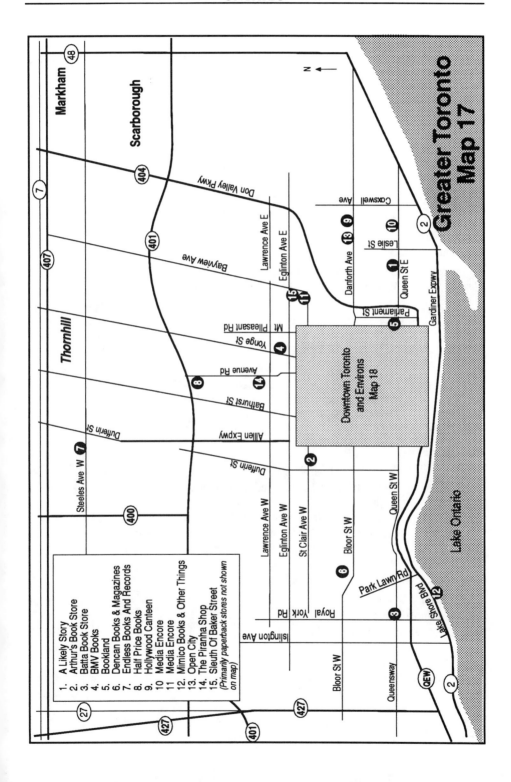

Greater Toronto
Map 17

1. A Likely Story
2. Arthur's Book Store
3. Batta Book Store
4. BMV Books
5. Bookland
6. Dencan Books & Magazines
7. Endless Books And Records
8. Half Price Books
9. Hollywood Canteen
10 Media Encore
11 Media Encore
12. Mimico Books & Other Things
13. Open City
14. The Piranha Shop
15. Sleuth Of Baker Street
(Primarily paperback stores not shown on map)

(Toronto)

Bookland   **Open Shop**
350 Queen Street East M5A 1T1   (416) 363-4820

Collection:	General stock of paperback and hardcover.
# of Vols:	50,000+
Hours:	Mon-Sat 10-5.
Travel:	Between Parliament and River. See Map 17.
Comments:	If you're into popular subjects or recent titles and/or enjoy comic books, this store may be one you'd want to visit. The store carries a mix of primarily paperbacks (toward the front and center of the store) and hardcover volumes along one side wall. Travelers seeking more scholarly titles are less likely to be impressed by this shop.

Books Plus   **Open Shop**
2442 Danforth Avenue M4C 1K9   (416) 691-3187

Collection:	General stock of mostly paperback, CDs and records.
Hours:	Mon-Thu 11-7. Fri 11-8. Sat 11-6. Sun 11-5.

Boz and Friends   **By Appointment**
350 Seneca Hill Drive, #806 M2J 4S7   Tel & Fax: (416) 494-9252
                                                     E-mail: bozbooks@home.com

Collection:	Specialty
# of Vols:	1,000
Specialties:	Charles Dickens (first and early editions) Dickensiana.
Services:	Appraisals, mail order, accepts want lists.
Owner:	Dan Calinescu
Year Estab:	1987

George Brown   **By Appointment**
PO Box 363, Station Q M4T 2M5   (416) 964-9134

Collection:	Specialty. Mostly used and some new.
# of Vols:	2,000-3,000
Specialties:	Art; history; North American Indians; primitive art; early travel and exploration in North America; painters of America and the West.
Services:	Appraisals, search service, accepts want lists.
Credit Cards:	No
Year Estab:	1988

CMG Books & Art   **Open Shop**
156 Davenport Road M5R 1J2   (416) 921-5870
Web page: www.cmgbooksandart.com   Fax: (416) 921-6296
                                                     E-mail: cmgbooks@total.net

Collection:	Specialty used and new.
Specialties:	Ethnographic art; art.
Hours:	Mon-Sat 10:30-5:15.
Services:	Appraisals, catalog.
Travel:	In Yorkville area, between Avenue and Yonge. See Map 18.
Credit Cards:	Yes

Owner: Charles Mus
Year Estab: 1991

Constant Reader Books for Children   **Open Shop**
111 Harbord Street M5S 1G7   (416) 972-0661

Collection: Specialty new and used.
Specialties: Children's
Hours: Tue-Sat 10:30-5:30. Sun 12-5. Closed holiday weekends.
Services: Search service, mail order.
Travel: 1½ blocks west of Spadina. See Map 18.
Credit Cards: Yes
Year Estab: 1989
Comments: Stock is approximately 35% used.

Contact Editions   **Open Shop**
759 Mount Pleasant Road M4S 2N4   (416) 322-0777
Web page: www.inforamp.net/~conedinc/   Fax: (416) 322-3226
                                                    E-mail: conedinc@inforamp.net

Collection: General stock of mostly hardcover.
# of Vols: 30,000
Specialties: Art; literature; modern first editions; history; Paris in the '20's.
Hours: Mon-Fri 10-6. Sat 9-6. Sun 9-5.
Services: Search service (in specialties only), accepts want lists.
Travel: Yonge St exit off Hwy 401. Proceed south on Yonge, then east on
                 Eglinton and right on Mt. Pleasant. Shop is just ahead on left. Map 18.
Credit Cards: Yes
Owner: Wesley J. Begg
Year Estab: 1990
Comments: The shop is large with a fine collection of mostly hardcover volumes in
                 good to excellent condition covering the general spectrum of subject
                 areas. The shop even had some "books about books" worth adding to a
                 book lover's collection. The mystery section, with several vintage
                 titles, was a pleasure to browse and our visit turned out to be most
                 fortuitous as the owner had just purchased several collections, one of
                 which provided us with a number of books we had long been searching
                 for. If you're a serious collector and have special interests, ask for
                 permission to visit the shop's rare book room.

Cover to Cover Bookshop   **Open Shop**
834 Yonge Street M4W 2H1   (416) 975-5123

Collection: General stock of hardcover and paperback.
# of Vols: 75,000
Specialties: History; literature; philosophy; literary criticism; military; art; fiction.
Hours: Mon-Wed 9-6:30. Thu & Fri 9-8. Sat 10-7. Sun and holidays 12-6.
Travel: Between Davenport & Bloor. See Map 18.
Credit Cards: Yes
Owner: Frank Velikonja

(Toronto)

Year Estab:	1994
Comments:	A nice shop on Toronto's major thoroughfare that carries a good balance of quality hardcover volumes and paperbacks displayed in a series of long aisles that are wide enough for easy browsing. The sections are well labeled and the books reasonably priced.

Dencan Books & Magazines   **Open Shop**
3113 Dundas Street West M6P 1Z9   (416) 763-2302

Collection:	General stock of paperback and hardcover.
# of Vols:	25,000-30,000
Specialties:	Vintage paperbacks; mystery.
Hours:	Mon-Fri 10:30-6. Sat 10:30-5:30. Sun by chance.
Travel:	Between Keele & Runnyemeade in the Junction area. See Map 17.
Credit Cards:	No
Year Estab:	1968
Comments:	Stock is approximately 75% paperback.

Dr. Hoff's Therapeutic Bibliotheca   **Mail Order**
35 Richard Avenue   M4L 1W8   (416) 466-6610
Web page: http://web.idirect.com/~booktrak/hoff/   E-mail: hoff@inforamp.net

Collection:	Specialty
# of Vols:	4,000+
Specialties:	Academic psychology, psychotherapy and psychoanalysis (1880-1980); philosophy and ethics (1880-1960); religion (Christian, 1820-1950); biblical studies.
Services:	Accepts want lists, mail order.
Credit Cards:	Yes
Owner:	Tory Hoff
Year Estab:	1994
Comments:	Collection may also be viewed by appointment.

Dragon Lady Paper Nostalgia   **Open Shop**
609 College Street M6G 1B5   (416) 536-7460
                                        E-mail: dragonladycomics@hotmail.com

Collection:	Specialty books and ephemera.
# of Vols:	2,000
Specialties:	Magazines; nostalgia.
Hours:	Sun, Mon, Tue, Thu 12-8. Wed 11-9. Fri & Sat 11-10.
Travel:	Between Palmerston and Ossington. See Map 18.
Credit Cards:	Yes
Owner:	John Biernat
Comments:	If you're a nostalgia buff and into the culture of the 1930's-1980's, you might want to drop in to this shop which, in addition to a large selection of popular magazines (sports, entertainment, fashion, etc.) also sells comic books, sheet music, and yes, we saw three bookcases with hardcover volumes whose titles fit into the general aura of the shop.

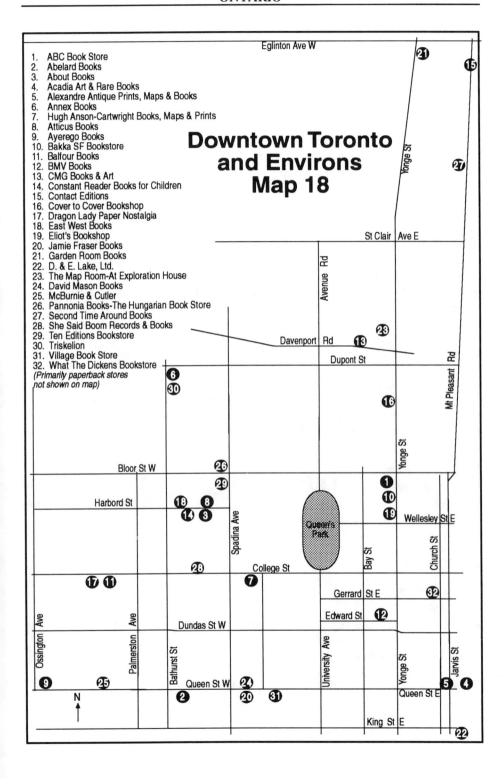

Downtown Toronto
and Environs
Map 18

1. ABC Book Store
2. Abelard Books
3. About Books
4. Acadia Art & Rare Books
5. Alexandre Antique Prints, Maps & Books
6. Annex Books
7. Hugh Anson-Cartwright Books, Maps & Prints
8. Atticus Books
9. Ayerego Books
10. Bakka SF Bookstore
11. Balfour Books
12. BMV Books
13. CMG Books & Art
14. Constant Reader Books for Children
15. Contact Editions
16. Cover to Cover Bookshop
17. Dragon Lady Paper Nostalgia
18. East West Books
19. Eliot's Bookshop
20. Jamie Fraser Books
21. Garden Room Books
22. D. & E. Lake, Ltd.
23. The Map Room-At Exploration House
24. David Mason Books
25. McBurnie & Cutler
26. Pannonia Books-The Hungarian Book Store
27. Second Time Around Books
28. She Said Boom Records & Books
29. Ten Editions Bookstore
30. Triskelion
31. Village Book Store
32. What The Dickens Bookstore
*(Primarily paperback stores
not shown on map)*

(Toronto)

Inno Dubelaar Books   **By Appointment**
53 Dixon Avenue M4L 1N4   (416) 694-1329
Web page: www.dubelaarnet/home/inno/   E-mail: inno@dubelaar.net

Collection:	General stock.
# of Vols:	4,000
Specialties:	Modern first editions; Canadiana; native studies; art; photography; decorative arts; sports; hockey; railroads, travel; West Indian literature.
Services:	Search service, accepts want lists, mail order.
Credit Cards:	Yes
Year Estab:	1995

East West Books   **Open Shop**
128 Harbord Street M5S 1G8   Tel & Fax: (416) 923-1725

Collection:	General stock of mostly used hardcover.
# of Vols:	20,000+
Specialties:	Asia; psychology; religion; philosophy; contemporary literature.
Hours:	Mon-Fri 11:30-6. Sat 11:30-5.
Services:	Occasional catalog.
Travel:	Between Spadina and Bathurst. See Map 18.
Credit Cards:	Yes
Year Estab:	1997
Comments:	If you're looking for books on the Far East, particularly China (history, literature, culture, etc.) your chances of finding that volume are quite good at this location. The balance of the collection is made up of a combination of paperback and hardcover books, shelved together, in what we would categorize as reading copies.

David Eves Books   **Mail Order**
4243-C Dundas Street West, Ste 135   M8X 1V3   (416) 695-1419
Web page: www.davidevesbooks.com   E-mail: deves@idirect.com

Collection:	General stock.
Services:	Accepts want lists.
Credit Cards:	No
Year Estab:	1997

Eliot's Bookshop   **Open Shop**
584 Yonge Street M4Y 1Z3   (416) 925-0268

Collection:	General stock of hardcover and paperback.
# of Vols:	50,000-60,000
Specialties:	Literature
Hours:	Mon-Sat 11-11. Sun 12-8
Travel:	Just north of Wellesley. See Map 18.
Credit Cards:	No
Owner:	Paul Panayiotidis
Year Estab:	1985

Comments: If one were to restrict one's visit only to the first floor of this shop, one would see a mixed collection of paperback and hardcover volumes nicely labeled but not necessarily out of the ordinary. Continue, though, up one flight of stairs, and you'll find more books, more hardcover volumes, more literature and more scholarly items. If you venture up to the third floor, you'll see still more books. While you ponder how the building takes the weight of all the volumes, you'll want to study the titles in each section, all carefully labeled, and you may, as we did, find some winners.

Endless Books And Records   **Open Shop**
2375 Steeles Avenue West, #31C M3J 3A8   (416) 736-9652
                                                       Fax: (416) 650-1091

Collection: General stock of hardcover and paperback.
# of Vols: 25,000
Hours: Tue & Wed 10-7. Thu & Fri 10-8. Sat & Sun 10-6.
Travel: Allen Expwy exit off Hwy 401. Proceed north on Expwy, then left (west) on Steeles. Shop is about two blocks ahead. See Map 17.
Credit Cards: Yes
Owner: Helen Pilgrim & Silvano Moschella
Year Estab: 1993
Comments: After carefully studying the Toronto map, we scheduled a stop here for the end of our first day in Toronto. Unfortunately, by 2:30pm, an unexpected snow storm caused us to retreat to the safety of our hotel. While we were able to spend additional time in Toronto, the shop was closed the next day and it's somewhat "out of the way" location precluded a visit during our remaining stay in the area. We regret being unable to view the shop's collection and hope that our readers, visiting on a sunnier day, will let us know what we missed.

Jamie Fraser Books   **Open Shop**
427A Queen Street West, 2nd Fl. M5V 2A5   (416) 598-7718
Web page: www.interlog.com/~fraserj/index.htm   E-mail: fraserj@interlog.com

Collection: Specialty paperback and hardcover.
# of Vols: 18,000
Specialties: Mystery and detective fiction; science fiction; fantasy; horror; pulps; vintage paperbacks.
Hours: Mon-Thu 11-6. Fri & Sat 11-7. Sun 12-5.
Services: Appraisals, search service, accepts want lists, mail order.
Travel: Just east on Spadina. See Map 18.
Credit Cards: Yes
Year Estab: 1990
Comments: As one who truly enjoys both vintage mystery and fantasy books, I found this particular stop in Toronto most pleasant. In addition to wonderful wonderful titles of rare materials in this genre, the shop also carries pulps, hard-to-find paperbacks and vintage mysteries. If this is your cup of tea, drink heartily.

(Toronto)

Friends Of Terpsichore   **Mail Order**
1608–25 Wood Street   M4Y 2P9   (416) 340-9958
Web page: www.toronto.com/terpsichore   Fax: (416) 348-0486
                                                    E-mail: mlos01@ibm.net

Collection:	Specialty new and used.
Specialties:	Dance and dance related.
Services:	Catalog, accepts want lists.
Credit Cards:	No
Owner:	Maria & Carlos Los
Year Estab:	1998

Garden Room Books   **Open Shop**
2097 Yonge Street M4S 2A4   (416) 932-8318

Collection:	Specialty new and mostly hardcover used.
# of Vols:	1,000-3,000
Specialties:	Horticulture; nature; northern outdoors.
Hours:	Mon, Tue, Fri-Sun 11-5:30. Other times by chance.
Services:	Search service, catalog.
Travel:	Yonge St exit off Hwy 401. Proceed south on Yonge. See Map 18.
Credit Cards:	Yes
Owner:	Michaela Keenan
Year Estab:	1994
Comments:	Book shop is inside a garden shop. Owner operates a second shop in Sault Ste. Marie (see above).

Great Escape Book Store   **Open Shop**
957 Kingston Road M4E 1S8   (416) 691-7150

Collection:	General stock of mostly paperback.
# of Vols:	25,000
Hours:	Tue-Sat 10-5. Sun 1-4.

Half Price Books   **Open Shop**
2042 Avenue Road M5M 4A6   (416) 544-1655

Collection:	General stock of new and used paperback and hardcover.
Hours:	Tue-Thu 10-6. Fri 10-9. Sat 10-6. Sun 12-5.
Travel:	Avenue Rd exit off Hwy 401. Proceed south on Avenue Rd. Shop is south of Wilson. See Map 17.
Credit Cards:	Yes
Year Estab:	1996
Comments:	Used stock is approximately 75% paperback. See other Half Price stores in neighboring Oshawa. There are approximately 50,000 used books between the four stores.

Harmony   **Open Shop**
711 Mount Pleasant Road M4S 2N4   (416) 440-1386

Collection:	General stock of mostly paperback, CDs and videos.

# of Vols:	1,500
Hours:	Tue-Sat 11-7. Sun 11-5.

Hillstar Bird Books   **By Appointment**
3 Sims Crescent M9V 2S9   (416) 744-3888
                                   E-mail: hillstar@sprint.ca

Collection:	Specialty
# of Vols:	900
Specialties:	Birds; natural history.
Services:	Search service, accepts want lists.
Credit Cards:	No
Owner:	Ronald Scovell
Year Estab:	1989

Hollywood Canteen   **Open Shop**
1516 Danforth Avenue M4J 1N4   (416) 461-1704
                             E-mail: hcanteen@interlog.com

Collection:	Specialty new and used. (See comments)
# of Vols:	10,000
Specialties:	Primarily film and some other related performing arts.
Hours:	Mon-Fri 11-7. Sat 10-6.
Travel:	Between Coxwell and Greenwood. See Map 17.
Credit Cards:	Yes
Owner:	Mike Orlando
Year Estab:	1979
Comments:	Most used books are in storage and are not available for general browsing. If searching for specific titles, contact the store first.

Horizon Books   **Mail Order**
6 Brucedale Crescent   M2K 2C7   Tel & Fax: (416) 226-4282
Web page: www.horizonbook.com   E-mail: errol@horizonbook.com

Collection:	Specialty
# of Vols:	3,000
Specialties:	Travel and exploration; gardening; natural history; ornithology.
Services:	Search service, catalog, accepts want lists.
Credit Cards:	Yes
Owner:	Errol Porter
Year Estab:	1991

Imago Press   **By Appointment**
836 Bloor Street West M6G 1M2   (416) 516-2966
Web page: www.imagopr.com   Fax: (416) 531-3197
                             E-mail: imago@interlog.com

Collection:	Specialty books and ephemera.
Specialties:	Poetry; classical studies; Canadian literary magazines; ontological discourse.
Credit Cards:	Yes
Year Estab:	1992

(Toronto)

Peter L. Jackson Military Books   **By Appointment**
23 Castle Green Crescent M9R 1N5   (416) 249-4796
                                                       Fax: (416) 241-7627
                                                       E-mail: pjackson@interlog.com

Collection:	Specialty
# of Vols:	2,000
Specialties:	Military and naval (all periods).
Services:	Appraisals, accepts want lists.
Credit Cards:	No
Year Estab:	1970

Joseph Patrick Books   **By Appointment**
PO Box 100, Postal Station V M6R 3A4   (416) 766-3357
Web page: www.abebooks.com   E-mail: jpbooks@idirect.com

Collection:	Specialty books and ephemera.
# of Vols:	10,000
Specialties:	Canadiana; religion (Catholic); philosophy.
Hours:	Mon-Thu 8:30-6.
Services:	Appraisals, catalog, accepts want lists.
Credit Cards:	Yes
Owner:	Joseph Gerald Sherlock
Year Estab:	1953
Comments:	A general collection is available online at www.abebooks.com.

D. & E. Lake, Ltd.   **Open Shop**
239 King Street East M5A 1J9   (416) 863-9930
Web page: http://booknet-international.com/ca/delake/   Fax: (416) 863-9443
                                                       E-mail: delake@istar.ca

Collection:	Specialty books, art and prints.
Specialties:	Antiquarian; early printed books; art; architecture; decorative arts.
Hours:	Mon-Sat 9:30-6. Sun 11-2:30.
Services:	Appraisals, catalog.
Travel:	Between Sherbourne and Jarvis. See Map 18.
Credit Cards:	Yes
Owner:	Don & Elaine Lake
Year Estab:	1978
Comments:	If your taste runs to fine books, particularly in the subjects listed above, a visit to this shop will provide you a happy experience as both the quantity and quality of the volumes are the answer to a collector's dreams.

Letters Bookshop   **By Appointment**
77 Florence St, Studio 104 M6K 1P4   (416) 537-5403
Web page: www.abebooks.com/home/LETTERSBOOKSHOP
                                                       E-mail: letters@interlog.com

Collection:	Specialty books and ephemera.

# of Vols:	35,000
Specialties:	Literature (raw and rare); poetry; small press; counter culture; bohemian malaise; anti-art; Arthur Cravan.
Services:	Appraisals, catalog, accepts want lists, mail order, collection development.
Credit Cards:	No
Owner:	Nicky Drumbolis
Year Estab:	1982

Neil D. MacDonald Fine Books   **By Appointment**
41 Spadina Road, Ste 1 M5R 2S9   (416) 961-2229
                                                        Fax: (416) 961-4446
                                               E-mail: neilbook@netcom.ca

Collection:	General stock.
# of Vols:	10,000
Specialties:	Antiquarian; Canadiana; early photography (books and photographs); early maps and prints.
Services:	Appraisals, catalog, search service, accepts want lists.
Credit Cards:	Yes
Owner:	Neil D. MacDonald & Megan Webster
Year Estab:	1992

The Map Room-At Exploration House   **Open Shop**
18 Birch Avenue M4V 1C8   (416) 922-5153
Web page: www.toronto.com/exploration   Fax: (416) 515-1728

Collection:	Specialty books and art.
Specialties:	Antique maps; nautical; nature; sports (with emphasis on pre-1900).
Hours:	Tue-Sat 11-5:30.
Services:	Appraisals, lists, repair and restoration (maps, books and art), search service, accepts want lists.
Travel:	West of Yonge St. See Map 18.
Credit Cards:	No
Owner:	Liana Sneyd
Year Estab:	1973

David Mason Books   **Open Shop**
342 Queen Street West, 2nd Fl. M5V 2A2   (416) 598-1015
Web page: www.abebooks.com   Fax:(416) 598-3994
                                               E-mail: dmbooks@netcom.ca

Collection:	Specialty
# of Vols:	50,000
Specialties:	Modern first editions; 18th & 19th century British and American literature; Canadian literature; Canadiana; travel; history (18th-20th century); children's; illustrated; sets; fine bindings.
Hours:	Mon-Sat 11-6.
Services:	Appraisals, catalog, accepts want lists.
Travel:	Just east of Spadina. (Note: The even numbers along Queen St do not correspond to the odd numbers across the street.) See Map 18.

(Toronto)

Credit Cards:	Yes
Year Estab:	1967
Comments:	One flight up, this shop has more books behind glass than most of the used book dealers we've visited. However, whether or not the books on display were behind glass or available for handling without the assistance of a staff member, we were impressed by both the quality and quantity of the stock. In addition to a strong representation in the specialties listed above, we saw several less obscure authors on display. Of course a "so called" common title in dust jacket or first edition ain't nothing to be sneezed at. Whether you're a scholar looking for a rare historic or scientific volume or a fan of a particular English or American writer whose works may be more difficult to locate, a visit here could prove most rewarding.

McBurnie & Cutler   **Open Shop**
698 Queen Street West M6J 1E7   (416) 504-8873
Web page: www.abebooks.com/home/   Fax: (416) 504-8418
                                          E-mail: mcburcut.books@on.aibn.com

Collection:	General stock.
# of Vols:	15,000-20,000
Specialties:	Music; Canadiana.
Hours:	Tue-Fri 11-6. Sat 11-7. Sun 12-6. Mon by chance.
Services:	Appraisals, subject lists, accepts want lists, mail order.
Travel:	3½ blocks west of Bathurst. See Map 18.
Credit Cards:	Yes
Owner:	Michael McBurnie & Tina Cutler
Year Estab:	1987
Comments:	The weather was generally good to us during our Canadian travels (it took us two visits to Canada to complete this volume), but our luck ran out when we ran into snow in Toronto on April 11th, the day we had planned to visit this shop. When we returned the next morning, we discovered that the shop was closed on Monday, despite the information we had been given earlier over the phone. (In a follow up phone call once we returned home we were advised that the Monday hours are "by chance.") We say that our luck ran out because from the little we were able to observe while behaving like children looking through a candy store window we believe that this shop carries quality hardcover volumes that could afford the serious book hunter an enjoyable visit. We regret being unable to return on Tuesday for a third attempt and hope that those of our readers who manage to visit on a sunny day, or when the shop is open, will be kind enough to let us know what we missed.

Media Encore (Half Price Books and Music)   **Open Shop**
1560 Bayview Avenue M4G 3B8   (416) 440-4253

Collection:	General stock of mostly used paperback and hardcover and remainders.

# of Vols:	30,000
Hours:	Apr-Dec: Mon-Sat 10-9. Sun 12-6. Jan-Mar: Mon-Wed 10-6. Thu-Sat 10-9. Sun 12-6.
Travel:	Corner of Belsize, two blocks north of Davisville and four blocks south of Eglington. See Map 17.
Credit Cards:	Yes
Year Estab:	1994
Comments:	Stock is approximately 85% used, 75% of which is paperback.

Media Encore   Open Shop
1939 Queen Street East M4L 1H7   (416) 699-5511

Collection:	General stock of hardcover and paperback used and remainders.
# of Vols:	5,000 (used)
Hours:	Jan-Apr: Mon-Wed 10-6. Thu-Sat 10-8. Sun 12-6. May-Sept: Mon-Wed 10-8. Thu-Sat 10-9. Sun 12-8. Oct-Dec: Mon-Wed 10-7. Thu-Sat 10-8. Sun 12-6.
Travel:	Between Woodbine and Lee. See Map 17.
Comments:	Stock is approximately 75% used and is evenly divided between hardcover and paperback.

Douglas Miller   Flea Market
St. Lawrence North Market   (416) 967-0535
Front and Jarvis Streets
Mailing address: 214 Queen Street East, 2nd Fl. Toronto ON M4V 2H4

Collection:	Specialty
Specialties:	Children's; illustrated; folklore.
Hours:	Sundays 5am-5pm. (Indoors)

Mimico Books & Other Things   Open Shop
2403 Lake Shore Boulevard West M8V 1C5   (416) 251-2728

Collection:	General stock of hardcover and paperback.
# of Vols:	15,000
Hours:	Daily 12-8.
Travel:	Between Royal York & Park Lawn. See Map 17.
Credit Cards:	Yes
Year Estab:	1997
Comments:	Taking our own advice, we phoned ahead on the day of our planned visit here to double check the store's 8pm closing time. When we arrived at 6pm, we found the hours posted in the window confirming the 8pm closing time along with a sign reading, "Sorry, We're Closed." Granted, one cannot adequately describe a shop by simply looking through the window. We can, however, note that we observed a fairly substantial number of paperback books taking up the front of the shop with hardcover volumes (which appeared to be of more recent vintage) lined up along the side walls. Should you find this shop open when you're in the neighborhood, we'd be happy to hear from you.

(Toronto)

Mooreshead Books   **Mail Order**
39 Mooreshead Drive M9C 2S2   E-mail: kath@idirect.com
Web page: www.abebooks.com/home/KATEH/

Collection:	General stock of mostly hardcover.
Specialties:	Mystery; biography.
Credit Cards:	No
Owner:	Kathleen Haushalter
Year Estab:	1999

Northern Books   **By Appointment**
Box 211, Station P M5S 2S7   Tel & Fax: (416) 531-8873
                                                 E-mail: norbooks@interlog.com

Collection:	Specialty
# of Vols:	3,000
Specialties:	Northern Canadiana; Arctic; wilderness; canoeing.
Services:	Appraisals, catalog, accepts want lists, search service.
Credit Cards:	No
Owner:	George Luste
Year Estab:	1984

Open City   **Open Shop**
1374 Danforth Avenue M4J 1M9   (416) 461-8087

Collection:	General stock of paperback and hardcover.
# of Vols:	10,000
Hours:	Mon-Fri 11-8. Sat 11-6. Sun 12-6.
Travel:	Between Greenwood and Coxwell. See Map 17.
Year Estab:	1986
Comments:	Stock is approximately 75% paperback.

Orion Book Store   **Open Shop**
544 Yonge Street M4Y 1Y8   (416) 923-5537

Collection:	General stock of mostly paperback.
# of Vols:	15,000
Hours:	Mon-Sat 11-11. Sun 12-9.

Pannonia Books-The Hungarian Book Store   **Open Shop**
344 Bloor Street West, Ste. 401 M5S 1W9   (416) 966-5156
Web page: www.panbooks.com   E-mail: pannonia@interlog.com

Collection:	Specialty new and used.
Specialties:	Hungary and Hungarian language books.
Hours:	Tue-Sat. Opens at 10am. Closing varies between 4-6pm.
Services:	Appraisals, catalog, search service.
Travel:	Near Spadina. See Map 18.
Credit Cards:	Yes
Owner:	Kate Karascony
Year Estab:	1957

The Piranha Shop
1550 Avenue Road M5M 3X5

Open Shop
(416) 789-3512
E-mail: piranhabt@home.com

Collection:	Specialty new and used.
# of Vols:	2,000+ (used)
Specialties:	Dogs
Hours:	Mon-Sat 10:30-6.
Services:	Appraisals, accepts want lists, mail order.
Travel:	1½ blocks north of Lawrence. See Map 17.
Credit Cards:	Yes
Owner:	Paul Wettlaufer
Year Estab:	1966

Planet X
2879 St Clair Avenue East M4B 1N4

Open Shop
(416) 285-4421

Collection:	Specialty books and comics.
# of Vols:	500+
Specialties:	Science fiction.
Hours:	Mon-Fri 12-7. Sat 11-6. Sun 12-5.

The Pleasant Bookstore
656 Eglinton Avenue East M4P 1P1

Open Shop
(416) 488-5998

Collection:	General stock of mostly paperback.
# of Vols:	25,000
Hours:	Mon-Fri 10-6. Sat 10-5.

Psychic Centre & Book Shop
2906 Danforth Avenue M4C 1M1

Open Shop
(416) 691-3335

Collection:	General stock of mostly paperback.
# of Vols:	30,000
Hours:	Mon-Thu 11-6. Fri 11-7. Sat 10-6.

Second Time Around Books
518 Mt. Pleasant Road M4S 2M2

Open Shop
(416) 483-3227

Collection:	General stock of paperback and hardcover.
# of Vols:	5,000-10,000
Specialties:	Magazines (primarily *Life*).
Hours:	Tue-Sat 10-6. Sun 12-5.
Travel:	One block north of Davisville. See Map 18.
Year Estab:	1992
Comments:	The appearance of so many shops like this one that are heavily paperback and have probably fewer than 1,000 hardcover volumes (most of which are of recent vintage and could be classified as reading copies) in neighborhoods in so many cities and towns clearly suggests that these shops serve their community in providing interesting and worthwhile reading materials. Whether one would plan a book hunting safari around such shops is an entirely different matter.

(Toronto)

She Said Boom Records & Books   **Open Shop**
372 College Street M5T 1S6   (416) 944-3224

Collection:	General stock of mostly used paperback and hardcover.
# of Vols:	10,000
Hours:	Mon-Tue, Wed, Sat 11-7. Thu & Fri 11-8. Sun 12-6.
Travel:	Between Spadina and Bathurst. See Map 18.
Credit Cards:	Yes
Year Estab:	1995
Comments:	Stock is approximately 70% paperback

Sleuth Of Baker Street   **Open Shop**
1600 Bayview Avenue M4G 3B7   (416) 483-3111
                                                    E-mail: sleuth@inforamp.net

Collection:	Specialty new and used.
# of Vols:	2,000 used (See Comments)
Specialties:	Mystery
Hours:	Mon-Thu 10-6. Fri 10-8. Sat 10-6. Sun and holidays 12-4.
Travel:	Between Eglington and Davisville. See Map 17.
Owner:	J.D. Singh & Marian Misters
Comments:	If you don't see what you're looking for, ask, as several thousand additional volumes (hardcover and paperback) are shelved off the main selling floor and are not available for customer browsing.

Subway Books   **By Appointment**
247 Albany Avenue M5R 3C7   Tel & Fax: (416) 538-3317
                                                    E-mail: subway@interlog.com

Collection:	General stock.
Specialties:	Modern first editions; Canadian literature and history; 1960's; black studies.
Services:	Mail order.
Credit Cards:	No
Owner:	D. Fetherling
Year Estab:	1980

Steven Temple Books   **By Appointment**
489 Queen Street West M5V 2B4   (416) 703-9908
Web page: www.abebooks.com/home/georgeschool   Fax: (416) 703-8872
                                                       E-mail: temple@istar.ca

Collection:	Specialty
# of Vols:	35,000
Specialties:	Literary first editions; Canadian literature; some general stock.
Services:	Appraisals, accepts want lists, mail order.
Credit Cards:	Yes
Year Estab:	1974

Ten Editions Bookstore   **Open Shop**
698 Spadina Avenue M5S 2J2   (416) 964-3803

Collection:	General stock and ephemera.
# of Vols:	20,000+
Specialties:	Canadiana; children's.
Hours:	Mon-Sat 11-6. Sun 1-5.
Travel:	One block south of Bloor, at intersection of Sussex and Spadina. See Map 18.
Credit Cards:	Yes
Owner:	Susan Duff
Year Estab:	1984
Comments:	Although the shelves in this shop reach up to the building's rather high ceiling, the owner has thoughtfully provided two sliding ladders along the side walls and several ladders in the back of the shop so that visitors can browse the titles on the upper shelves. We pity the person whose responsibility it is to stock the upper shelves. Of course, when we discovered three solid bookcases filled with vintage mysteries, we took to the highest shelves, risking life and dignity to retrieve some volumes that we were able to leave with. This is a serious shop with books to tempt folks with every taste and every pocketbook. It's certainly one that we would return to on our next trip to Toronto.

Tequilla Bookworm   **Open Shop**
490 Queen Street West M5V 2B3   (416) 504- 7335

Collection:	General stock of mostly paperback.
# of Vols:	1,000
Hours:	Mon-Thu 8am-midnight. Fri 8am-2am. Sat 10am-2am. Sun 11-11.

Triskelion   **Open Shop**
1081 Bathurst Street M5R 3G8   (416) 588-3727
                                            E-mail: trisk@globalserve.net

Collection:	General stock of mostly hardcover.
# of Vols:	30,000
Hours:	Mon-Wed & Sat & Sun 10:30-6. Thu & Fri 10:30-9.
Services:	Search service.
Travel:	Just south of Dupont. See Map 18.
Credit Cards:	Yes
Owner:	John & Stephanie Boyle
Year Estab:	1995
Comments:	A general shop with a mix of hardcover and paperback books, most of which are of fairly recent vintage and in good condition. The fact that this shop is immediately adjacent to another used book dealer suggests that a visit here gives the book traveler twice as good a chance of finding a volume of interest.

(Toronto)

Frederick Turner Bookseller   **By Appointment**
2 Sunnybrook Road M6S 1G2   (416) 769-9297

Collection:	Specialty
# of Vols:	10,000
Specialties:	Books arts.
Services:	Appraisals, search service, accepts want lists, mail order.
Credit Cards:	No
Year Estab:	1979

Used Books Etc.   **Open Shop**
22 Balliol Street M5S 1C1   (416) 489-5170

Collection:	General stock of mostly paperback.
Hours:	Mon-Fri 12-6. Sat 12-4.

Village Book Store   **Open Shop**
239 Queen Street West M5V 1Z4   (416) 598-4097

Collection:	General stock of hardcover and paperback.
# of Vols:	20,000
Specialties:	Art; literature.
Hours:	Mon-Sat 11-7. Sun 12-6.
Travel:	Between McCaul and University. See Map 18.
Credit Cards:	Yes
Owner:	Eric Wellington
Year Estab:	1961
Comments:	The shop carries a mix of hardcover volumes of recent as well as vintage titles in addition to paperbacks. If our comments here are brief, it's not because we've reached the end of the Toronto listings and are tired but rather that our visit here coincided with an unexpected April snow storm and our thoughts turned away from books and to getting to our hotel which was located outside of the city. We apologize to the owner if we've overlooked any of the store's more distinctive features.

What The Dickens Bookstore/Cafe   **Open Shop**
66 Gerrard Street East M5B 1G3   (416) 599-8211

Collection:	General stock of hardcover and paperback.
# of Vols:	10,000
Hours:	Mon-Fri 11am-7pm. Sat, Sun & holidays 12noon-6pm.
Services:	Accepts want lists, mail order.
Travel:	At northwest corner of Church and Gerrard Streets. See Map 18.
Credit Cards:	Yes
Owner:	Maureen Kahn & Randy Urquhart
Year Estab:	1994
Comments:	A mix of hardcover and paperback books, most of recent origin, located in a small coffee bar. While the titles we saw were broad enough to be of interest to the curious bibliophile, one is less likely to find a rare or esoteric title here.

Tweed

Bridgewater Trading Corp. Antique Market   **Antique Mall**
RR #3 K0K 3J0   (613) 478-3255

Hours: May 24-end of Oct: Daily 10-5. Remainder of year: Fri-Mon 10-5.
                  Closed in Feb.
Travel: Hwy 37 exit off Hwy 401. Proceed north on Hwy 37 to Tweed. Shop is
                  at north end of town.

Unionville

Sandpiper Books   **Mail Order**
88 Liebeck Crescent L3R 1Y5   (905) 946-9446

Collection: Specialty
Specialties: Visual arts.
Credit Cards: No

Uxbridge

Maple Ridge Books   **By Appointment**
7070 Concession 6, RR 2 L9P 1R2   (905) 852-0166
Web page: www.abebooks.com   Fax: (905) 852-0266
                                                  E-mail: mapleridgebooks@interhop.net

Collection: Specialty
# of Vols: 3,000
Specialties: Literary first editions; military fiction; travel & exploration; children's.
Services: Search service, catalog, accepts want lists.
Credit Cards: No
Owner: John Underhill
Year Estab: 1995

Vankleek Hill

Lisa & Andy's Used Books & Novelties   **Open Shop**
47 Main Street East   (613) 678-2657
Mailing address: PO Box 1031 Vankleek Hill   K0B 1R0   Fax: (613) 678-5598

Collection: General stock of paperback and hardcover.
# of Vols: 21,000
Hours: Dec-Apr: Mon-Sat 10-5. May-Nov: Mon-Sat 10-5. Sun 12-4.
Travel: Vankleek Hill exit off Hwy 417. Proceed northeast on Cty Rd 34. At
                  light, turn right onto Main St.
Credit Cards: No
Year Estab: 1995
Comments: Should you live within a 50-100 km radius of this shop and wish to buy
                  a used paperback or worn older hardcover volume for an interesting
                  read, chances are you'll find plenty of titles here to interest you. You'll
                  also find an assortment of novelties to amuse your children or friends.
                  If you're traveling a longer distance, though, unless you're a true

adventurer, you may not find the visit that exciting. On the other hand, we spotted an illustrated biography of Jack Dempsey written by Nat Fleicher of *Ring* magazine that probably would have warmed the hearts of boxing collectors.

Varna

McClymont Used Books   **By Appointment**
RR #1 N0M 2R0   (519) 233-3214

Collection:	General stock.
Specialties:	G.A. Henty; Canadiana; children's.
Services:	Accepts want lists, mail order.
Credit Cards:	No
Owner:	Ivan & Marg McClymont
Year Estab:	1978

Walsingham

Rose Of Sharon Antiquarian Books   **Open Shop**
24 Morgan Street 2024 RR 1 N0E 1X0   (519) 586-3760

Collection:	General stock of hardcover and paperback.
# of Vols:	5,000-10,000
Hours:	May 1-Nov 30: Tue-Fri 10-5. Sat 1-5.
Travel:	Nine km north of Long Point. Hwy 59 goes through the village of Walsingham. Once in village, turn east on Morgan.

Waterdown

Pickwick Books   **Open Shop**
325 Dundas Street East L0R 2H0   (905) 690-0632
                                                       Fax:(905) 632-0329

Collection:	General stock new and used paperback and hardcover.
# of Vols:	1,000+ (used)
Hours:	Mon-Wed, Sat 10-6. Thu 10-7. Fri 10-8. Sun 12-5.
Travel:	Waterdown exit off Hwy 6. Proceed north on Waterdown which becomes Mill. Shop is at corner of Mill and Dundas.
Comments:	Used stock is approximately 60% paperback.

Waterloo

The Bookworm   **Open Shop**
65 University East, #1 N1E 1K7   (519) 885-0473
                                                       E-mail: Kacollins@escarpment.com

Collection:	General stock of paperback and hardcover.
# of Vols:	15,000
Hours:	Mon-Thu 10-8. Fri 10-9. Sat 10-5. Sun 11-5.
Travel:	University Ave West exit off Hwy 86. Proceed west on University. After crossing Weber St, turn left into shopping plaza.
Credit Cards:	No

Owner:	Ron Collins
Year Estab:	1995
Comments:	Stock is approximately 70% paperback.

Ears 2 Hear Music & Books   **Open Shop**
37 King Street North N2J 2W9   (519) 884-4232
Web page: http://ears2hear.on.ca   E-mail: sales@ears2hear.on.ca

Collection:	General stock of books, records and CDs.
# of Vols:	4,000
Specialties:	Religion (Christian).
Hours:	Mon-Sat 10-6, except Thu & Fri till 9.
Travel:	Hwy 8 exit off Hwy 401. Proceed north on Hwy 8 to Kitchener, then exit onto Hwy 86 and continue to Bridgeport Rd exit in Waterloo. Right on Bridgeport, then left on King.
Credit Cards:	Yes
Owner:	Wesley Reimer
Year Estab:	1992
Comments:	Approximately 50% of the stock consists of books dealing with Christian theology.

Goodwill Thrift Shop   **Open Shop**
56 King Street North N2J 2X1   (519) 746-3770

Collection:	General stock of hardcover and paperback.
# of Vols:	1,000
Hours:	Mon-Thu 9:30-6. Fri 9:30-7. Sat 9:30-6.
Travel:	Entrance to store in on Princess, between Regina and King.

Salvation Army Thrift Shop   **Open Shop**
25 King Street South N2J 1N9   (519) 886-3020

Collection:	General stock of hardcover and paperback.
Hours:	Mon-Wed, Sat 10-5. Thu & Fri 10-8.
Travel:	Just south of Erb.

Whitby

Henderson Books   **Open Shop**
122 Brock Street South L1N 4J8   (905) 430-3756

Collection:	General stock of mostly paperback, greeting cards and gifts.
# of Vols:	7,000 (used)
Hours:	Mon-Fri 9-5. Sat 10-5.
Travel:	Brock St exit off Hwy 401. Proceed north on Brock St.
Credit Cards:	Yes
Owner:	Walter, Ruth & Linda Henderson
Year Estab:	1995
Comments:	Overwhelmingly paperback with a couple of shelves of hardcover volumes of little distinction.

Winchester

Chatter's   **Open Shop**
493 Main Street   (613) 774-0253
Mailing address: PO Box 360 Winchester ON KOC 2KO

Collection: General stock of mostly new and some used.
Hours: Tue-Sat 10-5.

Windham Centre

Caresa Antiques, Books & Cherishables   **Open Shop**
RR #1, Concession #9 N0E 2A0   (519) 443-5856
                                                              E-mail: caresa@kwic.com

Collection: General stock.
# of Vols: 2,000
Specialties: Children's; Canadiana.
Hours: Daily 12-6. Mornings by chance.
Travel: Delhi Concession 9 exit off Hwy 24. Proceed west on Delhi Conces-
                     sion 9. Shop is about six km ahead.
Credit Cards: No
Owner: Suzanne Moore
Year Estab: 1988

Windsor

Bahr's Books   **Open Shop**
4683 Tecumseth Road East N8W 1K8   (519) 945-0800

Collection: General stock of paperback and hardcover.
# of Vols: 12,000
Hours: Mon-Fri 11-8. Sat & Sun 12-6.
Travel: Hwy 2 is Temcumseth. Shop is on the east side of Windsor.
Credit Cards: No
Year Estab: 1989
Comments: Stock is approximately 70% paperback.

Biblioasis   **Open Shop**
519 Ouellette Avenue M9A 4J3   (519) 256-7367
                                                        E-mail: biblioasis@attcanada.net

Collection: General stock of mostly hardcover.
# of Vols: 12,000+
Specialties: Canadian literature; history.
Hours: Mon-Thu 10-6. Fri 10-7. Sat 10-6.
Services: Search service, accepts want lists, mail order.
Travel: Dougall exit (Tunnel exit) off Hwy 401. Proceed on Dougall which
                     becomes Ouellette. From US: From tunnel, Park exit. Left on Park and
                     left on Ouellette.
Credit Cards: Yes
Owner: Dan Wells

Year Estab: 1998
Comments: Stock is approximately 75% hardcover.

The Bookroom   **Open Shop**
2161 Wyandotte Street West N9B 1K1   (519) 258-2726
                                          E-mail: abeer@mnsi.net
Collection: General stock of mostly used hardcover and paperback.
# of Vols: 5,000
Hours: Tue, Wed, Sat, Sun 12-6. Thu & Fri 12-9.
Travel: Hwy 401 to end where it becomes Hwy 3. Continue on Hwy 3 which
                   becomes Huron Church Rd, then left on College, right on Felix, left on
                   Mill and right on Wyandotte.
Credit Cards: Yes
Owner: Anne Beer
Year Estab: 1989
Comments: Used stock is evenly divided between hardcover and paperback.

Works on Paper   **Open Shop**
315 Pelissier Street, 2nd Fl.   (519) 258-8583
Mailing address: PO Box 24084 Windsor ON N8Y 4Y9

Collection: Specialty
# of Vols: 5,000
Specialties: Art; Canadian literature; literature; history; British countryside;
                   children's; biography; memoirs; Anglo-Saxon revival.
Hours: Thu-Sun afternoons.
Travel: Ouellette Ave exit off Hwy 401. Proceed north on Ouellette, then left
                   on Tecumseth Rd and right on Pelissier. Shop is on 2nd floor of the
                   Capitol Theatre Building.
Credit Cards: No
Owner: Betty Wilkinson
Year Estab: 1994

Woodstock

Read More Collectibles (Mostly Books)   **Open Shop**
599 Dundas Street N4S 1C9   (519) 539-3052

Collection: General stock of mostly paperback.
# of Vols: 5,000+
Hours: Mon-Fri 10-5. Sat 10-4, except during summer 10-1.

Finding a book here is like looking for a needle in a haystack.

Prince Edward Island

Alphabetical Listing By Dealer

Alphabetical Listing By Location

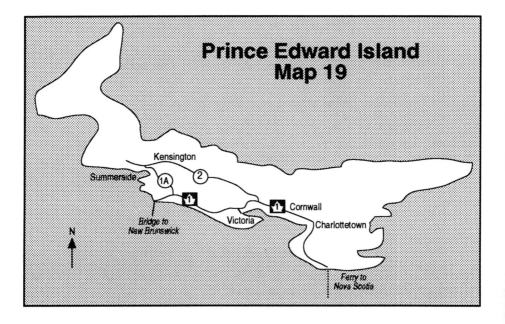

Charlottetown

The Book Emporium   **Open Shop**
169 Queen Street C1A 4B4   (902) 628-2001

Collection:	General stock of new and used paperback and hardcover.
# of Vols:	10,000
Hours:	Mon-Thu 9:30-5:30. Fri 9:30-8. Sat 9:30-5. Jul & Aug: Mon-Fri 9:30-8. Sat 9:30-5:30.
Travel:	See The Bookman below.
Credit Cards:	Yes
Owner:	Helen Huynh
Year Estab:	1991
Comments:	Primarily paperback with a few hardcover volumes. You're not likely to find a book here not normally available elsewhere.

The Bookman   **Open Shop**
177 Queen Street C1A 4B4   (902) 892-8872

Collection:	General stock of hardcover and paperback.
# of Vols:	10,000
Hours:	Mon-Sat 9:30-5:30. Sun 1-5. Mid Jun-mid Sept: Mon-Sat 9-9. Sun 12-5.
Travel:	Downtown, between Kent and Grafton.
Comments:	A nice shop with an interesting mix of older hardcover volumes (some quite rare and displayed on shelves with a cautionary warning to browsers regarding their not being handled), a nice selection of newer hardcover volumes, most in dust jackets, a fair number of remainders and enough paperbacks to satisfy most fans of that type of literature. The shop is easy to browse and is less than 50 feet away from another used book dealer. (See The Book Emporium above.)

Gallery 18   **Open Shop**
18 Queen Street, Ste. 111 C1A 4A1   (902) 628-8869
Web page: www.virtuo.com/gallery18/   E-mail: gallery@isn.net

Collection:	General stock, prints and ephemera.
# of Vols:	1,000
Specialties:	Prince Edward Island; Canadiana; modern first editions; maps.
Hours:	Year-round. Call for seasonal hours.
Travel:	At foot of Queen St, in the lobby of the Prince Edward Hotel.
Credit Cards:	Yes
Owner:	Aubrey R. Bell
Year Estab:	1996
Comments:	Although closed at the time of our visit, looking through the shop's windows, we were able to view three bookcases filled with hardcover volumes that appeared to be a mix of older (perhaps antiquarian or rare??) and slightly newer volumes sporting dust jackets, plus a collection of prints, lithographs, maps and posters.

Cornwall

Booktales   **Open Shop**
Cornwall Plaza C0A 1H0   (902) 566-3484
Collection: General stock of mostly paperback.
Hours: Mon-Wed 10-7. Thu & Fri 10-9. Sat 10-7.

Kensington

Abegwit Books   **Open Shop**
Commercial Street   (902) 836-4334
Mailing address: RR #1 Kensington Malpeque PE C0B 1M0
                                            E-mail: rregular@auracom.com
Collection: General stock of mostly paperback.
# of Vols: 10,000+
Hours: Tue-Sat 9-5.

Summerside

Avonlea Bookstore   **Open Shop**
240 Water Street C1N 1B3   Tel & Fax: (902) 888-2665
                                            E-mail: rmrk@pei.sympatico.com
Collection: General stock of new and mostly paperback used.
# of Vols: 5,000
Hours: Mon-Sat 9-5.
Services: Appraisals, search service, accepts want lists, mail order.
Travel: From Confederation Bridge, take Hwy 1, then Hwy 1A into Summerside
                   where it becomes Water St. At light at Waterfront Plaza bear right to
                   continue on Water St.
Credit Cards: No
Owner: Richard Kays
Year Estab: 1994
Comments: A mix of paperback and hardcover books with an emphasis on the
                   paperback. The hardcover items, though fewer in number, were in
                   generally good condition, of mixed vintage and worth viewing.

Victoria

Hilary Price Books   **Open Shop**
6 Main Street   (902) 658-2329
Mailing address: PO Box 34 Victoria PE C0A 2G0
Web page: www.abebooks.com/home/h.jamesprice
                                            E-mail: hjprice@pei.sympatico.ca
Collection: General stock of hardcover and paperback.
# of Vols: 5,000
Specialties: Mystery (paperback).
Hours: Jun-Sept: Daily 10-6.
Services: Accepts want lists, mail order.

Travel: From Confederation Bridge, continue on Hwy 1, taking turn off to Victoria. At water, turn left.

Credit Cards: No

Year Estab: 1994

Comments: Although not normally open until June, the owner was kind enough to allow us to visit on a chilly April afternoon when only a portion of the shop's inventory was on hand. The shop is located in a barn-like building one block from the water's edge. For the most part, the modest number of hardcover volumes we saw were in generally good condition, nicely organized and reasonably priced. In some sections paperbacks and hardcover titles were intershelved and several unusual volumes could be seen along with the more common variety.

Quebec
Map 20

Québec

Alphabetical Listing By Dealer

Alphabetical Listing By Location

Beauport
(Map 20, page 272)

Michel Villeneuve, Libraire Enr.   **By Appointment**
2392 du Vieux-Moulin G1E 6E1   Tel & Fax: (418) 661-6907
Web page: www.bibliopolis.net/villeneuve   E-mail: michelvilleneuve@sprint.ca

Collection: Specialty
# of Vols: 10,000-15,000
Specialties: Canadiana; local history; genealogy; French Canadian literature.
Services: Catalog, accepts want lists.
Credit Cards: Yes
Year Estab: 1982

Beloeil (Vieux)
(Map 21, page 279)

Au Royaume du Livre   **Open Shop**
225 St Jean Baptiste J3G 2V6   (450) 464-8184

Collection: General stock. (Primarily French)
Hours: Mon-Wed 11-6. Thu & Fri 11-9. Sat 11-5. Sun 12-5.
Services: Search service, accepts want lists.
Credit Cards: No
Owner: Roxane Chapdelaine
Year Estab: 1993

Bury

Canterbury Books, QC   **Mail Order**
1240 Gould Station Road   J0B 1J0   Tel & Fax: (819) 657-4668
Mailing address: (Call for US mailing address)
Web page: www.abebooks.com/home/CANTERBURYBOOKS
                                          E-mail: canterbook@sympatico.ca
Collection: General stock of hardcover and paperback.
# of Vols: 20,000
Services: Search service, accepts want lists.
Credit Cards: Yes
Owner: Bob & Pat Bosson
Year Estab: 1992
Comments: Stock is approximately 75% hardcover.

Chicoutimi

Bouquinerie Jacques-Cartier   ******
366 Savard Street   G7J 2T1
                                                       (418) 696-1534

** *Information about this dealer has not been verified.*

Dollard-des-Ormeaux
(Map 21, page 279)

Book Market   **Open Shop**
3393 des Sources   H9B 1Z8   (514) 683-9890

Collection:	General stock of 75% paperback.
# of Vols:	75,000+
Hours:	Mon-Wed 10-6. Thu & Fri 10-9. Sat 10-6. Sun 12-5.

Drummondville
(Map 20, page 272)

Librairie O Vieux Bouquins   **By Appointment**
PO Box 8   J2B 6V6   (819) 477-2993
                                                        Fax: (819) 477-6877
                                              E-mail: duhamel@cgocable.ca

Collection:	Specialty (English and French)
# of Vols:	60,000
Specialties:	Canadiana; New France; Quebec; Franco Americans; hockey.
Services:	Appraisals, catalog, search service.
Credit Cards:	Yes
Owner:	Serge-Patrick Duhamel
Year Estab:	1974

Gatineau
(Map 20, page 272)

Loisir des Usagers   **Open Shop**
27 Gréber   (819) 246-5606
Mailing address: 333 St. Joseph Hull QC J8Y 3Z1

Collection:	General stock of mostly hardcover. (Primarily French)
# of Vols:	30,000
Hours:	Mon-Wed 10-6, Thu & Fri 10-9. Sat 10-5. Sun 12-5.
Services:	Search service, accepts want lists, mail order.
Travel:	From downtown Ottawa, take Macdonald Cartier bridge. Turn right on Laurier Blvd, then continue east on Fournier Blvd, then turn onto Gréber Blvd.
Credit Cards:	Yes
Owner:	Christiane Gourde & Marc Bureau
Year Estab:	1982

Grenville
(Map 20, page 272)

Antiquities Art Gallery   ***By Appointment**
55 Maple Street J0V 1J0   (819) 242-9551

Collection:	General stock of hardcover and paperback.
# of Vols:	5,000
Specialties:	Art

*Hours:**	Jul & Aug: Open Sundays
Services:	Appraisals, search service, accepts want lists.
Credit Cards:	Yes
Owner:	Gloria Welden Thorburn
Year Estab:	1995
Comments:	Stock is approximately 75% hardcover.

Havelock

Bibliography of the Dog   **Mail Order**
625 Route 203 J0S 2C0   (450) 826-0711
                                                          Fax: (450) 826-0713

Collection:	General stock.
Specialties:	Dogs
Services:	Catalog
Owner:	Nigel Aubrey-Jones
Year Estab:	1956

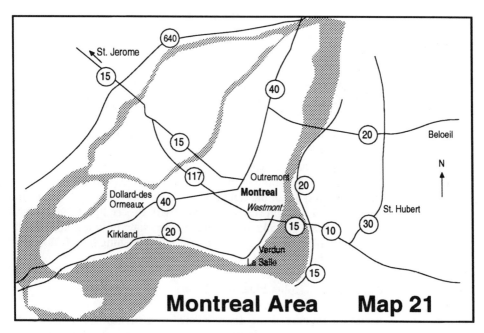

Montreal Area   Map 21

Hull
(Map 20, page 272)

Loisir des Usagers   **Open Shop**
333 St. Joseph J8Y 3Z1   (819) 778-0341
                                                          Fax: (819) 772-9107
                                                 E-mail: Pyromark@netcom.com

Collection: General stock of mostly hardcover. (Primarily French)

# of Vols:	40,000
Hours:	Mon-Wed 10-6. Thu & Fri 10-9. Sat 10-5. Sun 12-5.
Services:	Search service, accepts want lists, mail order.
Travel:	From downtown Ottawa, take Portage bridge. Turn left on Alexandre Taché Blvd. Continue for about one km, then turn right on St. Joseph.
Credit Cards:	Yes
Owner:	Christiane Gourde & Marc Bureau
Year Estab:	1982

Kirkland
(Map 21, page 279)

Book Market   **Open Shop**
2935 St Charles Boulevard   H9H 3B5   (514) 694-1546

Collection:	General stock of mostly paperback.
Hours:	Mon-Wed 10-76. Thu & Fri 10-9. Sat 9:30-5:30. Sun 12-5.

La Salle
(Map 21, page 279)

Livres Bronx Books   **Open Shop**
34–6th Avenue   H8P 2K8   (514) 368-3543
Web page: www.abebooks.com/home/bronxbooks   E-mail: bronxbooks@openface.ca

Collection:	General stock of paperback and hardcover, ephemera and records.
# of Vols:	15,000
Specialties:	Counterculture; UFOs; modern first editions; military; history.
Hours:	Tue-Sun 10-9.
Services:	Appraisals, search service, catalog, accepts want lists.
Travel:	From downtown Montreal, turn south on Atwater and follow it under the tunnel, staying in the right line. Take turnoff for Hwy 15 south and then first exit on right (La Verendrye Blvd). Proceed past five bridges, then left on Shevchenko. Continue to river, staying in left lane. At the river (La Salle Blvd), turn left and veer left at flashing light (Edourard). 6th Ave is two blocks ahead.
Credit Cards:	No
Owner:	Roy Berger & Robin Finesmith Young
Year Estab:	1997
Comments:	While the owners of this shop, located in a suburb of Montreal, take pride in considering their stock to be heavily counter culture in nature, our view, more simply stated, is that you'll find lots of paperbacks here, a modest number of hardcover volumes and quite a few records, comics and magazines. While we were not tempted by any of the above, someone with tastes more akin to that of the owners might walk out of this shop with a smile on his or her face.

Lennoxville
(Map 20, page 272)

Black Cat Books   **Open Shop**
47 Park J1M 1K1   (819) 346-1786
E-mail: cfish@blackcatbooks.com

Collection: General collection of hardcover and paperback. (English and French)
Specialties: Eastern townships, Canadiana; literature.
Hours: Tue & Wed 11-5. Thu & Fri 11-7. Sat 11-5. Sun by chance.
Services: Accepts want lists, mail order.
Travel: Three miles south of Sherbrooke. Entrance is from the Café Java.
Credit Cards: No
Owner: Janice LaDuke & Cynthia Fish
Year Estab: 1998
Comments: Stock is evenly divided between hardcover and paperback and is approximately 85% English.

Montréal
(Map 22, page 284 & Map 21, page 279)

Anthologies-Cafe Boooks   **Open Shop**
1420 Stanley Street H3A 1P7   (514) 287-9929
E-mail: marylou@inforoute.net

Collection: General stock of paperback and hardcover.
# of Vols: 40,000-50,000
Hours: Daily 10:30-6, except Wed-Fri till 9.
Services: Mail order.
Travel: Between St. Catherine and Maisonneuve.
Credit Cards: Yes
Owner: Gordon Campbell
Year Estab: 1993
Comments: A general shop with mostly recent hardcover and paperback titles. While we were unable to spot anything that piqued our curiosity, we readily recognize the nature of the book business and since this store is directly across the street from another dealer, a dual visit to these two establishments seems like a sound investment of your time.

ART45   **By Appointment**
3440 du Musee H3G 2C7   (514) 843-5024

Collection: Specialty
Specialties: Art; architecture.
Credit Cards: No
Owner: Serge Vaisman
Year Estab: 1976

Au Paradis du Livre   **Open Shop**
5153 Wellington H4G 1Y2   (514) 767-2589
Collection: General stock of hardcover and paperback. (French and English)

(Montréal)

# of Vols:	30,000
Hours:	Mon-Wed 10:30-5:30. Thu & Fri 10:30-9. Sat 10-5.
Travel:	In Verdun, between 6th Ave & Desmarchais. (See Map 21.)
Comments:	Stock is evenly divided between English and French. Non fiction books are mostly hardcover.

Au Tourne-Livre   **Open Shop**
707 Mont Royal East   H2J 1W7   (514) 598-8580

Collection:	General stock of hardcover and paperback. (French)
Travel:	Two blocks east of St. Denis.

Bibliomania Bookshoppe   **Open Shop**
1841A St. Catherine Street West   H3H 1M2   (514) 933-8156

Collection:	General stock of mostly used hardcover and paperback.
# of Vols:	30,000 (used)
Specialties:	Art; architecture; decorative arts; film; music; fashion; antiques; cookbooks; fine bindings.
Hours:	Mon-Sat 12-6:30, except Thu & Fri till 9. Sun 12-6.
Services:	Mail order.
Travel:	Guy St exit off Hwy 720 (Ville-Marie Expwy). Exit will lead onto Réne Lévesque Blvd. Continue west on Réne Lévesque, then right (north) on Atwater and right (east) on St. Catherine. Shop is between St. Mathieu and St. Marc.
Credit Cards:	Yes
Owner:	Joseph Block
Year Estab:	1982
Comments:	Our kind of shop in that the vast majority of the books were in good to excellent condition, primarily hardcover, well organized and easy to browse. Most categories were represented nicely. This is a place where, unless your tastes are very narrow, you should enjoy visiting. Note: additional stock, ephemera and magazines can be seen by appointment.

Bidonlivre   **Open Shop**
3428 St. Denis   H2X 3L3   (514) 844-0892

Collection:	General stock. (Primarily French)
# of Vols:	12,000
Specialties:	Film
Hours:	Mon-Fri 11-9. Sat 11-9. Sun 12-8.
Services:	Appraisals, search service, accepts want lists, mail order.
Travel:	At corner of St. Denis and Sherbrooke.
Credit Cards:	Yes
Owner:	M. Grzelak
Year Estab:	1984
Comments:	Collection is 80% French, with sections in Spanish, German and English.

Bookstore of the Americas
4555 St. Laurent Boulevard   H2T 1R2
Web page: www.abyayala.com

* **Mail Order**
(514) 849-4908
Fax: (514) 259-4687
E-mail: abyayala@abyayala.com

Collection: Specialty new and used.
# of Vols: 8,000-10,000 (used)
Specialties: Latin America; books in Spanish (general collection); First Nations. Books are in French, English and Spanish.
Services: Accepts want lists.
Credit Cards: Yes
Owner: Steven Kaal
Year Estab: 1995
*Comments:**   The owner maintains an open shop at the above location. However, only a limited number of used books, primarily in Spanish, are available for browsing at the shop.

Bouquinerie Saint-Denis
4075 St. Denis H2W 2M7
Web page: marchedulivre.qc.ca

Open Shop
(514) 288-5567
Fax: (514) 522-3408
E-mail: marche@marchedulivre.qc.ca

Collection: General stock of used and new. (French)
Specialties: Art
Hours: Daily 10-10.
Services: Appraisals, mail order.
Credit Cards: Yes

Le Bouquiniste P. Chapus
2065 St. Denis   H2X 3K8
Web page: www.lebouquiniste.com

Open Shop
(514) 842-9204
Fax: (514) 842-9293
E-mail: pchapus@lebouquiniste.com

Collection: Specialty (French)
# of Vols: 13,000
Specialties: French literature; Canadiana; science; humanities; art; history; antiquarian illustrations.
Hours: Mon-Sat 11-8. Call for Sun hours.
Services: Appraisals, search service.
Travel: Between Sherbrooke and Ontario.
Credit Cards: Yes
Owner: Pierre Chapus
Year Estab: 1993

Chapitre un Librairie
4109 St. Catherine Street East   H1V 1X1

Open Shop
(514) 523-5345

Collection: General stock. (French)
Hours: Mon-Wed 10-7. Thu & Fri 10-9. Sat & Sun 10-6.
Services: Book repair.
Credit Cards: No
Owner: Christine Piat & Dominique Robert
Year Estab: 1993

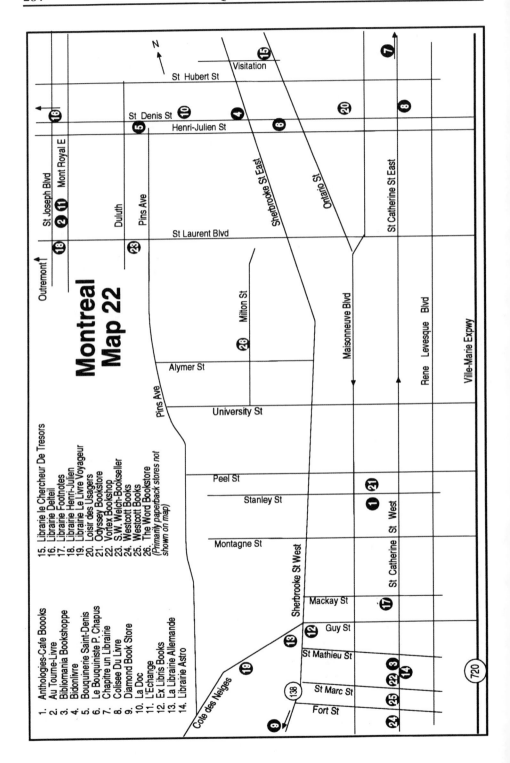

Montreal
Map 22

1. Anthologies-Cafe Books
2. Au Tourne-Livre
3. Bibliomania Bookshoppe
4. Bidonlivre
5. Bouquinerie Saint-Denis
6. Le Bouquiniste P. Chapus
7. Chapitre un Librairie
8. Colisee Du Livre
9. Diamond Book Store
10. La Doc
11. L'Echange
12. Ex Libris Books
13. La Librairie Allemande
14. Librairie Astro
15. Librairie le Chercheur De Tresors
16. Librairie Delteil
17. Librairie Footnotes
18. Librairie Henri-Julien
19. Librairie Le Livre Voyageur
20. Loisir des Usagers
21. Odyssey Bookstore
22. Vortex Bookshop
23. S.W. Welch-Bookseller
24. Westcott Books
25. Westcott Books
26. The Word Bookstore
(Primarily paperback stores not shown on map)

Cheap Thrills   **Open Shop**
2044 Metcalfe   H3A 1X8   (514) 844-8988

Collection: General stock of mostly paperback.
Hours: Mon-Wed & Sat 11-6. Thu & Fri 11-9. Sun 12-5.

Cheap Thrills   **Open Shop**
1433 Bishop   H3G 2E4   (514) 844-7604

Collection: General stock of mostly paperback.
Hours: Mon-Wed & Sat 11-6. Thu & Fri 11-9. Sun 12-5.

Colisee Du Livre   **Open Shop**
908 St. Catherine Street East   (514) 845-1792

Collection: General stock of hardcover and paperback. (French)
Hours: Daily 10-10.
Travel: East of St. Andre St.

François Côté, Libraire   **
2111 Jeanne-d'Arc Avenue, #4 H1W 3V6   (514) 899-1118

Débédé   **
3882 St. Denis H2W 2M2   (514) 499-8477

Diamond Book Store   **Open Shop**
5035 Sherbrooke Street West   H4A 1S8   (514) 481-3000

Collection: General stock of hardcover and paperback.
# of Vols: See Comments.
Hours: Mon-Fri 9:30-6. Sat 9:30-5. Sun 10-5.
Travel: From Hwy 15, proceed east on Sherbrooke. Shop is between Grey and
                   Claremont.
Owner: R. Russell
Comments: A store in transition. At the time of our visit, we saw an assortment of
                   non-descript volumes, some apparently remainders, with little concern
                   for condition, in a rather worn looking establishment. We were ad-
                   vised, though, that the owner had plans to renovate the shop and trans-
                   fer some of the stock from his other shop that was in the process of
                   being closed down.

La Doc   **Open Shop**
3778 St. Denis H2W 2M1   (514) 499-0654

Collection: General stock. (French)
Hours: Mon-Wed 10-6. Thu & Fri 10-9. Sat & Sun 10-6.

L'Echange   **Open Shop**
713 Mont Royal East   H2J 1W7   (514) 523-6389

Collection: General stock of paperback and hardcover. (French)
Hours: Daily 10-10.
Travel: Two blocks east of St. Denis.
Credit Cards: Yes

*** Information about this dealer has not been verified.*

(Montréal)

Year Estab: 1976
Comments: Stock is approximately 60% is paperback.

Ex Libris Books   **Open Shop**
1628B Sherbrooke Street West H3H 1C9   (514) 932-1689
                                                    E-mail: rcampbell@securenet.net

Collection: General stock.
# of Vols: 10,000-15,000
Specialties: History; science; medicine; history of ideas; Judaica.
Hours: Mon-Thu 11-6. Fri 11-9. Sat 11-5.
Services: Appraisals, catalog, accepts want lists.
Travel: From Hwy 15, turn east onto Sherbrooke St. Shop is just west of Guy.
Credit Cards: Yes
Owner: Robert Campbell
Year Estab: 1995
Comments: Particularly strong in the specialties listed above with titles you're not
                 likely to see elsewhere. The shop's general collection is also quite
                 respectable. A good example of a quality bookstore carrying titles in
                 mostly English but also some French.

Wilfrid M. de Freitas–Bookseller   **Mail Order**
PO Box 883, Stock Exchange Tower H4Z 1K2   (514) 935-9581
Web page: www.deFreitasbooks.com   Fax: (514) 931-8999
                                                    E-mail: Wilfrid@deFreitasBooks.com

Collection: General stock.
Specialties: First editions; Winston Churchill; Lewis Carroll; golf; tennis; travel
                 guides (Baedeker); Gilbert & Sullivan; A. Conan Doyle; W. Somerset
                 Maugham.
Services: Catalog, accepts want lists in specialty areas above.
Credit Cards: No
Year Estab: 1977

R.P. Goodman Military Books   **By Appointment**
PO Box 173, Station H   H3G 2K7   (514) 697-9892
                                                            Fax: (514) 697-0705
                                                    E-mail: pgoodman@securenet.net

Collection: Military (from ancient world to post 1945).
# of Vols: 10,000
Services: Appraisals, search service, accepts want lists, mail order.
Credit Cards: No

Helen R. Kahn-Antiquarian Books   **By Appointment**
PO Box 323, Victoria Station H3Z 2V8   (514) 844-5344
Web page: www.hrkahnbooks.com   Fax: (514) 499-9274
                                                    E-mail: hrk@hrkahnbooks.com

Collection: Specialty
Specialties: Voyages; travel; Canadiana; Americana.

Services: Appraisals, catalog, accepts want lists.
Credit Cards: Yes
Year Estab: 1997

Michel Lanteigne, Bookseller   **By Appointment**
5468 St. Urbain, # 4   H2T 2X1   (514) 273-4963
Web page: www.abebooks.com/home/LANTEIGNE   Fax: (514) 270-8360
                                                      E-mail: intral1@sprint.ca
Collection: General stock.
# of Vols: 5,000+
Specialties: Mystery first editions; naval and military history; children's.
Services: Appraisals, occasional catalog, accepts want lists for mystery only,
           mail order.
Credit Cards: No
Year Estab: 1986

La Librairie Allemande   **Open Shop**
3434 Côte des Neiges   H3H 1T8   (514) 933-1919
                                                            Fax: (514) 933-3275
                                          E-mail: lalibrairieallemade@attcanada.net
Collection: Specialty new and used
Specialties: Books in German.
Hours: Mon-Fri 10-6. Sat by appointment.
Services: Mail order.
Travel: Between Sherbrooke and Penfield.
Credit Cards: Yes
Owner: Marion Heinze

Librairie Astro   **Open Shop**
1844 St. Catherine Street West   H3H 1M1   (514) 932-1139
                                                            Fax: (514) 932-5020
                                             E-mail: astro@game-master.com
Collection: General stock of new and used paperback and hardcover and comics.
Hours: Mon-Wed 11-7. Thu & Fri 11-9. Sat 10-8. Sun 12-6.
Travel: See Bibliomania Bookshoppe above.
Owner: Paul Stock
Comments: If you're into the world of comic books (used and new), you should
           enjoy a visit here. The shop also carries paperbacks, CDs and a modest
           assortment of quite recent popular hardcover books.

Librairie Le Chercheur De Trésors   **Open Shop**
1339 Ontario Street East   H2L 1R8   (514) 597-2529
                                                         E-mail: folio@total.net
Collection: General stock.
# of Vols: 12,000
Specialties: Canadiana; French Canadian modern first editions; art; history; litera-
           ture in French.
Hours: Mon-Sat 12-6.

(Montréal)

Services:	Appraisals, catalog, accepts want lists.
Travel:	East of St. Hubert.
Credit Cards:	Yes
Owner:	Richard Gingras
Year Estab:	1978
Comments:	A casualty of Canada's Easter Monday holiday during which some (but hardly all) retail businesses are closed. Based on the frustrating effort of trying to determine what a shop might be like inside by peering through the front door, all we can say is that we wish we could have seen more as such views "do not an observation make."

Librairie Delteil   **Open Shop**
7348 St. Denis   H2R 2E4   (514) 277-8235

Collection:	General stock of hardcover and paperback. (French)
# of Vols:	20,000
Hours:	Mon-Fri 12-6, except Thu till 9. Sat 12-5.
Comments:	Stock is evenly divided between hardcover and paperback.

Librairie Footnotes   **Open Shop**
1454 Mackay Street   H3G 2H7   (514) 938-0859

Collection:	General stock of mostly used paperback and remainders.
# of Vols:	20,000
Hours:	Mon-Fri 10-6:30. Sat 12-5.
Travel:	Between Maisonneuve and St. Catherine.

Librairie Henri-Julien   **Open Shop**
4800 Henri-Julien   H2T 2E1   (514) 844-7576
Web page: www.henri-julien.com   E-mail: jfsylvain@henri-julien.com

Collection:	General stock of hardcover and paperback. (Primarily French)
# of Vols:	16,000
Specialties:	Philosophy; art; literature; history.
Hours:	Tue-Sat afternoons.
Travel:	One block south of St. Joseph Blvd.
Credit Cards:	Yes
Owner:	Michel Lefebvre
Year Estab:	1987
Comments:	Stock is approximately 50% hardcover.

Librairie Le Livre Voyageur   **Open Shop**
5400 Côte des Neiges   (514) 736-0999
Mailing address: 1487 Logan Montreal QC H2L 1X6
Web page: www.mtl.net/livre.voyageur

Collection:	General stock. (French)
Specialties:	Canadiana; spiritualism; religion (Christianity), literature; poetry.
Hours:	Daily 11-6.

Services: Appraisals, search service.
Credit Cards: Yes
Owner: Bruno LaLonde
Year Estab: 1996

Loisir des Usagers   **Open Shop**
365 Emery   (819) 845-4888
Mailing address: 333 St. Joseph Hull QC J8Y 3Z1   Fax: (819) 772-9107
                                          E-mail: Pyromark@netcom.ca
Collection: General stock of mostly hardcover. (Primarily French)
# of Vols: 30,000
Hours: Mon-Wed 10-6. Thu & Fri 10-9. Sat 10-5. Sun 12-5.
Services: Search service, accepts want lists, mail order.
Travel: Two blocks northwest of intersection of Maisonneuve and St. Denis.
Credit Cards: Yes
Owner: Christiane Gourde & Marc Bureau
Year Estab: 1987

Odyssey Bookstore   **Open Shop**
1439 Stanley Street H3A 1P4   (514) 844-4843
Web page: www.odysseybooks.qc.ca   E-mail: info@odysseybooks.qc.ca
Collection: General stock of hardcover and paperback.
# of Vols: 15,000
Hours: Mon-Fri 10-8. Sat & Sun 12-6.
Services: Appraisals, mail order.
Travel: Westsbound on Hwy 720 (Ville-Marie Expwy): Montagne/St Jacques
                   exit. Turn right and proceed south to St. Jacques, then left on Peel, left
                   on Maisonneuve and left on Stanley. Eastbound coming off the Jacques
                   Cartier Bridge, continue straight after bridge to Maisonneuve, then
                   turn left on Maisonneuve and continue to the City Centre. Turn left on
                   Stanley.
Credit Cards: Yes
Owner: Bernard Wolf
Year Estab: 1986
Comments: A quite respectable shop with a mix of most reasonably priced hard-
                   cover and paperback books. The books were in generally good condi-
                   tion. Most subjects were represented but not necessarily in great depth.
                   We managed to exchange some American dollars for a volume that
                   proved to be of interest to us.

Ronald Smith, Libraire   **
1604 Notre-Dame West H3J 1M1   (514) 278-6847

TBCL The Book Collector's Library   **By Appointment**
PO Box 127 C.S.L. H4V 2Y3   (514) 484-5536
Web page: www.abebooks.com/home/TBCL   E-mail: tbcl@securenet.net
Collection: Specialty
# of Vols: 5,000

** *Information about this dealer has not been verified.*

(Montréal)

Specialties:	Modern first editions; antiquarian; Virginia Woolf; Bloomsbury group; *livres d'artiste*; autographs.
Services:	Appraisals, search service, mail order, accepts want lists.
Credit Cards:	No
Owner:	Sharon Shulman
Year Estab:	1975

Francisco Uribe, Libraire   ******
4593 Draper Avenue   H4A 2P5   (514) 487-1260

Alfred Van Peteghem–Books   **By Appointment**
7894 Berri Street   H2R 2G9   (514) 271-2825
                                                                     Fax: (514) 271-0633

Collection:	Specialty books and ephemera.
# of Vols:	2,000
Specialties:	Canadiana; Americana; history; native studies.
Services:	Appraisals, catalog.
Credit Cards:	No
Year Estab:	1972

Vortex Bookshop   **Open Shop**
1855 St. Catherine Street West   H3H 1M2   (514) 935-7869
                                                            E-mail: vortex@securenet.net

Collection:	General stock of hardcover and paperback.
# of Vols:	15,000
Specialties:	Modern first editions; illustrated; scholarly out-of-print in most academic fields.
Hours:	Daily 11-8.
Services:	Appraisals, search service, accepts want lists, mail order.
Travel:	See Bibliomania Bookshoppe above.
Credit Cards:	Yes
Owner:	Normand Pichette
Year Estab:	1996
Comments:	Unfortunately on the day of our visit the shop was not open (despite the Open/Ouvert sign on the door). Based on an extremely unscientific glance through the door, all we can say is that we would have liked to have visited the shop as there appeared to be an interesting selection of hardcover volumes on hand. Should you visit here, please let us know what we missed.

Charles Vyvial, Bookseller   **By Appointment**
4501 Harvard Avenue   H4A 2X3   (514) 488-1816
                                                        E-mail: bookhunter@proxyma.net

Collection:	General stock.
Specialties:	Art; architecture; antique references; travel and exploration; photography; illustrated.

** *Information about this dealer has not been verified.*

Services: Mail order.
Credit Cards: Yes
Year Estab: 1994

S.W. Welch-Bookseller
3878 St. Laurent Boulevard H2W 1Y2
Web page: www.swwelch.com

Open Shop
(514) 848-9358
E-mail: info@swwelch.com

Collection: General stock of hardcover and paperback.
# of Vols: 10,000-15,000
Hours: Daily 11-9. Longer hours in summer.
Services: Appraisals, search service, accepts want lists, mail order.
Travel: Between Pins and Duluth.
Credit Cards: Yes
Owner: Stephen Welsch
Year Estab: 1985
Comments: A most ordinary shop with paperbacks and hardcover volumes shelved side by side on appropriately labeled shelves. Mostly popular titles, including some comics. Unless you're very lucky, your chances of finding a rarity here are underwhelming.

Westcott Books
2065 St. Catherine Street West H3H 1M6

Open Shop
(514) 846-4037
E-mail: westcott@sprint.ca

Collection: General stock of mostly hardcover.
# of Vols: 17,000-22,000
Specialties: Literature; history; travel; first editions; scholarly.
Hours: Daily 10am to 10:30pm (or later).
Services: Accepts want lists, mail order.
Travel: Guy St exit off Hwy 720 (Ville-Marie Expwy). Exit will lead onto Réne Lévesque Blvd. Continue west on Réne Lévesque, then right (north) on Atwater and right (east) on St. Catherine.
Credit Cards: Yes
Owner: Terry Westcott
Year Estab: 1993
Comments: How nice to find a small shop that carries a good collection of mostly hardcover used books representing a wide range of categories and of various vintages. While the shop may lack depth in many categories, the books we saw were of sufficient interest to suggest that a visit here would not be a mistake.

Westcott Books
1917 St. Catherine Street West H3H 1M6

Open Shop
(514) 937-4494
E-mail: westcott@sprint.ca

Collection: General stock of mostly hardcover.
# of Vols: 5,000-7,000
Specialties: Literature; history; travel; first editions; scholarly.
Hours: Daily 11:30-7 (or later).
Services: Accepts want lists, mail order.

(Montréal)

Travel:	See Westcott Books above.
Credit Cards:	Yes
Owner:	Terry Westcott
Year Estab:	1993
Comments:	Smaller than its sister shop a block away but quite similar in nature, the primary difference being that the books here seemed to be newer and in better condition.

The Word Bookstore   **Open Shop**
469 Milton Street   H2X 1W3   (514) 845-5640

Collection:	General stock of hardcover and paperback.
# of Vols:	20,000
Specialties:	Literature, particularly Canadian literature.
Hours:	Mon-Wed 10-6. Thu & Fri 10-9. Sat 11-6.
Credit Cards:	No
Owner:	Adrian & Lucille King-Edwards
Year Estab:	1975
Comments:	Another casualty of Easter Monday. About all we could gather from looking through the front window was that the side walls appeared to be filled with paperbacks, trade paperbacks and hardcover volumes, all intershelved, with more hardcover volumes toward the rear of the store, many with dust jackets. Based on the store's location close to McGill University, we assume that a good percentage of the volumes here are ones that would be of interest to the university population.

Outremont
(Map 21, page 279)

Guy de Grosbois, Libraire   **Open Shop**
1220 Bernard Avenue, #15   H2V 1V6   (514) 490-0170

Collection:	Specialty (French)
# of Vols:	4,000
Specialties:	Theater; fine art; decorative arts; books on books.
Hours:	Mon-Sat 1-6. Other times by chance.
Services:	Accepts want lists; mail order.
Travel:	At Park Ave.
Credit Cards:	Yes
Year Estab:	1997

Mimosa Pinson   **Open Shop**
1224 Bernard Avenue   H2V 1V6   (514) 277-8645

Collection:	General stock and prints.
Hours:	Tue, Wed, Fri 11-6. Thu 11-8. Sat 11-5.
Credit Cards:	Yes
Owner:	Maryse Atallah
Year Estab:	1995

Québec
(Map 23, page 294 & Map 20, page 272)

Argus, Livres Ancien   **Open Shop**
160 Saint Paul Street GIK 3W1   (418) 694-2122

Collection:	General stock and ephemera. (Primarily French)
# of Vols:	10,000
Specialties:	Art; architecture.
Hours:	Mon-Sat 10-5.
Services:	Appraisals, search service, accepts want lists, mail order.
Travel:	Located in the Old Port area.
Credit Cards:	Yes
Owner:	Claudine Villeneuve
Year Estab:	1990

Roger Auger, Libraire   **By Appointment**
33 Sault-au-Matelot Street, #101   Tel & Fax: (418) 692-5236
Mailing address: 246 Station B Quebec G1K 7A6   E-mail: augerlib@total.net

Collection:	Specialty (French and English)
# of Vols:	2,000
Specialties:	Canadiana
Services:	Appraisals, search service, catalog, accepts want lists.
Credit Cards:	Yes
Year Estab:	1981

Librairie à La Bonne Occasion   **Open Shop**
24B René Lévesque Boulevard East   G1R 2B1   (418) 647-0477
                                                  E-mail: anaron@clic.net

Collection:	General stock of paperback and hardcover. (Primarily French)
# of Vols:	22,000
Specialties:	Science; Canadiana.
Hours:	Mon 12-5. Tue, Wed, Sat 10:30-5. Thu & Fri 10:30-90.
Services:	Appraisals
Travel:	Downtown, near Parliament building.
Credit Cards:	Yes
Owner:	Denys Néron & Joanne Champagne
Year Estab:	1984

Librairie Du Faubourg   **Open Shop**
718 St. Jean Street G1R 1P9   (418) 529-8287

Collection:	Specialty (French and English)
# of Vols:	10,000
Specialties:	History; beat generation; art.
Hours:	Mon-Sat 10-6. Sun 12-6.
Services:	Mail order.
Travel:	Between St. Augustine & Ste. Marie.
Credit Cards:	Yes
Owner:	Alain Pinel

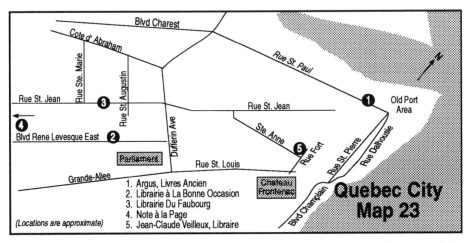

1. Argus, Livres Ancien
2. Librairie à La Bonne Occasion
3. Librairie Du Faubourg
4. Note à la Page
5. Jean-Claude Veilleux, Libraire

(Locations are approximate)

Note à la Page   **Open Shop**
106 Réne Lévesque West   G1R 2A5   (418) 529-7070

Collection:	General stock. (Primarily French)
# of Vols:	6,000
Hours:	Tue & Wed 10-6. Thu & Fri 10-9. Sat 10-5. Sun 11-5.
Services:	Accepts want lists, mail order.
Credit Cards:	Yes
Year Estab:	1997

Jean-Claude Veilleux, Libraire   **Open Shop**
8 Fort Street G1R 4M1   (418) 694-9949
                                    E-mail: jeanclaudeveilleux@videotron.ca

Collection:	Specialty (French and English)
# of Vols:	25,000 (See Comments)
Specialties:	Canadiana
Hours:	Mon-Sat 9:30-5.
Services:	Appraisals, catalogs, search service.
Travel:	Located near Château Frontenac.
Comments:	Only about 3,000 books are available for browsing in the store.

Rimouski

Alain Doucet, Libraire   **Mail Order**
C.P. 1341 G5L 8M2   (800) 203-8953
Web page: www.icrdl.net/basques/adl/   Fax: (418) 723-3118
                                          E-mail: adoucet@quebectel.com

Collection:	Specialty
# of Vols:	1,000
Specialties:	Canadiana; French literature.
Services:	Appraisals, search service, catalog, accepts want lists.
Credit Cards:	No
Year Estab:	1996

Rivière-du-Loup

Boutique Turelis Enr.   ******
407 LaFontaine Street   G5R 3B6   (418) 862-0332

Sainte Agathe des Monts
(Map 20, page 272)

La Retrouvaille   **Open Shop**
89 St. Vincent   J8C 2A8   (819) 326-3717

Collection:	General stock of mostly paperback. (French)
Hours:	Mon-Sat 10-5:30, except Thu & Fri till 9. Sun 11-5.
Services:	Search service.
Credit Cards:	Yes
Owner:	Jean-Paul Huneault
Year Estab:	1995

Sainte Foy
(Map 20, page 272)

Bouquinerie Du Bonheur   **Open Shop**
3291 Sainte-Foy Road, #4 G1X 3V2   (418) 656-9828
Web page: www.circulation.qc.ca/bonheur   Fax: (418) 656-6765
                                               E-mail: ricg@circulation.qc.ca

Collection:	General stock and magazines. (French)
# of Vols:	600,000
Hours:	Mon-Fri 9-9. Sat & Sun 9-5.
Services:	Search service, book repair.
Credit Cards:	No
Owner:	Gilles Labrie, Manager
Year Estab:	1993

Service De Recherche GLF   **Mail Order**
C.P. 8853   G1W 3R5   (418) 653-8042
                                                        Fax: (418) 653-1354
                                                       E-mail: glf@cmq.qc.ca

Collection:	General stock of hardcover and paperback. (French)
Specialties:	Magazines; journals.
Services:	Search service.
Owner:	Gerard L. Fortin
Year Estab:	1983

Saint Hubert
(Map 21, page 279)

Librairie de La Montée   **Open Shop**
5317 Mtee St. Hubert J3Y 1V8   (450) 926-8822

Collection:	General stock. (French and English)
# of Vols:	25,000

** Information about this dealer has not been verified.

Specialties:	Science fiction.
Hours:	Tue & Wed 10-6. Thu & Fri 10-9. Sat 10-5. Sun 11-5.
Services:	Accepts want lists.
Credit Cards:	No
Owner:	Joel Lefrancois
Year Estab:	1994

St. Jérôme
(Map 20, page 272)

Lire Et Relire   **Open Shop**
690 St. Georges   J7Z 5C6   (450) 431-4580
E-mail: danielle.l@qc.aira.com

Collection:	General stock of used and new. (French)
# of Vols:	50,000
Hours:	Mon-Wed 10-6. Thu & Fri 10-9. Sat 10-5. Sun 12-5.
Services:	Search service, accepts want lists, mail order.
Travel:	St. Jérôme exit off Hwy 15. Continue toward city center, then left on St. George.
Credit Cards:	Yes
Owner:	Danielle Leblanc
Year Estab:	1991
Comments:	Stock is approximately 75% used.

St. Lambert

Normand Houde, Libraire   **

609A Notre Dame   J4P 2K8   (450) 466-6758
E-mail: nshoude@sympatico.ca

Saint Malachie
(Map 20, page 272)

Caron Canadiana   **Open Shop**
1178 Principale   (418) 642-2635
Mailing address: 104 Rang 3 Saint Malachie QC G0R 3N0
E-mail: caron6x@globetrotter.net

Collection:	General stock of paperback and hardcover. (Primarily French)
Specialties:	Canadiana
Hours:	Tue-Thu 8:30-5. Fri 8:30-9. Sat & Sun by appointment.
Services:	Search service, catalog, accepts want lists.
Travel:	From Hwy 20, continue south on Hwy 277. Once in Saint Malachie, the bookshop and cafe are located across from the Catholic church.
Credit Cards:	Yes
Owner:	Jean-François Caron
Year Estab:	1992
Comments:	Shop also features a cafe.

** *Information about this dealer has not been verified.*

St. Saveur
(Map 20, page 272)

Lire Et Relire
222A Principale Street
Mailing address: 690 St. Georges St. Jérôme J7Z 5C6
daniellie.l@qc.aira.com

Open Shop
(450) 227-0482
E-mail:

Collection:	General stock of used and new. (French)
# of Vols:	50,000
Hours:	Mon-Fri 10-6. Sat 10am-11pm. Sun 12-6.
Services:	Search service, accepts want lists, mail order.
Travel:	Exit 60 off Hwy 15. Turn left at the exit and take first street on right. Turn right at second light onto De La Gare St, then right on Principale. The shop is across from the church on the lower level.
Credit Cards:	Yes
Owner:	Danielle Leblanc
Year Estab:	1992

Stanstead

Giacomo Falconi, Bookseller
455 Dufferin Street   J0B 3E0

Mail Order
(819) 876-5471
E-mail: giafal@together.net

Collection:	Specialty (French)
Specialties:	Antiquarian (European and American); Canadiana; eastern provinces.
Credit Cards:	Yes
Year Estab:	1979
Comments:	Collection can also be viewed by appointment.

Trois Rivières
(Map 20, page 272)

L'Exèdre Librairie Inc
910 St-Maurice G9A 3P9

Open Shop
(819) 373-0202
Fax: (819) 373-0675
E-mail: exedre@tr.cgocable.ca

Collection:	General stock of new and used. (French)
# of Vols:	15,000
Specialties:	History
Hours:	Mon-Wed 9-5:30. Thu & Fri 9-9. Sat 10-5.
Owner:	Benoit St. Aubin
Year Estab:	1981
Comments:	Stock is approximately 40% used.

Val Morin
(Map 20, page 272)

Le Bookstore @ the Laurentian Centre					**Open Shop**
5991 Morin Street J0T 2R0					(819) 322-1668
Web page: centrelaurentian.hypermart.net					Fax: (819) 322-5216
					E-mail: garybike@intlaurentides.qc.ca

Collection:	General stock of hardcover and paperback. (English and French)
# of Vols:	20,000+
Hours:	Daily 9-6, except Fri till 9.
Services:	Appraisals, search service, accepts want lists, mail order.
Travel:	Northbound on Hwy 15: Exit 76. Turn right at end of ramp and right on Curé Corbeil. Continue for two km to the end, then left on Morin St. Southbound on Hwy 15: Hwy 117 exit. Proceed south on Hwy 117 for eight km then left on Morin St.
Credit Cards:	Yes
Owner:	Gary McKeehan
Year Estab:	1994
Comments:	If you're the outdoor type and enjoy skiing (downhill or cross country) or snow shoeing in the winter and/or bicycling in the spring and summer, this is a shop where you'll be able to rent the equipment you need and, at the same time, purchase some paperback books for relaxing reader or find an older hardcover book from a different age. While the shop does not pretend to carry rare or necessarily hard-to-find volumes, one never knows what one might come across. Note: Shortly after our visit, the shop underwent an expansion which increased the display space for books and added a cafe area.

Westmount
(Map 21, page 279)

Sindell and Company					**By Appointment**
4635 Sherbrooke Street West H3Z 1G2					(514) 934-5957
					Fax: (514) 934-2380
					E-mail: sindellco@securenet.net

Collection:	Specialty books and ephemera.
# of Vols:	500 (books), 5,000 pieces (ephemera)
Specialties:	Manuscripts; stocks and bonds; transportation; telecommunications; television; mining.
Services:	Catalog, accepts want lists.
Credit Cards:	Yes
Owner:	Peter S. Sindell
Year Estab:	1975

Saskatchewan

Alphabetical Listing By Dealer

Alphabetical Listing By Location

Moose Jaw

Reader's Book Shop   **Open Shop**
422 Main Street North S6H 3K2   (306) 692-0737

Collection: General stock of mostly paperback.
# of Vols: 15,000
Hours: Mon-Sat 9:45-5:30.

Moosomin

Yesteryear Books   **Open Shop**
620 Main Street   (306) 435-3123
Mailing address: PO Box 400 Moosomin SK S0G 3N0   Fax: (306) 435-4144
                                          E-mail: yybooks@sk.sympatico.ca

Collection: General stock of hardcover and paperback and ephemera.
# of Vols: 20,000
Specialties: Charles Dickens.
Hours: Summer: Mon-Fri 9-5:30. Winter: Tue-Sat 9-5:30.
Services: Appraisals, search service, accepts want lists, mail order.
Travel: From Hwy 1 in Moosomin, turn south on Main St and cross tracks. Shop
                   is two blocks after crossing the tracks.
Credit Cards: Yes
Owner: John & Doris Bishop
Year Estab: 1996
Comments: Stock is approximately 75% hardcover.

Prince Albert

Tramp's Music and Books   **Open Shop**
1127 Central Avenue S6V 4V7   (306) 764-3816

Collection: General stock of mostly paperback.
# of Vols: 3,000
Hours: Mon-Sat 9-6, except Thu till 9.

Venturoso Used Books   **Open Shop**
924 Central Avenue   (306) 764-1780
Mailing address: PO Box 220 Muskoday SK S0J 3H0

Collection: General stock of paperback and hardcover and some ephemera.
# of Vols: 60,000
Hours: Jun-Sept: Mon-Fri 10:30-6. Sat 10:30-5:30. Oct-May: Mon-Fri 10:30-
                   5:30. Sat 10:30-5.
Services: Accepts want lists, mail order.
Travel: Hwy 2 to 15th St. Turn right on 15th St (follow City Centre signs), then
                   left on Central. Shop is 5½ blocks ahead on right.
Credit Cards: No
Owner: Ron & Marion Bear
Year Estab: 1992
Comments: Stock is approximately 60% paperback.

Regina

Buy The Book And Record Store   **Open Shop**
2718–13th Avenue S4T 1N3   (306) 924-5051

Collection:	General stock of paperback and hardcover.
# of Vols:	30,000
Hours:	Mon-Sat 10-6.
Services:	Mail order.
Travel:	1½ blocks west of Albert St (Hwy 6) in the Cathedral area.
Credit Cards:	No
Owner:	Chris Prpich
Year Estab:	1996
Comments:	In addition to its large paperback stock, the shop also carries lots of hockey related materials and other sports magazines as well as a good supply of *National Geographics* and LPs. The hardcover volumes we saw were a mix in terms of vintage and condition with a nice representation of Canadian writers.

Dragon's Eye Books   **Open Shop**
240B College Avenue East S4N 0V6   306-569-7171

Collection:	General stock of mostly paperback.
# of Vols:	3,000-5,000
Hours:	Mon, Tue, Sat 12-6. Wed-Fri 12-8.

Grandpa's Books & Comics   **Open Shop**
2741 Avonhurst Drive S4R 3J3   (306) 543-9907

Collection:	General stock of mostly paperback and comics.
# of Vols:	5,000-10,000 (books)
Hours:	Mon-Sat 10:30-5:30 Sun ususally 1-4, but best to call ahead. Some seasonal variation.

Reader's Book Shop   **Open Shop**
2104B Grant Road S4S 5C8   (306) 586-1414

Collection:	General stock of mostly paperbacks and comics.
# of Vols:	15,000
Hours:	Mon-Sat 10-6, except Thu till 8. Sun 12-4.

Regina Book Exchange   **Open Shop**
1332–11th Avenue S4P 0G7   (306) 522-5433

Collection:	General stock of mostly paperback.
# of Vols:	500,000 +
Hours:	Tue-Sat 9:30-6, except Thu till 8.
Travel:	Westbound on Hwy 1 which becomes Victoria Ave. Continue on Victoria, then right on Toronto and left on 11th Ave. Eastbound on Hwy 1. Turn north on Albert St, then right on Victoria, left on Toronto and left on 11th.
Credit Cards:	Yes
Comments:	Approximately 2,000 hardcover volumes.

Richard Spafford-Bookseller   **Open Shop**
1230 Broad Street S4R 1Y3   (306) 525-4910
                                                                   Fax: (306) 525-4971

Collection: General stock of hardcover and paperback.
# of Vols: 30,000
Specialties: Canadian and American Plains; Western Canada; Western Americana;
                   fur trade; Indians; Inuit.
Hours: Mon-Sat 9:30-5:30, except Thu till 9. Sun 12-5. (See Comments)
Services: Appraisals, catalog.
Travel: From Victoria (Hwy 1), turn north on Broad. Shop is on left, between
                   6th & 7th Avenues, in Value Mall.
Credit Cards: Yes
Year Estab: 1970
Comments: Unless someone decides to change the color scheme (always a possi-
                   bility), look for a shopping mall located inside a blue building with a
                   yellow roof. The bookstore, located at the entrance to the mall, offers a
                   plethora of paperbacks, comic books for children, *Playboy* magazines
                   for the more mature and some very interesting hardcover titles that,
                   while not profuse in all fields, did suggest to our eyes that a careful
                   perusal of titles would reveal some older items (antiquarian?) and
                   which should pique the interest of many a traveling book person. Note:
                   an additional 20,000 volumes, primarily in the shop's specialty areas,
                   are located in a nearby warehouse and can be viewed by appointment.

Tramp's Music and Books   **Open Shop**
1828 Scarth Street S4P 2G3   (306) 757-8616

Collection: General stock of new, mostly paperback used and comics.
Hours: Mon & Tue 9:30-6. Wed-Fri 9:30-9. Sat 9:30-6. Sun 12-6.

Saskatoon
(Map 25, page 304)

A Book Hunter   **Open Shop**
626 Main Street S7H 0J6   (306) 664-1050
Web page: www.wayneshaw.home.com   E-mail: wayneshaw@home.com

Collection: General stock of hardcover and paperback.
# of Vols: 50,000+
Specialties: Fine bindings; Western Canadiana; literature (Canadian, American, Brit-
                   ish); history; politics; nature; philosophy; religion; sports; children's.
Hours: Mon-Sat 9:30-5:30.
Travel: From Hwy 16, proceed west on Circle Drive, then right on 8th St, left
                   on Broadway and right on Main.
Owner: Wayne Shaw
Year Estab: 1981
Comments: This shop's two front windows give visitors an early taste of what
                   they'll find once they enter the shop; both windows are covered over
                   with shelves filled with books. Upon entering the shop, the visitor

finds several rooms and alcoves filled from floor to ceiling with mostly older volumes in mixed condition. While the shelves are labeled, we did note, on more than one occasion, that books perhaps belonged elsewhere. More books, plus lots of old magazines (primarily *Life* and *National Geographic* but others as well) are to be found in a basement. While time would not permit us to check prices on many of the volumes, we suspect that particularly for some of the more collectible items, bargains could be had. For someone who really wants to see it all, a great deal of patience will be required.

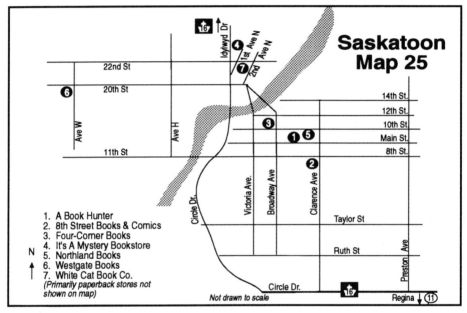

Four-Corner Books   **Open Shop**
832 Broadway Avenue S7N 1B6   (306) 384-4425
Web page: www.abebooks.com   E-mail: hbcalder@sk.sympatico.ca

Collection:	General stock of paperback and hardcover.
# of Vols:	20,000-25,000
Specialties:	Literature; First Nations; art; travel.
Hours:	Mon-Wed 10-6. Thu & Fri 10-9. Sat 10-6. Sun 12-5.
Travel:	See A Book Hunter above. Shop is between Main and 10th St.
Credit Cards:	No
Owner:	Pat Borgerson & Holly Borgerson Calder
Year Estab:	1997
Comments:	We visited this shop a few months prior to its move to this new location. At the time we noted a nicer than average "neighbohood" bookshop with a healthy balance of paperback and hardcover volumes. While the hardcover items were of mixed vintage, most appeared to be fairly recent and in generally good condition.

8th Street Books & Comics
1010–8th Street East S7H 0R9

Open Shop
(306) 343-6624
Fax: (306) 244-5689
E-mail: patman@dlcwest.com

Collection: General stock of paperback and hardcover.
Hours: Mon-Sat 10-6, except Thu & Fri till 9. Sun 12-6.
Services: Accepts want lists.
Travel: See A Book Hunter above. Continue east on 8th St. Shop is at southeast corner of 8th St & Clarence Avenue.
Credit Cards: Yes
Owner: Pat Thompson & Karl Tischler
Comments: Stock is approximately 70% paperback.

It's A Mystery Bookstore
Charter House Mall
331 First Ave. N S7K 1X5

Open Shop
Tel & Fax: (306) 384-6464

Collection: General stock of new and used paperback and hardcvoer.
Specialties: Mystery.
Hours: Mon-Sat 10-5:30, except Thu till 9.
Travel: At 25th St.
Credit Cards: No
Owner: Isabel Jungwirth
Year Estab: 1998
Comments: Used stock is mostly paperback.

Northland Books
630–10th Street East S7H 0G9

Open Shop
(306) 242-9466
Fax: (306) 242-2682
E-mail: northland@shaw.wave.ca

Collection: General stock.
# of Vols: 35,000
Specialties: Canadiana; Prairies; Arctic; North American Indians; Canadian ethnic groups.
Hours: Tue-Sat 12-5.
Services: Appraisals, occasional catalog.
Travel: From Hwy 16, proceed west on Circle Drive, then right on 8th St, left on Broadway and right on 10th St.
Credit Cards: Yes
Owner: Garry & Janice Shoquist
Year Estab: 1968
Comments: We had looked forward to visiting this shop but as luck would have it, when we arrived we found a notice on the door advising would be visitors that the owners were out of town and would not be back for another week. It would, in our judgement, be a disservice to try to describe the shop based on a simple look through the front door. Readers who visit Saskatoon are invited to let us know what we missed.

(Saskatoon)

Reader's Book Shop   **Open Shop**
140A 2nd Avenue North S7K 2B2   (306) 933-9426

Collection:	General stock of mostly paperback.
# of Vols:	10,000
Hours:	Mon-Sat 10-6.

Tramp's Music and Books   **Open Shop**
20–2105 8th Street S7H 0T8   (306) 477-1511

Collection:	General stock of paperback and hardcover.
# of Vols:	15,000
Hours:	Daily 10-midnight.
Travel:	Between Preston and Cumberland.
Comments:	Stock is approximately 75% paperback.

Westgate Books   **Open Shop**
3 2305–22nd Street West S7M 0V6   (306) 382-5252

Collection:	General stock of paperback and hardcover.
# of Vols:	50,000+
Hours:	Mon-Fri 10-9. Sat 10-6. Sun 12-5.
Services:	Appraisals, accepts want lists.
Travel:	At Avenue W.
Credit Cards:	No
Owner:	William Holoboff
Year Estab:	1972
Comments:	The shop does carry hardcover books, although one has to look for them as three quarters or more of the shop's space seems to be devoted to paperbacks, comics and magazines. Most of the hardcover volumes were of fairly recent vintage with plenty of fiction, some non fiction and some reference and how-to items.

White Cat Book Co.   **Open Shop**
129–2nd Avenue North S7K 2A9   (306) 652-2287
Web page: www.abebooks.com/home/whitecat   E-mail: whitecat@sk.sympatico.ca

Collection:	General stock of paperback and hardcover.
# of Vols:	30,000
Specialties:	Canadiana
Hours:	Mon-Sat 10-6.
Services:	Appraisals, search service, accepts want lists. mail order.
Travel:	22nd St exit off Hwy 16. If northbound, then right on 22nd and left on 2nd Ave.
Credit Cards:	Yes
Owner:	John Parsons
Year Estab:	1996
Comments:	Well lit and easy to browse, this shop carries of mix of paperback and hardcover books. Most of the hardcover books we saw were in good to better condition and of recent vintage.

Swift Current

Reader's Book Shop   **Open Shop**
Swift Current Mall   (306) 778-6447
307 1 Springs Drive S9H 3X6

Collection: General stock of mostly paperback.
# of Vols: 6,000
Hours: Mon-Sat 9:30-6.

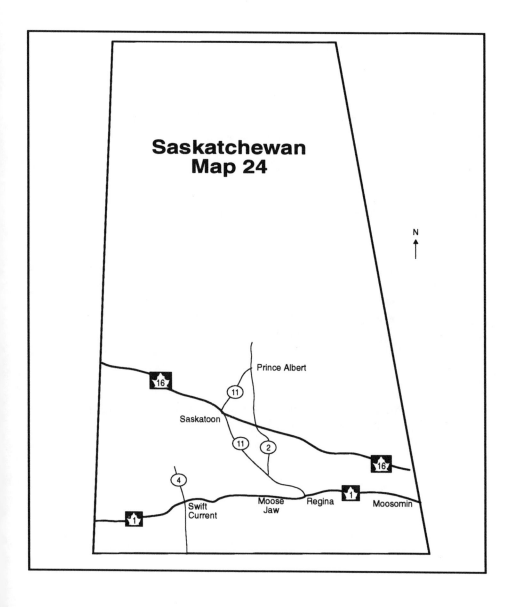

Yukon

Whitehorse

The Broke Bookworms   **Open Shop**
4230–4th Avenue Ste 1   Y1A 1K1   (867) 633-6214

Collection: General stock of hardcover paperback and hardcover.
# of Vols: 5,000+
Hours: May-Sept: Daily 9-9. Oct-Apr: Daily 11-7.
Travel: Across from Yukon Inn.

Well Read Books   **Open Shop**
4194B 4th Avenue Y1A 1J8   Tel & Fax: (867) 393-2987
Web page: www.wellreadbooks.yk.net   E-mail: wellreadbooks@canada.com

Collection: General stock of mostly paperback.
# of Vols: 12,000
Hours: Mon-Wed & Sat 10-6. Thu & Fri 10-9, Sun 12-5. (Closed Mon Sept-
                  May.)
Credit Cards: Yes
Owner: Jan Stick, Karen Walker & Hans Herdes
Year Estab: 1999

Zack's   **Open Shop**
Porter Creek Mall   (867) 393-2614
Mailing address: 203 Main Street Whitehorse YK Y1A 2B2

Collection: General stock of new and used hardcover and paperback.
Hours: Wed-Sun 12-6, except Fri till 7.
Travel: On Wann Rd just off Alaska Hwy.
Credit Cards: No
Owner: Chris Sorg
Year Estab: 1999
Comments: Stock is evenly divided between new and used books and used stock is
                  evenly divided between hardcover and paperback.

Dealer Index

(By Business Name)

I've heard of reaching for a book but this is ridiculous.

319

Specialty Index

The Used Book Lover's Guide Series

Your guide to over 7,500 used book dealers.

Central States Guide
1,250 dealers
465 pp • $18.95
ISBN 0-9634112-6-8

Canadian Guide
850 dealers
334 pages • $19.95
ISBN 1-891379-00-3

New England Guide
(2nd Rev Ed)
750 dealers *
$19.95
Due Spring, 2000
ISBN 1-891379-03-8
*estimate

Midwest Guide
(Rev Ed)
1,300 dealers
511 pp • $19.95
ISBN 0-9634112-9-2

Mid-Atlantic Guide
(Rev Ed)
1,100 dealers
439 pp • $18.95
ISBN 0-9634112-7-6

Pacific Coast Guide
(Rev Ed)
1,350 dealers* $19.95
Due Winter, 1999
ISBN 1-891379-02-X
*estimate

South Atlantic Guide
(Rev Ed)
950 dealers
375 pp • $17.95
ISBN 0-9634112-8-4

Keeping Current

As a service to our readers, we're happy to make available, at cost, Supplements for each of our guides.

The Supplements, published annually, provide our readers with additional listings as well as information concerning dealers who have either moved or gone out of business.

Much of the information in the Supplements comes to us from loyal readers who, in using our guides, have been kind enough to provide us with this valuable data based on their own book hunting experiences.

Should you wish to receive the next Supplement for the book(s) you currently own, complete the Order Form on the next page and enclose $2.50 for each Supplement, plus postage. Please note the date of any earlier Supplement/s you may have. **The new Supplements will be mailed as they become available.**

ORDER FORM

Book Hunter Press
PO Box 193 • Yorktown Heights, NY 10598
(914) 245-6608 • Fax: (914) 245-2630
bookhuntpr@aol.com • www.bookhunterpress.com

GUIDES	Price	# of Copies	Disc.	Unit Cost	Total
New England/2nd Rev Ed Due Spring '00	19.95				
Mid-Atlantic/Rev Ed	18.95				
South Atlantic/Rev Ed	17.95				
Midwest/Rev Ed	19.95				
Pacific Coast/Rev Ed Due Winter '99	19.95				
Central States	18.95				
Canada	19.95				
ANNUAL SUPPLEMENTS *	(See Keeping Current on previous page)				
New England	2.50				
Mid-Atlantic	2.50				
South Atlantic	2.50				
Midwest	2.50				
Pacific Coast	2.50				
Central States	2.50				
Canada	2.50				

The latest Supplement is automatically included with NEW orders.

Subtotal

Shipping

(NYS residents only) Sales Tax

(Canadian customers) 7% GST

TOTAL

SPECIAL DISCOUNTS
Any combination of books
2-5 copies: 20%
6 or more copies: 40%

SHIPPING & HANDLING
Guides: Single copy: Book rate: $3.50. Priorty(US) $6.50. Airmail (Canada) $7.00.
Add'l. copies: USA: Add $1.00 per copy. Foreign: Add $2.50 per copy.
Supplements: 50 cents each.

Name_____

Company_____

Address_____

City_____ State/Prov_____ Zip/PC_____

Phone_____ E-mail _____

MC Card _____ Visa _____ Exp Date _____

Card # _____

Signature_____